Unity and Harmony

Ecology and Justice

An Orbis Series on Integral Ecology

Advisory Board Members
Mary Evelyn Tucker
John A. Grim
Leonardo Boff
Sean McDonagh

The Orbis Series on Integral Ecology publishes books seeking to integrate an understanding of Earth's interconnected life systems with sustainable social, political, and economic systems that enhance the Earth community. Books in the series concentrate on ways to:

- reexamine human–Earth relations in light of contemporary cosmological and ecological science.
- develop visions of common life marked by ecological integrity and social justice.
- expand on the work of those exploring such fields as integral ecology, climate justice, Earth law, ecofeminism, and animal protection.
- promote inclusive participatory strategies that enhance the struggle of Earth's poor and oppressed for ecological justice.
- deepen appreciation for dialogue within and among religious traditions on issues of ecology and justice.
- encourage spiritual discipline, social engagement, and the transformation of religion and society toward these ends.

Viewing the present moment as a time for fresh creativity and inspired by the encyclical *Laudato si'*, the series seeks authors who speak to ecojustice concerns and who bring into this dialogue perspectives from the Christian communities, from the world's religions, from secular and scientific circles, or from new paradigms of thought and action.

Ecology & Justice Series

UNITY AND HARMONY

Toward an Ecospirituality

Victorino Pérez Prieto

ORBIS BOOKS
Maryknoll, New York 10545

Founded in 1970, Orbis Books endeavors to publish works that enlighten the mind, nourish the spirit, and challenge the conscience. The publishing arm of the Maryknoll Fathers and Brothers, Orbis seeks to explore the global dimensions of the Christian faith and mission, to invite dialogue with diverse cultures and religious traditions, and to serve the cause of reconciliation and peace. The books published reflect the views of their authors and do not represent the official position of the Maryknoll Society. To learn more about Maryknoll and Orbis Books, please visit our website at www.orbisbooks.com.

English translation copyright © 2025 by Orbis Books.

Originally published in Spanish as *Hacia una ecoteología*, copyright © 2023 by Victorino Perez Prieto, published by Fragmenta Editorial, Barcelona, Spain.

In the case of Spanish references to books originally published or otherwise available in English, the quoted material is translated from the Spanish and is not a direct quote from texts that may be available in English.

This edition published by Orbis Books, Box 302, Maryknoll, NY 10545-0302.

All rights reserved.

No part of this publication may be reproduced or transmitted in any form or by any means, electronic or mechanical, including photocopying, recording, or any information storage or retrieval system, without prior permission in writing from the publisher.

Queries regarding rights and permissions should be addressed to: Orbis Books, P.O. Box 302, Maryknoll, NY 10545-0302.

Manufactured in the United States of America.

Library of Congress Cataloging-in-Publication Data

Names: Pérez Prieto, Victorino author
Title: Unity and harmony : toward an ecospirituality / Victorino Pérez Prieto.
Other titles: Hacia una ecoteología. English
Description: Maryknoll, NY : Orbis Books, [2025] | Series: Ecology & justice series | Includes bibliographical references and index. | Summary: "A spirituality of ecology based on the truth that "everything is connected"— Provided by publisher.
Identifiers: LCCN 2025020628 (print) | LCCN 2025020629 (ebook) | ISBN 9781626986367 trade paperback | ISBN 9798888660911 epub
Subjects: LCSH: Ecotheology | Ecology—Philosophy | Ecology—Religious aspects—Catholic Church | Complexity (Philosophy)
Classification: LCC BT695.5 .P425 2025 (print) | LCC BT695.5 (ebook) | DDC 261.8/8—dc23/eng/20250718
LC record available at https://lccn.loc.gov/2025020628
LC ebook record available at https://lccn.loc.gov/2025020629

Contents

Foreword
Ilia Delio ix

1. Complexity and Ecosophy: The Reality of a Seamless Fabric in the Face of a Fragmentary Perspective 1
    Superficiality and Unconsciousness versus Awareness of Reality 2
    Fragmentary Perspective versus Unity: The Seamless Fabric of Reality 6
    Relationship, Complexity, and Ecosophy 7
    Quantum Physics, Spirituality, Theology, and the Originating Source of Beings 9

2. Science and the Philosophy of Complexity 21
    Complexity in Science 22
    Meteorology, the Uncertainty Virus, and the "Butterfly Effect" 23
    New Complexity Science versus the Old Reductionistic-Mechanistic Science: The Entropy Principle and Thermodynamics—The Basis of Complexity Theory 25
    The Science of Complexity from Eddington and Heisenberg to Prigogine: From Chemistry, Physics, and Biology to Economics and Politics 31

Complexity in Philosophy: From the Perennial
    Philosophy to Contemporary Philosophy   35
   *Complexity Opens Up Avenues for Metaphysical
    Reflection*   35
   *The Millennial Challenge of "Perennial Philosophy":
    From Laozi, Shankara, Plotinus, Spinoza, and
    Meister Eckhart to Huxley, Jung, and Panikkar*   38
   *Complexity in Contemporary Philosophy: Husserl,
    Zubiri, Amor Ruibal, Van Rensselaer Potter, and
    Alfred North Whitehead*   46
Complexity and Interrelatedness of the Whole of
    Reality in Edgar Morin and Raimon Panikkar   55
   Edgar Morin: Complexity and Aspiration to Totality   55
   *Raimon Panikkar: The Integration of the Whole of
    Reality in All Its Dimensions—Everything Is Related*   74

3. **Environmentalism and Interrelationality in the
   Bible and in Other Religions and Cultures**   97
   The Unity and Harmony of Reality
    in Eastern and Primitive Cultures   98
    In Hinduism and Buddhism   98
    *In Primitive Religions and in
     Current Religions of Indigenous Peoples*   102
   The Current Challenge of Environmentalism and
    Holistic Sensitivity. Ecologists, Prophets
    of Our Times   107
    "Ecology," "Environmentalism," and "Environmentalists"   108
    *Ecopacifism and Ecofeminism: Alter-Globalism,
     Environmentalism, and the Third World*   110
    *Holistic Sensitivity, the New Paradigm;
     An Interrelational Worldview*   114
   The Bible and Ecology: Between Contemplation
    of the Harmony of the Universe and the
    Denunciation of Destructive Sin   115
    The Bible Is Inherently Green   115
    Jesus of Nazareth, an "Ecologist": The Cosmic Christ   129

4. Green Christian Faith Betrayed. Theology and the Churches in the Face of Ecological Challenge. Pope Francis and *Laudato Si'* — 141

Green Christian Faith Betrayed: Christian Theology and the Churches in the Face of Ecological Challenge — 142
Christians and Their Share of the Blame for the Assault on the Environment — 142
Contemporary Christian Theology in the Face of Ecological Challenge — 145
Churches in the Face of the Ecological Challenge — 152
Pope Francis and *Laudato Si'*: Environmentalism and Complexity — 158
Pope Francis and His Challenge to Thought and to a World in the Midst of Destruction — 159
Laudato Si': *A Unique Encyclical in the History of the Church's Magisterium* — 163
Ecological and Social Critiques and Challenges of Laudato Si' — 167
The New Cosmovision of Laudato Si' — 173
Two Complementary Texts to the Encyclical: The Post-Synodal Apostolic Exhortation "Dear Amazonia" ("An Ecological Dream") and Pope Francis's Book, A Great Hope: The Stewardship of Creation — 180

5. Toward an Ecotheology and an Ecospirituality — 189

Toward an Ecotheology from a Relational Conception of Reality — 190
Ecotheology and Complexity — 190
A New Way of Conceiving God and Our Relationship with Him — 194
Toward a Non-dual Ecosophical Ecospirituality — 212
We Need to Open "The Third Eye" for a Total Non-dual Vision of Reality — 212

Learning from Three Great Ecological Mystics: Francis of
 Assisi, John of the Cross, and Pierre Teilhard
 de Chardin 221
A Brief Conclusion 239

Bibliography 241

Index 261

Foreword

Ilia Delio

In 1990, a group of distinguished scientists, including the late Carl Sagan and physicist Freeman Dyson, wrote a letter appealing to the world's spiritual leaders to join the scientific community in protecting and conserving an endangered global ecosystem. They wrote that we are close to committing "crimes against creation." We are on the brink of humanitarian and ecological catastrophes, and the risks they pose are not arrayed equitably. If global warming continues, deaths from global warming will double in just twenty-five years. With the loss of shelf ice in Greenland and Antarctica, sea levels could rise by more than twenty feet, devastating coastal areas worldwide. Heat waves will be more frequent and more intense. Droughts and wildfires will occur more often. By 2050 the Arctic Ocean could be ice free in summer and more than one million species worldwide could be driven to extinction.

How did we arrive at this point of ecological crisis? In his controversial article "The Historical Roots of Our Ecologic Crisis," historian Lynn White said that the source of our environmental problems is religious in nature. Christianity, he claimed, with its emphasis on human salvation and dominion over nature, made it possible to exploit nature in a mood of indifference to the feelings of natural objects. White argued that no religion had been more anthropocentric than Christianity and none more rigid in excluding all but humans from divine grace and in denying any moral obligation to lower species. We will continue to have an ecological crisis, he said, until we reject the Christian axiom that nature has no reason for existence except to serve us.

In 2015 Pope Francis wrote a landmark encyclical, *Laudato si'*, that placed the ecological crisis at the center of the Church's mission and theology. Integrating scientific, theological, and metaphysical insights, he called for situating humanity within an ecological network of relationships. In a recent letter, he said that the need to bring science and theology into an integrated framework is now imperative. "Listening to the sciences," he states, "continually offers us new knowledge. Consider what we are told about the structure of matter and the evolution of living beings: there emerges a far more dynamic view of nature compared to what was thought in Newton's time."[1] Similarly, Saint John Paul II, in his remarkable letter to Fr. George Coyne, SJ, spoke of the need to bring science and religion together in mutual exchange: "Science can purify religion from error and superstition; religion can purify science from idolatry and false absolutes. Each can draw the other into a wider world, a world in which both can flourish."[2]

In *Laudato si'* Pope Francis describes reality as a seamless garment, where everything is connected, related and intertwined. It is not a coincidence that this new book by Victorino Pérez Prieto is published on the tenth anniversary of *Laudato si'*, in which Pope Francis emphasizes the need for a new ecospirituality. Pérez Prieto is a renowned Spanish theologian whose works on science and religion, while unknown in the English-speaking world, have been widely acclaimed in Europe. This is his first

---

[1] Pope Francis, "The End of the World? Crises, Responsibilities, Hopes," Message of the Holy Father to Participants in the General Assembly of the Pontifical Academy for Life, March 3–5, 2025.

[2] Pope John Paul II, "Letter of His Holiness John Paul II to Father George Coyne, SJ, Director of the Vatican Observatory," June 1, 1988.

book in English translation, and it is both impressively erudite and illuminative.

A student of the great mystic theologian Raimon Panikkar, Victorino offers numerous examples from the sciences, mystics, theology and philosophy to support *Laudato si*'s call to interrelatedness. Theology can no longer be understood exclusively as a human phenomenon and must be seen within the overlapping domains of cosmos and nature. He establishes a profound vision: humans exist as part of a sublime communion with which we share deep interdependence. His fundamental thesis asserts that nothing exists outside the relationships of the whole. Reality possesses a seamless-fabric quality that forms the foundation of cosmic wholeness. When we understand this wholeness as energy's fundamental nature, we begin to appreciate life's inherent dynamism.

Pérez Prieto brilliantly illuminates complexity science as the study of this seamless whole—a core principle underlying evolution. He explains the universal laws of thermodynamics in terms of energy and entropy, positioning the second law as the foundation of complexity. Complexity—literally meaning "woven together"—describes cosmic life as a developmental process moving toward greater unity and consciousness. Based on the second law of thermodynamics, complexity involves the dissipation of energy and the emergence of new patterns of order. At the biological level, complexity refers to matter organizing within energy fields, creating new properties and causal forces that transcend their components. The cosmos consists of interweaving energy fields, with humans embedded within countless layers of entangled energy. Complex systems may represent the most fundamental aspect of life in our expanding universe.

This complexity reflects the principle that the whole exceeds the sum of its parts—we inhabit a universe of undivided wholeness. As David Bohm wrote, "We are all linked by a fabric of unseen connections. This fabric is constantly changing and evolving.

This field is directly structured and influenced by our behavior and by our understanding."[3] He further notes, "What is needed is to learn afresh, to observe, and to discover for ourselves the meaning of wholeness."[4] This pursuit forms the foundation of Prieto's work: learning to perceive and comprehend the whole of which we are a part. Without developing a new awareness of this wholeness and our place within the ecological web of interrelationships, we risk compromising planetary health and degrading the entire community of life it sustains.

Our understanding of the natural world—the biosphere—is now deeply connected to our view of Earth as a single planet. This perspective emerges not only from scientific knowledge but also from our perception of the living world as a magnificent yet vulnerable habitat facing potential catastrophe. Pierre Teilhard de Chardin recognized our planetary unity: despite diverse beliefs, cultures, and conflicts, we form one humanity, sharing a common destiny and collective responsibility for Earth's future and our own survival.

Building on Austrian scientist Eduard Suess, who introduced the term "biosphere" in 1875 and authored *The Face of the Earth* (1883–1909), Teilhard envisioned a new planetary consciousness—an energy of love that unifies and increases complexity while advancing life toward greater vitality. In his essay "Human Energy," Teilhard describes love's energy manifesting across all life forms, from pre-molecular structures to human individuals. This love functions as a centralizing force occupying the space between interior and exterior reality, symbolized by what he terms "Omega." The deeper one connects with Omega internally, the more one manifests it externally. For Teilhard, this loving energy

---

[3] Quoted in Penney Peirce, *Frequency: The Power of Personal Vibration* (New York: Atria Books, 2009), 168.

[4] David Bohm, *Wholeness and the Implicate Order* (New York: Routledge, 1980), 30.

must transform into active earth-building, a process he identifies with God's emergence.

Victorino Pérez Prieto draws deeply from Raimon Panikkar's rich synthesis, particularly his concept of "cosmotheandrism"—a threefold dimension of reality encompassing the cosmic, human, and divine as an interconnected trinitarian structure. Panikkar explicitly articulated what Teilhard only implied: humanity urgently needs a new guiding myth. As Panikkar observed: "Myths naturally evolve and change, and this is true also for the myth of modern cosmology. When the symbolic myth of a civilization is destroyed, that civilization collapses."[5] Our contemporary global crisis fundamentally stems from conflicting cosmologies. The struggle between these different worldviews cannot be resolved through the triumph of one over others—such victory can never foster genuine peace. Panikkar argued that traditional theistic frameworks have become inadequate for addressing our current human and planetary condition. What we require is a new mythos—a more profound conceptual horizon from which a relevant narrative for our age can emerge. This emerging cosmology represents something far more fundamental than merely another "scientific revolution" within Western thought. The critical question is whether modern cosmology can offer a vision of reality in which humanity can develop its boundless potential and achieve the fullness of life to which all aspire.

Professor Pérez Prieto contributes to this search for a new guiding myth by emphasizing the need for ecological wisdom—where knowledge is deepened by love and thought enriched by action—a new way of living within what Teilhard called the "divine milieu." He develops a rich synthesis of ideas, from Franciscan mysticism to deep ecology and complexity, in order to arrive at a robust and coherent ecospirituality. This ideal, however,

---

[5] Raimon Panikkar, *The Rhythm of Being: The Gifford Lectures* (Maryknoll, NY: Orbis Books, 2013), 371.

has become increasingly difficult to achieve in our time. The denaturing of human personhood in our post-Cartesian era of restless desire has generated profound cognitive dissonance and disconnection, manifesting as greed, apathy, and selfishness. In our world driven by excessive wealth and artificial intelligence, we face a troubling question: Have we become irretrievably denatured? As Teilhard observed, "Not all directions are good for our advance: one alone leads upward, that which through increasing organization leads to greater synthesis and unity. . . . Life moves toward unification. Our hope can only be realized if it finds its expression in greater cohesion and greater human solidarity."[6]

This book serves as an invitation to discover greater cohesion and human solidarity on a resource-depleted planet. We need profound transformation—not merely personal conversion but systemic reformation. The organization of systems across all dimensions of life—including politics, education, and religion—must be realigned according to nature's fundamental principles. Any other approach will ultimately fail. This book therefore arrives at a critical juncture in our planetary history. As Thomas Berry poignantly reminded us: "We will go into the future as a single sacred community, or we will all perish in the desert."[7]

---

[6] Pierre Teilhard de Chardin, *The Future of Man,* trans. Norman Denny (New York: Image Books, 2004), 64.

[7] Thomas Berry, *Befriending the Earth: A Theology of Reconciliation Between Humans and the Earth* (Mystic, CT: Twenty-Third Publications, 1991), 29.

1

Complexity and Ecosophy: The Reality of a Seamless Fabric in the Face of a Fragmentary Perspective

The cosmos is a chaosmos. The physical world is the product of an organizing disintegration; it is not possible to conceive of it without referring to an incomprehensible tetragram of order-disorder-interactions-organization. . . . Complexity is not everything, but it is, all the same, what can best open itself up to intelligence and reveal the inexplicable.
          EDGAR MORIN, Mes démons

What I am trying to do is precisely to overcome the fragmentation of knowledge and the fragmentation of human life and, consequently, my answer is always: all or nothing.
      RAIMON PANIKKAR, "Reflexiones autobiográficas"

It is necessary to emphasize the wealth of reality, which overflows any single language, any single logical structure. Each language can express only part of reality. Music, for example, has not been exhausted by any of its realizations. . . . The world of sound is richer than any musical language.
        ILYA PRIGOGINE, Order out of Chaos

> *When I discovered the parallels between the worldviews of physicists and mystics. . . . I had the strong feeling that I was merely uncovering something that was quite obvious and would be common knowledge in the future. . . . The reluctance of modern scientists to accept the profound similarities between their concepts and those of mystics is not surprising. . . . Fortunately, this attitude is now changing.*
>
> FRITJOF CAPRA, *The Tao of Physics*

> The secret of science transcends the scientific . . .
> Physicists now speak like mystics . . .
> The confusion now between physics and spirit . . .
> Only fantastic theories stand a chance of being true.
> "It's not sufficiently mad," thus Bohr criticized a theory.
>
> ERNESTO CARDENAL, *Cosmic Canticle*

SUPERFICIALITY AND UNCONSCIOUSNESS VERSUS AWARENESS OF REALITY

Raimon Panikkar often said that "the greatest epidemic in our world is superficiality." Contrary to the outrage this statement might incite, considering that there are other much more serious problems in the world—hunger, the death of millions of children, the injustice and violence committed daily against the poor and women, war, the grave and increasing attacks committed by humans against Mother Earth—this is not a trivial expression. *Superficiality* has to do with living on the surface of

Reality,[1] not seeing Reality in depth, not thinking overmuch, as opposed to having a *deeper* philosophical and aesthetic perspective. It also has to do with the ethical and spiritual, with a way of seeing the world and being in the world. It involves living *unconsciously*, unaware of what Reality *is*. Buddhism teaches that the essence of love lies in understanding and knowledge. As the great Buddhist master Thich Nhâ't Hanh says, "With full awareness, we see that the other person suffers, and it is precisely this that motivates us to do something so that he or she does not suffer." In this way, in-depth knowledge "is the very essence of love." "Without understanding, love is not possible."[2]

The French philosopher Gilles Deleuze says that if anyone asks what philosophy is for, one must say that philosophy comprises "the struggle against stupidity;" "stupid thinking" is the abjection of thought. Philosophy consists of overcoming the mental laziness associated with the status quo by appealing to a "new Earth."[3] Superficiality is an attack on what it means to be truly human.

An old and well-known Latin maxim states that *nulla æsthetica sine ethica*: there is no aesthetics/beauty without an ethical/moral commitment to the social reality in which one lives. This statement

---

[1] Reality is the most repeated word in this book. It will usually be capitalized, as I learned to do from Panikkar and Morin, who writes in his last book that "Reality hides behind our realities" (*Leçons d'un siècle de vie,* Paris: Denöel, 2021, 147). The capital *R* is a way of elevating its importance from the everyday concept of the same: everything that exists is part of Reality; the rational and the transrational, the animate and the inanimate, the material and the spiritual, the immanent and the transcendent. God himself, if he exists, is "real" and necessarily part of Reality.

[2] Thich Nhâ't Hanh, *Bouddha et Jésus sont des frères* (Gordes: Reliés, 2001), 35 and 36; in English, *Going Home: Buddha and Jesus as Brothers* (New York: Riverhead Books, 1999).

[3] *Cf.* Gilles Deleuze, *Nietzsche y la filosofía* (Barcelona: Anagrama, 2006), 65; in English, *Nietzsche And Philosophy* (New York: Columbia University Press, 2006).

cost José María Valverde (poet and professor of aesthetics at the University of Barcelona) and José Luis Aranguren (professor of ethics at the University of Madrid) their professorships in the final years of Franco's regime. Superficiality means to live on the surface, in banality and foolishness; to live on the margins of the reality that surrounds us, on the margins of what Reality truly *is*. Superficiality means living focused only on one's own selfish material interests, without caring what happens to other human beings and to the world around me, to the Earth of which I am a part; and we are children of Adam (*adamâ*, children of the earth). Superficiality means being indifferent to the joys and sorrows of my brothers and sisters, to the joy and pain of our world; it is to be indifferent to what happens to the rest of Reality.

Superficiality, then, means living in a state of unconsciousness. It means not being aware of what we are—in *relation* to everything. We are earth and spirit, whatever that might mean for us. We are *consciousness*; if we live in *unconsciousness*, we are not. Without a religious or secular *spirituality*, we cannot be fully human. Spirituality is the only place where believers of all religions and non-religious people who seek to live their existence with depth, intensity, veneration, and honesty can find ourselves. That place is the path of Christian *salvation* or *liberation*, but also that of Eastern *illumination* and secular *fulfillment*. This is why Raimon Panikkar writes:

> The history of spirituality coincides with the history of human beings. In the end, it *is the most real and effective dimension of human history*, since the true human endeavor is not so much the making of wars, nations, or cultures, as the *making of oneself* and one's "salvation." . . . The thirst for "beyond" has ultimately been the greatest force that has always impelled humanity to walk in this world.[4]

---

[4] Raimon Panikkar, *Espiritualidad hindú. Sanâtana dharma* (Barcelona: Kairós, 2004), 57.

Mysticism seeks an integral experience of Reality, a life in fullness—the consciousness *of deep communion with all of Reality*. Raimon Panikkar defines it as the "full experience of life," to which every human being is called. It is the experience of the human being who is "mystical spirit, as well as rational animal and corporeal being." Not a "specialization," but the integral vision of human beings; the "integral experience of life" or Reality, rather than ecstatic experiences or conceptual elucubrations.[5]

Mysticism is the *deep and attentive look* at Reality—looking deeply. To live fully is to live *consciously*, with *full attention*. It is to *open our eyes* and *awaken* to Reality, beyond any reductionist vision of it. It means daring to see Reality even beyond our ideas and beliefs, our fears and desires; to see beyond reason, for the scope of the real overflows the intelligible, since reason is limited and Reality is greater than our reason. This seems very clear to me, despite the fact that Hegel went so far as to say that "everything *real* is *rational* and everything *rational* is *real*" (*Elements of the Philosophy of Right*). It is not a matter of renouncing reason, but of relativizing it in order to reach the *transrational*. For this reason, the mystical experience presupposes having not only the eyes of the face fully awake but also the "three eyes of knowledge"—the sensitive/empirical eye, the rational/philosophical eye, and the spiritual/contemplative eye (*third eye*)—in order to fully enjoy life.[6]

---

[5] Raimon Panikkar, *De la mística. Experiencia plena de la vida* (Barcelona: Herder, 2005), 20-23; in English, *Mysticism, Fullness of Life* (Maryknoll, NY: Orbis Books, 2014).

[6] As we will see below, in the Christian tradition the concept of three eyes of knowledge is especially prevalent in the medieval thinkers Hugo of St. Victor and St. Bonaventure. *Cf.* Victorino Pérez Prieto, "Los tres ojos del conocimiento en San Buenaventura. De la reductio Bonaventuriana al pensamiento complejo de Edgar Morin y la perspectiva cosmoteándrica de Raimon Panikkar," in *Perspectivas sobre el pensamiento de san Buenaventura de Bagnoregio y otros estudios*, ed. Julio César Barrera, Luis Fernando Benítez, and Andrés Felipe López (Bogotá: Universidad de San Buenaventura, 2018).

FRAGMENTARY PERSPECTIVE VERSUS UNITY: THE SEAMLESS FABRIC OF REALITY

Superficiality has as much to do with banality, whether moral or spiritual, as with a *fragmentary perspective* of seeing Reality, as opposed to the vision of its Unity as non-duality. *Unity only exists in the difference* that we perceive at every moment. Superficiality is a perspective in which I see myself as an individual isolated from the rest of Reality, considering it to be at my service. It means seeing myself as a *subject* and everything else as an *object* that exists for my enjoyment. It is the perspective of the American *self-made man*, the man who believes he has made himself,[7] when in reality we are all dependent beings, dependent from the moment of our birth until we die, always needing others and our environment to exist. Even the fifth-century Simeon the Stylite, ridiculed in Luis Buñuel's film *Simón del desierto* (*Simon of the Desert*), needed at least water and vegetables to be brought to the column on which he was perched in the middle of the desert near Aleppo (Syria) in order to subsist. Only the foolish claim that they owe nothing to anyone, or that they have made *themselves* without the help of others, when in truth numerous people collaborate on our life's journey. This is the greatness and wonder of our existence: to recognize how we *are* all *interrelated*, interacting and weaving webs and warps from which we emerge stronger.

---

[7] This American expression seems to have originated in 1832 in the U.S. Senate. It was later linked to Benjamin Franklin, described as "the most original *self-made man*." But, in the history of the United States, the idea of the *self-made man* as an American cultural archetype or ideal was criticized by some and even considered "a pernicious myth." *Cf.* Irvin G. Wyllie, *The Self-Made Man in America: The Myth of Rags to Riches* (New York: The Free Press, 1966) and John John Swansburg, "The Self-Made Man: The Story of America's Most Pliable, Pernicious, Irrepressible Myth," Slate, 2017, https://www.slate.com/articles/news_and_politics/history/2014/09/the_self_made_man_history_of_a_myth_from_ben_franklin_to_andrew_carnegie.html

Complexity and Ecosophy

Superficiality is the opposite of seeing Reality as the *seamless fabric* that it truly is: a Reality in which everything is completely *interrelated/interconnected*. Fragmentary superficiality is the opposite of *the unity and harmony of Reality*. And that does not depend on my will, on what I see or do not see, on what I think or do not think. For as Antonio Machado wisely said in one of his poem-aphorisms:

> The eye you see is not
> an eye because you see it,
> it is an eye because it sees you.[8]

Einstein himself said, in a well-known and oft-repeated phrase, that "Our separation from others is an optical delusion of consciousness,"[9] and this delusion is a prison for us; our task must be to free ourselves from this prison to embrace all Reality.

RELATIONSHIP, COMPLEXITY, AND ECOSOPHY

This individualistic perspective, besides being egomaniacal and immoral, is contrary to the vision of Reality that has been presented by science for over a century: *Reality is relational*. Within it, everything is connected; we ourselves, though unique and

---

[8] Antonio Machado, "Proverbios y cantares I," in *Poesías completas* (Madrid: Espasa-Calpe, 1973), 197.

[9] The full paragraph reads: "A human being is a part of the whole, called by us "Universe," a part limited in time and space. He experiences himself, his thoughts and feelings as something separated from the rest—a kind of optical delusion of his consciousness. This delusion is a kind of prison for us, restricting us to our personal desires and to affection for a few persons nearest to us. Our task must be to free ourselves from this prison by widening our circle of compassion to embrace all living creatures and the whole of nature in its beauty. Nobody is able to achieve this completely, but the striving for such achievement is in itself a part of the liberation and a foundation for inner security." Available at https://www.thymindoman.com/einsteins-misquote-on-the-illusion-of-feeling-separate-from-the-whole/

immeasurable beings, true microcosms, are pieces of an immense cosmic puzzle, of the macrocosm. This complex Reality is manifested in quantum physics and the theory of complexity, as we read at the beginning in the quote by Edgar Morin: "Complexity *is not everything*, but it is, all the same, *what can best* open itself up to intelligence and *reveal the inexplicable.*" Or, as we also read in Ilya Prigogine's quote, Reality "*overflows any single language, any single logical structure,*" since, like music, "has not been exhausted by any of its realizations . . . the world of sound is richer than any musical language." In the end, it will be a matter of *overcoming* "*the fragmentation* of knowledge and the fragmentation of human life," as Raimon Panikkar said.

Complexity does not mean complicated or strange, but comes from *complexus*, "that which is woven together." Bruno Latour, French anthropologist, sociologist, and philosopher of science, popularized the expression that Reality is a *seamless fabric*: nothing exists outside the relationships of Reality. The natural and social worlds are the product of networks of relations between actors, both human and non-human; we must surpass the contrapositions of object/subject and society/nature.[10]

This is also the basis of an authentic *ecology/ecosophy*, or Earth wisdom—discovering the relationship *of everything to everything* in our world, from chemical and biological structures to human social networks; discovering that relationship in Reality and seeking to live in harmony with it. Here we can see the

---

[10] This is the *Actor-network theory*, known by the acronym ANT. It originated in the mid-1980s among Bruno Latour, Michel Callon and John Law. It was mainly Latour who popularized it; *cf.* Bruno Latour, *Reassembling the Social: An Introduction to Actor-Network Theory* (Oxford: Oxford University Press, 2007). Latour's best-known work is *We Have Never Been Modern* (Cambridge, MA: Harvard University Press, 1993) (the original French title is *Nous n'avons jamais été modernes. Essais d'anthropologie symétrique* (Paris: La Découverte, 1991). In it, he uses case studies to prove the fallacy of the modern oppositions of object/subject and society/nature.

environmental movement as a prophetic reality of our times and acknowledge its presence in the Judeo-Christian Bible.

Pope Francis himself speaks of Reality as a *fabric* in his encyclical *Laudato si'*. His most novel contribution in this revolutionary encyclical, as we will see, is not just denouncing the assault on the environment and proposing ecological solutions; it is also the first time that a pope has dared to speak of the new and old worldview that shows that everything is interrelated. And he does so via the most oft-repeated expressions throughout the text, after *ecology* and *environment*: "Everything is connected," "everything is related," "everything is interrelated," "we are intertwined," etc. The whole of reality forms a "seamless fabric." We are part of a "universal family, a sublime communion," with which we are in a profound "interdependence."

QUANTUM PHYSICS, SPIRITUALITY, THEOLOGY, AND THE ORIGINATING SOURCE OF BEINGS

This relational vision of Reality is the one provided by the new physics—specifically quantum physics, which conceives matter more as packets of energy, called *quanta,* than as substance/particles. These "energy packets" are also called wave packets; that is why *quantum* physics or *quantum mechanics* is also called *wave mechanics*.[11]

As Fritjof Capra eloquently expresses, quantum physics "manifests a profound harmony between scientific language and mysticism." In contrast to the *mechanistic model,* twentieth-century science overcomes this *fragmentation* and returns to the idea of *unity* expressed in early Greek and Eastern philosophies. The Eastern worldview is *organic*: all things and events perceived

---

[11] *Cf.* the relatively simple but well-done "Introduction" with which I entered this fascinating world many years ago: Tony Hey and Patrick Walters, *The Quantum Universe* (Cambridge: Cambridge University Press, 1987).

by the senses are connected/interrelated, and are but different aspects of the same ultimate Reality. As Capra writes:

> The profound harmony between scientific language and the corresponding ideas in Eastern mysticism is impressive evidence that the philosophy of mystical traditions, also known as the "perennial philosophy," provides the most consistent philosophical background to our scientific theories.[12]

Werner Heisenberg—the great German physicist, father of the uncertainty principle that is the fundamental concept of quantum physics, and winner of the 1932 Nobel Prize in Physics—wrote: "The great scientific contribution in theoretical physics since the last war may be an indication of a certain relationship between philosophical ideas in the tradition of the Far East and the philosophical substance of quantum theory."[13]

As we shall see, the relational vision of Reality revealed to us by quantum physics and complexity is thus the one that has been shown to us for centuries by the *perennis philosophia* and the spirituality of all the great religious traditions. Reality *is One*, total and undivided.

This relational vision of Reality provided by the new physics is also that of a theology which the Irish theologian Diarmuid O'Murchu explicitly called "quantum theology."[14] Conscious of

---

[12] Fritjof Capra, *El tao de la física* (Málaga: Sirio, 2000), 15; in English, *The Tao of Physics* (Boulder: Shambhala, 2010). *Cf.* Leonardo Boff, *El Tao de la liberación. Una ecología de la transformación* (Madrid: Trotta, 2006); in English, *The Tao of Liberation: Exploring the Ecology of Transformation* (Maryknoll, NY: Orbis Books, 2009).

[13] Werner Heisenberg, *Physics and Philosophy* (London: Harper Perennial, 1963), p. 725, quoted by Capra, *The Tao of Physics*.

[14] Diarmuid O'Murchu, *Teología cuántica. Implicaciones espirituales de la Nueva Física* (Quito: Abya Yala, 2014); in English, *Quantum Theology* (New York: Crossroad Publishing, 2004).

his breakthrough ideas, he thanked his brothers in the Congregation of the Missionaries of the Sacred Heart for "respecting the foolish and often unconventional dreams of his heart."

In his long introduction to the Spanish edition, José María Vigil says:

> The growing accumulation of knowledge . . . occasionally undergoes qualitative leaps that imply a radical change. . . . These are the scientific revolutions. . . . One of those radical qualitative leaps in the history of science was quantum physics. It was a shock that forced a complete and radical reformulation of all our traditional concepts. Old categories, unquestioned assumptions, and first principles of knowledge considered unprovable axioms were disqualified and rendered obsolete. A new way of looking invaded everything. . . . It is quantum physics that exposes this transformation with greater radicality, to the point of leaving us defenseless, dispossessed of all logic. . . . It breaks the rules of the unquestionable traditional logic with which we have always functioned and still function.[15]

O'Murchu highlights many of these disconcerting discoveries provided by quantum physics, which radically change the vision we have had for centuries. Thus, while we have traditionally understood matter to be the leftovers of the cosmos—something lifeless, purely passive, sterile—and this concept invaded philosophy, theology, and spirituality, quantum physics tells us this concept is completely wrong. "Such matter does not exist," says O'Murchu. As long as we continue to think and talk like this about the matter of this world, without drastically correcting the concept behind that word, we will deceive ourselves and live in a mirage. Matter is energy, which springs forth in a quantum

---

[15] *Ibid.* 10-11.

universe that makes all things consist from within at every level. Matter is force, it tends toward informed self-organization, it is the germinator of life . . . and of mind and spirit. As Morin says, we are not in a *cosmos*, but in a *chaosmos*, as we shall see later; a *cosmogenesis*, essentially and universally evolutionary. The universe is the result of an evolution in which an infinity of factors converge. Our fixist image of the world—as static, created like this directly by God—is left behind, insists O'Murchu. Moreover, *anthropocentrism*, the human being as the measure of all things, falls apart.

This vision of the new cosmology "does not sit well with the religious interpretation of the purpose of the cosmos," adds Vigil in his introduction. "The central message of the religious narrative elaborated in the times of the other cosmology seems misplaced, or even frankly incorrect." We are not "in the image and likeness" of God *as opposed to* all other living beings, the species that owns the planet and the cosmos. We come from within, not from outside the Earth; we come from below. That is why Vigil concludes:

> We have the right—and the obligation—to reconcile the discourse of our religion (its symbolic heritage, its stories, as well as our theology and spirituality) with the story of the cosmos that science offers us, so that we are not forced into a state of schizophrenia between our religiosity and our condition as people of today.[16]

O'Murchu confesses beautifully at the beginning of the book:

> Dare I compare myself with some of the pioneering figures of twentieth-century science—Albert Einstein, Niels Bohr, Werner Heisenberg, Erwin Schrödinger—but every time I read their personal memoirs I feel a strong

---

[16] *Ibid.* 15.

resonance. Yes, mine, too, is a searching, questioning, exploratory heart just as theirs is a discerning, spiritual, and theological adventure—at least at the subconscious level. Indeed, it is probably quite accurate to suggest that it is in the moments of mystical awakening that these two strands meet. And that is not simply an encounter of like minds; much more to the point, it is a meeting of burning hearts.[17]

Brazilian theologian Leonardo Boff, a connoisseur of contemporary theology and science, recently wrote:

> One of the most persistent quests among scientists, generally coming from the Earth and life sciences, is that of the unity of the Whole. This quest is called the *Grand Unified Theory* or *Quantum Field Theory*, or the pompous *Theory of Everything*. No matter how much effort they have made, they all end up frustrated, abandoning this pretension as impossible. The universe is too complex to be apprehended by a single formula.
>
> However, research on subatomic particles and primordial energies has led us to perceive that they all refer to the so-called *quantum vacuum*, which is not a vacuum at all but rather the fullness of all potentialities. All beings and the entire universe have emerged from this *bottomless bottom*.... Others call it the *Original Source of Beings* or the *All-nourishing Abyss*.
>
> One of the greatest cosmologists, Brian Swimme, calls it the *Ineffable* and the *Mysterious* (*The Hidden Heart of the Cosmos*). Well, these are characteristics that religions attribute to the Ultimate Reality, which is known by a thousand names: Tao, Yahweh, Allah, Olorum, God. The Void, pregnant with

---

[17] *Ibid.* 17.

Energy if it is not God (God is always greater), is its best metaphor and representation.[18]

The intimate relationship between *complexity*, *ecology*, and *mysticism* is what we will try to express here. We will turn to science and philosophy, but also to theology and spirituality/mysticism, taking into account the *Original Source of Beings* or the *Abyss* mentioned by Leonardo Boff, the presence of the Divinity in any of its conceptions. As a theologian of today who wants to be honest in his work, I want to seriously consider a brilliant statement by one of the greatest and best-known Christian theologians of all times—paradoxically, a theologian who lived over seven hundred years ago and who has a reputation for being reactionary among many people today, but who was ahead of his time: Thomas Aquinas. He says, "A mistake about creation results in a mistake about God" (*Summa contra Gentiles*, 1,2, c.3). Developing a theology for today involves approaching and humbly taking into account what today's sciences tell us, albeit without yielding to the scientism of some scientists, which is reductive of Reality. From mysticism, I also want to learn from the mystics, who have been able to penetrate Reality better than even the most prestigious scientists, as some of the greatest physicists of the twentieth century have acknowledged; for the mystics do this *directly*, and not through intermediaries, as scientists do. This is what Ken Wilber says in one of his most beloved books (*Quantum Questions: Mystical Writings of the World's Great Physicists*), from which I have learned much of what I know about the matter over the years. Wilber says in the Introduction (italics by the author):

---

[18] Leonardo Boff, "El Cristo Cósmico: Una espiritualidad del universo," https://www.atrio.org/2016/09/el-cristo-cosmico-una-espiritualidad-del-universo.

I would simply ask, you of orthodox belief, you who pursue disinterested truth, you who—whether you know it or not-are molding the very face of the future with your scientific knowledge . . . to you I ask: *what does it mean that the founders of your modern science*, the theorists and researchers who pioneered the very concepts you now worship implicitly, the very scientists presented in this volume, what does it mean that they *were, every one of them, mystics*?[19]

Suspicious, like myself, of any useless concordism between science and religion, Wilber says of the mystical experience and the scientific work of today's physicist:

> In the *mystical* consciousness, Reality is *apprehended directly and immediately*, meaning *without any* mediation, any symbolic elaboration, any conceptualization, or any abstractions; subject and object become one in a timeless and spaceless act. . . . Mystics universally speak of contacting reality in its "suchness." . . .
>
> Now, when the *physicist* "looks at" quantum reality or at relativistic reality, he *is not looking at the* "things in themselves," at noumenon, at direct and nonmediated reality. Rather, the physicist is looking at *nothing but a set of highly abstract differential equations.* . . . Physics deals with shadows; to go beyond shadows is to go beyond physics; to go beyond physics is to head toward the *meta-physical* or *mystical*—and *that* is why so many of our pioneering physicists were mystics. The new physics contributed nothing positive to this mystical venture, except a

---

[19] Ken Wilber, *Cuestiones cuánticas. Escritos místicos de los físicos más famosos del mundo* (Barcelona: Kairós, 1987), 12; in English, *Quantum Questions: Mystical Writings of the World's Great Physicists* (Boulder: Shambhala, 1984).

spectacular failure, from whose smoking ruins the spirit of mysticism gently arose.[20]

The contributions of Heisenberg, Schrödinger, Eddington, and other great physicists to quantum theory show that the classical ideal of scientific *objectivity* is no longer feasible. In this sense, modern physics also shatters the myth that science is something completely *objective*, alien to values and spiritual experiences. The patterns and structures that scientists observe in nature are intimately related to the patterns and structures that exist in their minds; to their concepts, their thoughts, and their values. Thus, the scientific results they obtain and the technological applications they investigate will be conditioned by their own mental structures. This is what Raimon Panikkar calls the "myth of science," for many unquestionable, as are all myths.

> Many will agree that we must not allow ourselves to be dominated by the machine and that we must progress in spirit to keep up with material development. But few will dare to touch *the taboo of modern science*. . . . This is the myth. *We have relativized everything*: from what the Aztecs thought to what Jesus Christ said. *But we have not relativized our science*. . . . The successes of science and its symbiosis with modern technology have made people believe that *there is no salvation outside of science*.[21]

Scientists, therefore, have not only an intellectual responsibility toward their research but also a moral responsibility. Thus humbly writes Erwin Schrödinger, winner of the 1933 Nobel Prize in Physics:

---

[20] *Ibid.* 22-23.
[21] Raimon Panikkar, *Paz y desarme cultural* (Santander: Sal Terræ, 1993), 100; in English, *Cultural Disarmament: The Way to Peace* (Louisville: Westminster John Knox Press, 1995).

The *scientific picture of the world* around me is very deficient. It provides a great deal of factual information, reduces all experience to a wonderfully consistent order, but *is sepulchrally silent* about every aspect related to the heart, *with everything that really matters to us*. It cannot tell us a single word about what it means for something to be red or blue ... painful or pleasurable; it knows nothing of the beautiful or the ugly, the good or the bad, of God and eternity.[22]

And for this reason, we could also read with feeling the magnificent verses of Ernesto Cardenal's *Cosmic Canticle* at the start of this chapter, in which he also quoted another great quantum physicist, Niels Bohr (1885-1962, Nobel Prize in Physics in 1922):

> The secret of science transcends the scientific . . .
> Physicists now speak like mystics . . .
> The confusion now between physics and spirit . . .
> Only fantastic theories stand a chance of being true.
> "It's not sufficiently mad," thus Bohr criticized a theory.

In short, this is why a passage in the Upanishads said, more than two thousand years ago, "From the *unreal*, lead me to the *real*! From *darkness*, lead me to *light*!" The millenary texts of Hinduism speak of higher and *lower knowledge*; they relate the latter to the various sciences and the *higher* to *religious consciousness*. In-depth knowledge of Reality can never be adequately described

---

[22] Wilber, *Cuestiones cuánticas. Escritos místicos de los físicos más famosos del mundo*, 128.

in words, because it is beyond the realm of the senses and the intellect, from which all our words and concepts are derived. That is why the Upanishads also state:

> The eye does not reach there.
> The word does not go, nor the mind.
> We don't know it, we don't understand it.
> How could I unite to *teach it?*

Buddhists speak of *relative knowledge* (conditional truth) and *absolute knowledge* (transcendental truth). One of their greatest teachers, Nagarjuna (150-250), says that reason cannot grasp the essence of the absolute, One Reality. And more than half a millennium earlier, Laozi, who calls this Reality the Tao, says the same thing in the first maxim of the *Book of Tao (Daodejing)*: "The Tao that can be expressed is not the true Tao." This knowledge is an experience arising from a non-ordinary state of consciousness, which we might call a "meditative" or "contemplative" state. In this meditation, the mind has emptied itself of thoughts and concepts, thus preparing itself to function intuitively, completely open to Reality, without conceptual conditioning.

This book—written during the long pandemic lockdown of March-May 2020, but also the fruit of many studies, conferences, and previous publications of mine—follows a path from matter to spirit, from the empirical to the spiritual, from the bottom up and the top down in continuous motion. As can be seen from the many quotes by Raimon Panikkar, I am very much indebted to the thinking of this great teacher and friend. He once told me, "I am happy to serve as a springboard for you to jump higher."[23] He shone down from high above, and I will barely

---

[23] Prologue to Victorino Pérez Prieto, *Más allá de la fragmentación de la teología, el saber y la vida: Raimon Panikkar* (Barcelona: Tirant lo Blanch, 2008), 15.

reach his level; but, as a wise medieval saying goes, walking "on the shoulders of a giant," I hope to "see further" and contribute something new with this text, where I present some ideas that go beyond Panikkar.

I start from complexity in science and philosophy, particularly the thought of Edgar Morin and Raimon Panikkar. I then shift to an ecological perspective, and the vision of Reality as a harmonious unity in difference, from the challenge of ecologists, theology, and spirituality; Eastern thought and religiosity; early and Indigenous peoples and the Judeo-Christian Bible; ecopacifism, ecofeminism, and the holistic perspective. All to arrive at an *eco-theology* and *eco-spirituality* in the company of three great Christian mystical ecologists: Francis of Assisi, John of the Cross, and Pierre Teilhard de Chardin. In both chapters, I will approach Pope Francis's encyclical *Laudato si'*; a text that knows how to unite a denunciation of the assault on the planet and ecological proposals with a vision of Reality as an indissolubly united Whole—the *seamless garment* of Reality, of which we are a part, as a harmonious unity in difference.

I hope the non-believer/religious reader, who I hope will also read these pages, will not quit after the first chapters but make it to the end. For this book is born from a desire to learn without prejudice. Thus, it attempts to overcome both the old faith/science conflicts and the assumed European/Western "superior culture" pitted against all the other "backward" cultures. I set out from the conviction that it is a mistake to oppose faith and science, because each complements the other. Against *heteronomy*, the dependence and submission of one to the other—the case for a long time in the West with science in regard to religion—and *autonomy*, a freedom fairly won by science, but which led both to walk separately and even in conflict, I am in favor of what Raimon Panikkar calls *ontonomy*: the relationship of everything to everything, of the different spheres of knowledge and ways of knowing mutually complementing each other. Moreover, I am trying to overcome the conflict between Christianity, which has also considered itself superior, and the other religions, knowing that they have much to learn from one another.

2

Science and the Philosophy of Complexity

The second law of thermodynamics is the most metaphysical of all the laws of physics.

HENRI BERGSON, *Creative Evolution*

The entire universe is a cocktail of order, disorder, and organization. We are in a universe from which we cannot eliminate the randomness, the uncertainty, the disorder.

EDGAR MORIN, *Introduction to Complex Thought*

It is no exaggeration to speak of the transformation of concepts as a true metamorphosis of science. . . . We believe that these questions were not just scientific questions, and that this metamorphosis of science is not always scientific in nature.

ILYA PRIGOGINE, *Order Out of Chaos*

Reality is one, divine, substantial to the manifold world of things and lives and minds. But the nature of this one Reality is such that it cannot be directly and immediately apprehended except by those who have chosen to fulfil certain conditions, making themselves loving, pure in heart, and poor in spirit.

ALDOUS HUXLEY, Introduction to
the Perennial Philosophy

Physics is not metaphysics, nor can metaphysics be identified with philosophy. . . . However, the plurality of the notions of metaphysics, ontology, wisdom, and philosophy is inherent to physical, metaphysical, and philosophical thought, because the human and cosmic condition is far from being uniform and rejects the univocity. . . . There is no metaphysics without physics. . . . But, on the other hand, there is no physics without metaphysics.

RAIMON PANIKKAR, The Narrow Gate of
Knowledge: Sense, Reason and Faith

COMPLEXITY IN SCIENCE

Thermodynamics is the mother of all the theories of complexity.

E. D. SCHNEIDER AND D. SAGAN,
The Thermodynamics of Life:
Physics, Cosmology, Ecology and Evolution

Why must we approach science for philosophical, theological, and spiritual reflection? Specifically, why do so via a science like thermodynamics, which seems so distant from not having specialized knowledge in physics? Over a decade ago, during my final project for a master's degree in Current Philosophical Issues at the University of Santiago de Compostela, where I had expressed my interest in complexity, the professor I had chosen as director, Luis Miguel Varela—a professor at the university, where he was then Dean of the Faculty of Physics—told me

Science and the Philosophy of Complexity

that I could not seriously approach complexity if I did not start from a knowledge of thermodynamics. I could not start simply from philosophy, but had to begin from the sciences, particularly from physics and especially from thermodynamics. Fortunately, I listened to him because I wanted to learn and was very satisfied with that decision. This whole book is closely related to my work during that year in Compostela, spent between the faculties of Philosophy and Physics, and it would not be possible without it. That genuine effort, particularly hard for someone who did not come from a background in mathematics, has opened up many avenues for me to this day.

I increasingly realized something I had suspected for some time: it is impossible to develop a truly contemporary thought—philosophical, theological, or otherwise—without an in-depth dialogue with the new vision of the world arising from the sciences of life, the Earth, and the cosmos. This forced me to study different sciences: quantum physics, the new biology, astrophysics, chaos and complexity theory. This dialogue with the new cosmology and with ecology forces us to change the paradigm: from the old *essentialist* Western paradigm, based on substance, on essence, to a *relational* and complex paradigm, where everything is in relationship. Thus, the relationality that I was discovering in science better established what I knew of Reality, of the human being, and of God/the Divinity, the Foundation, the Origin. . . . That is the reason for the following pages, ones I consider essential.

Meteorology, the Uncertainty Virus, and the "Butterfly Effect"

For a long time, describing something as *complex* meant designating it as difficult to understand or realize; the "explanation" of what could not be explained in any other way, the lack of theory, replaced the inadequacy of its explanations. However, *complexity* itself became an object of study and research in the last century in physics, chemistry, and biology, and a quite satisfactory explanation of what Reality is: *complexus* (fabric). But what is complexity?

In a 1963 report to the New York Academy of Sciences, mathematician Edward Lorenz explained the inability to predict the weather using mathematical formulas and relating variables such as temperature and humidity: small changes in initial conditions produced staggering differences. It was possible to predict the course of the stars, but not something as simple as knowing for certain if it would rain the following day. The reason was that the appearance of minute alterations in the data generates changes and produces unthinkable phenomena. Thus, the traditional *certainty* of mathematics could not compensate for the *uncertainty* of meteorology; the virus of uncertainty had invaded the very body of the exact sciences. This articulated something known for a long time: Reality is neither mechanical nor linear, but *random*.

Lorenz rewrote an ancient Chinese saying—that the flapping of a butterfly's wings can be felt on the other side of the world—and coined a phrase that became famous: "A butterfly flaps its wings in California and it snows in the Himalayas." This is *the butterfly effect*: the intercommunication of the entire universe; everything that happens anywhere and on any occasion in the cosmos affects the rest of reality. In a very simplified way, this is the meaning of complexity theory.

But shortly afterward, Nobel laureate Ilya Prigogine (1917–2003) applied it to the *theory of dissipative structures*, or out-of-equilibrium structures: the world does not strictly follow the model of a clock with a mechanism that makes it function in a predictable and determined way as classical physics said; instead, Reality is *a mixture of order and disorder*. The processes of reality depend on an enormous set of uncertain circumstances, which determine that any small variation at one point of the planet generates a considerable effect at the other end of the Earth.[1]

---

[1] *Cf.* Ilya Prigogine and Isabelle Stengers, *La nueva alianza. Metamorfosis de la ciencia* (Madrid: Alianza, 1990); in English, *Order Out of Chaos: Man's New*

Science and the Philosophy of Complexity

Prigogine rightly says that the so-called *paradigm of complexity* is a true Copernican revolution in science, and better still in the sciences, since it affects not only physics, chemistry, and biology, but also social and economic systems and thought itself.

Edgar Morin—who laid the foundations of *complex thinking*—voiced the phrase we read at the beginning of this section: "The entire universe is a *cocktail* of *order, disorder,* and *organization.*" The *cosmos*—harmony—is, in reality, *chaos-cosmos*, a mixture of order-disorder-organization in constant evolution, produced by entropy. That is why Morin writes:

> Even in the favorable hypothesis of a Teilhardian universe which develops its own richness in an ascensional way, there is hemorrhage, waste, mess of which we must be conscious. The encounters produce more destruction and dispersion than organization. To constitute an organization, erect an order, keep a life alive, so many "useless" agitations, so many "fruitless" expenses, so many squandered energies, so many dispersive hemorrhages are needed![2]

New Complexity Science versus the Old Reductionistic-Mechanistic Science: The Entropy Principle and Thermodynamics—The Basis of Complexity Theory

Until the nineteenth century and almost the beginning of the twentieth century, most of the empirical sciences had as their mode of knowledge specialization and abstraction: *the reduction of a whole to knowledge of its parts*; for they were based on

---

Dialogue with Nature (London: Verso, 2018). Also, Ilya Prigogine, *Introducción a la termodinámica de los procesos irreversibles* (Madrid: Selecciones Científicas, 1974), Appendix III, "Estructuras disipativas."

[2] Edgar Morin, *La Naturaleza de la Naturaleza*, vol. I, El Método (Madrid: Cátedra, 2008), 106–107; in English, *The Nature of Nature*, vol. I, Method: Towards a Study of Humankind, (New York: Peter Lang, 1992).

the assumption that the reality of all that exists was marked by *determinism* and the *application of Cartesian mechanical logic*. But first the old thermodynamics, then revisions to it, and later quantum mechanics demonstrated the failure of this Cartesian deterministic-mechanistic order and the need for a new order, more in line with what Reality actually is. Thus, Prigogine says:

> Starting from a nature similar to an automaton, subject to mathematical laws that calmly and proudly determine its future forever... today we find ourselves in a completely different theoretical situation.... It is no exaggeration to speak of this transformation of concepts as a true *metamorphosis* of science....
>
> We believe that these questions were not just scientific questions, and that this metamorphosis of science is not always scientific in nature... Science is part of the cultural complex in which, each generation, man tries to find *a form of intellectual coherence*.[3]

Here, we can agree with Professor Luis Miguel Varela that thermodynamics is the best approach to complexity; along with him, we make our own the statement by Schneider and Sagan that we read at the start: "Thermodynamics is *the mother of all theories of complexity*." We could say, then, that the entrance to the *labyrinth of complexity science* necessarily passes through *thermodynamics*. Thus, the best approach to complexity is thermodynamics, a branch of physics that became the basic interpretative framework for how the world works, for understanding our known reality. Above all, the *second law of thermodynamics*, which governs the universe. Thermodynamics examines the properties of macroscopic bodies in relation to heat and temperature.

---

[3] Prigogine and Stengers, *La nueva alianza. Metamorfosis de la ciencia*, 29.

Let us recall its three laws or principles:[4]

Zeroth law: *bodies in* thermal *contact can exchange energy* in the form of heat. Two bodies in thermal equilibrium with a third are also in *thermal equilibrium* with each other.

First law. *Principle of conservation of energy. Energy is neither created nor destroyed*, but either conserved or transformed through physical processes. This principle is one of the most fundamental and significant in physics. This law identifies heat as a form of energy; an idea that seems elementary to us today, but which took time to make its way and was not formulated until the 1880s, with the research of Mayer and Joule.

Second law. *Principle of entropy or dissipation of energy.* Not all disorganized energy (heat) can be converted into organized energy (work). Not all disorder can be converted into order without a *loss of energy*; when converting heat into mechanical work, there are losses.[5] This law is *the core of thermodynamics*.

Third law. *Absolute zero temperature cannot be achieved.*

The universe's energy is constant, but entropy tends to move toward a maximum. The amount of energy is always the same, but it tends to be transformed into *increasingly less usable* forms of energy. Thus, the logic of the *entropy principle* is the Ariadne's thread of Reality: the microcosm and the macrocosm are in necessarily constant motion and evolution.

---

[4] *Cf.* Michael M. Abbott and Hendrick C. Van Ness, *Termodinámica* (Mexico: McGraw-Hill, 1975); Eric D. Schneider and Dorion Sagan, *Into the Cool: Energy Flow, Thermodynamics, and Life* (Chicago: University of Chicago Press, 2006); and Ilya Prigogine, *Introduction to the Thermodynamics of Irreversible Processes* (New York: Wiley, 1968)

[5] R. Clausius formulated the second law in 1865 and took the name from the Greek *etropé*, "transformation."

These principles of thermodynamics can be interpreted as saying that in the world in which we live, *energy* is constant and *entropy* (useless energy) increases at every instant; nothing remains the same. The *dissipation* of energy cannot be stopped or reversed; it is not recyclable. Nature and the cosmos are a gigantic reservoir of energy, but we cannot dispose of it unconditionally. The principle of entropy is the engine of evolution: we survived in a world in which wear and tear constantly increase with every advance. Entropy *does not kill*, but demands ever greater organization, which is manifested in progressive biological complexity.

The state of thermodynamic equilibrium of a body is one in which, as long as the environment remains invariable, all macroscopic properties of the system cease to depend on time. *The thermodynamic process*, which allows work to be obtained from the system, *is a set of states that a system adopts over time as a result of interactions*—thermal, mechanical, electrical, matter transfer, etc.—*with the environment and internal mechanisms*. In essence, all our efforts are directed toward the creation of new states by departing from thermodynamic equilibrium.

Thermodynamics speaks of *irreversible and reversible processes*. In irreversible processes, restoring both the system and its environment to their original states is impossible; real processes are normally like this. *Reversible processes*—ideal ones, in which it would be possible to return the system to its initial state—do not exist. *Carnot's theorem*[6] elaborates on the attempt to make processes as irreversible as possible in the production of energy. For this reason, Prigogine goes so far as to say that "thermodynamics is the first non-classical science": irreversibility as a source of order and organization, as opposed to the reversibility of elementary behaviors as proclaimed by the old

---

[6] French engineer considered the founder of thermodynamics. In 1824 he published *Reflections on the Motive Power of Fire*, where he explained the first two principles of thermodynamics. His work was later developed by two great masters: R. Clausius and W. Thomson (Lord Kelvin).

physics.⁷ Prigogine himself would culminate the work in the twentieth century with his *thermodynamic structure of Reality*.

Professor Luis Miguel Varela says that in this thermodynamic structure of reality, reality seems to be nothing more than *a set of thermodynamic states*, particularly of hierarchically organized *dissipative structures*. No wonder that two great scientists like Albert Einstein and Arthur Eddington stated that *the second law of thermodynamics* is "the principal law of all science" (Einstein), and that it is the "supreme metaphysical law of the whole universe" (Eddington).⁸ For Prigogine,

> Equilibrium thermodynamics was the first response of physics to the problem of nature's complexity. This response was expressed in terms of the dissipation of energy, the forgetting of initial conditions, and evolution toward disorder.⁹

Henri Bergson (1859–1941), a spiritualist philosopher critical of positivism, but deeply knowledgeable of the new physical theories of his time, stated in his most important book, *Creative Evolution*:

> The second law of thermodynamics is *the most metaphysical of the laws of physics*, since it points out without interposed symbols, without artificial devices of measurement, the direction in which the world is going.¹⁰

It seems, then, that the principles of thermodynamics transcend the frontiers of science in which they were forged, to describe

---

⁷ Prigogine and Stengers, *La nueva alianza. Metamorfosis de la ciencia*, 41 and 151.

⁸ *Cf.* Jeremy Rifkin, *Entropy: A New World View* (New York: Viking Press, 1980), 78.

⁹ Prigogine and Stengers, *La nueva alianza. Metamorfosis de la ciencia*, 167.

¹⁰ Henri Henri Bergson, *La evolución creadora* (Madrid: Espasa-Calpe, 1973), 217; in English, *Creative Evolution* (Westport: Greenwood Press, 1944).

the physical foundations of all natural processes and give us something like a *universal grammar* of the structure of Reality: of physicochemical, biological, psychical, social, cultural, and economic systems.

The old *reductionist-mechanistic* and *pre-complex* approach to science (Descartes, Newton, Leibniz . . .) assumed that the world was a perfectly regulated machine: the *Newtonian machine of the world*. To understand this reality, it was sufficient to break down the systems it presented into smaller, more measurable values and then put them together again. In this way, physics could understand the workings of the universe by understanding the most elementary mechanics: *there is nothing in the whole that is not in the parts*. They believed the universe was static, that structures are established prior to any consideration and do not evolve with time; they are separable from the rest of the universe, and the laws governing them are the same as those governing the constituent parts; the net effects are the deterministic result of the adding causes. Newton (*Philosophiæ naturalis*, 1687) conceives the universe as a perfectly geared clock, and Leibniz (*Nova Methodus*, 1684) interprets it by means of a "differential calculus."[11]

But today we know that reality is not so simple. While there are *simple systems* that can be decomposed into a sum of parts where the whole is equal to the sum of the parts—as with gases—there are also *complex systems* that cannot be broken down into a sum of parts without the loss of essential properties—as with vertebrate animals—and where *the whole is more than the mere sum of the parts; which implies that there is something in the whole that is not in the parts*. On the other hand, classical thermodynamics itself began to consider that things were not as simple as the whole of classical physics and cosmology claimed. Inevitable heat transfer between objects makes equilibrium processes increasingly

---

[11] *Cf.* Giuseppe Gembillo, *Da Einstein a Mandelbrot. La filosofia degli scienziati contemporanei* (Florence: Le Lettere, 2009).

intricate, affecting both their states and phases. Furthermore, one thing is the *organized* energy, the work, and another is the energy *that is lost* with that work.

Therefore, we must state, as Prigogine did, that "Newtonian science constituted one synthesis, and thermodynamics constitutes another"; we need to "*abandon the Newtonian concept* that a scientific theory should be universal, deterministic, objective in inasmuch as it contains no reference to the observer, complete inasmuch as it attains a fundamental level of description that escapes the clutches of time." Classical science emphasized permanence, while modern science has emphasized *change* and *evolution*; we now know that "stability and simplicity are exceptions." Thus, "the omniscient demon is dead" and we are in *indeterminacy*:

> Since the appearance of quantum mechanics fifty years ago, the idea of the simplicity of the microscopic has become unsustainable. We discovered that irreversibility plays an essential role in nature and is at the origin of many *processes of spontaneous organization*. . . . The *omniscient demon is dead*. . . . We find ourselves in a *world that is indisputably random*, a world in which . . . *irreversibility and microscopic indeterminacy* are the rule.[12]

The Science of Complexity from Eddington and Heisenberg to Prigogine: From Chemistry, Physics, and Biology to Economics and Politics

It was the astrophysicist Arthur Eddington (1882–1944) who, in the 1930s, definitively questioned not only the mechanistic Cartesian world but also the most advanced nineteenth-century physics: *It is the thermodynamic structure of Reality itself that demands*

---

[12] Prigogine and Stengers, *La nueva alianza. Metamorfosis de la ciencia*, 38–39.

organization-complexity. Eddington introduced a fundamental concept in thermodynamics, "time's arrow":

> Let us draw an arrow arbitrarily. If as we follow the arrow we find more and more of the random element in the state of the world, then the arrow is pointing towards the future; if the random element decreases the arrow points towards the past. That is the only distinction known to physics. This follows at once if our fundamental contention is admitted that *the introduction of randomness is the only thing which cannot be undone*. I shall use the phrase *time's arrow* to express this one-way property of time which has no analogue in space.[13]

The *arrow of time* is the irreversible direction of time in the processes of energy transformation, due to the increase of entropy required by the second law of thermodynamics: the very thermodynamic structure of reality requires organization-complexity. *Complexity* is the characteristic of a system that *exists*, and therefore *dissipates energy* in a regimen of non-equilibrium. It destroys one equilibrium to create a new one and produces disorder to create a new order; the production of entropy is unavoidable. We know from everyday experience that we cannot burn the same piece of wood twice to generate heat and energy; it is necessary to go search for more, to spend energy, to go further and further. . . . In the face of a *reductionist* approach, *complexity* understands that the quality of the complex cannot be understood by resorting to the analysis of the parts; there are *emergent characteristics* of evolving systems in an uncertainty that increases with constant complexification.[14]

---

[13] *Cf.* Arthur Stanley Eddington, *The Nature of the Physical World* (New York: Macmillan, 1928); reference taken from Paul Davies, "La flecha del tiempo," *Investigación y Ciencia*, no. 314 (November 2002).

[14] *Cf.* Giuseppe Gembillo, "Fuoco! La chimica 'fonte' della complessità," *Complessità* IV, no. 1–2 (2009).

In 1927, Nobel laureate Werner Heisenberg (1901–1976) presented the *indeterminacy* or *uncertainty principle*: The values of certain physical quantities cannot be known simultaneously with arbitrary precision. Heisenberg thus establishes the limit beyond which the concepts of classical physics cannot be used. Certain pairs of physical variables (for example, the position and momentum of a given object) cannot be determined simultaneously and with arbitrary precision; the more certainty one seeks in determining the position of a particle, the less one knows momentum and, therefore, its velocity. For Heisenberg, this new approach to the heat problem of thermodynamics represented the transition from the old reductionist physics to the new complex physics.

Fundamental in this process were the pioneering discoveries of the Frenchmen Lavoisier (1743–1794) regarding oxygen (*Elements of Chemistry*) and Fourier (1768–1830) on the "propagation of heat in solid bodies."[15] Boltzmann and Planck completed these theories and experiments, and Prigogine brought them to their culmination. He expressly depicts the *birth of complexity*, true to the maxim of the ancients: *Ignis mutat res*; heat transforms things, it changes matter. His studies on the principle of conservation and *dissipation of energy*, the theory of *dissipative structures* and *fluctuations*, and *nonlinear thermodynamics*, were decisive.[16] Edgar Morin went so far as to write: "Cosmogenesis is a *thermogenesis*"; heat associates "energy and disorder, transformation and dispersion."[17]

The most important feature that defines emergent complexity comes from the entropic principle: the creation of order in one part of the world can only occur at the expense of destroying order in other parts of the world. Since energy is neither created nor destroyed, but only transformed (first law), from the

---

[15] *Cf.* ibid.
[16] *Cf.* Appendix III, "Dissipative Structures."
[17] *El Método*, Morin, *La Naturaleza de la Naturaleza*, I, 67.

thermodynamic point of view, *the construction of something can only occur with the destruction of another thing* (second law). This is indispensable for the evolution in which matter has been immersed since the very beginning of the cosmos. The slogan seems to be *Complicate life or die*; however, greater complexity implies greater problems than those it tries to solve. This is easy to understand in the evolution of our planet's ecosystem, especially through human actions. Evolution is a path of no return for everyone, and energy processes are the physical-material basis of all physicochemical, biological, and social processes.[18] The degree of complexity indicates the evolutionary level of a system, its *thermodynamic status*: how far it is from equilibrium and the entropy it produces in order to survive. The universe seems to have an intrinsic tendency toward dynamism, fluctuation, and complexification, which causes a continuous evolutionary organization.

It increasingly appears that the same laws govern all levels of Reality: chemistry, biology, ecology, economics, politics, and philosophy are nothing but continuations of physics. From here we arrive at the *network theory*, the *statistical theory of stable processes, statistical mechanics, the thermodynamics of irreversible processes, computer simulations*, etc.[19] Reality seems to be nothing more than a *set of thermodynamic states*. But are human creation and spirituality also reduced to this?

This allows us to approach complexity from the perspective of philosophy and spirituality.

---

[18] *Cf.* Guillermo Agudelo and José Guillermo Alcalá, "La complejidad," in *Evolución: Un nuevo paradigma*, ed. Máximo Sandín (Madrid: Instituto de Investigación sobre Evolución Humana, 2003).

[19] Brian Castellani and Lasse Gerrits recently created an impressive map of the complexity sciences: Brian Castellani and Lasse Gerrits, *Map of the Complexity Sciences* (York: Art & Science Factory, 2021). https://www.art-sciencefactory.com/complexity-map_feb09.html.

COMPLEXITY IN PHILOSOPHY: FROM THE PERENNIAL PHILOSOPHY TO CONTEMPORARY PHILOSOPHY

Although they may despise metaphysics, contemporary philosophers are eager to formulate its first principles.

ALFRED NORTH WHITEHEAD,
Process and Reality

Complexity Opens Up Avenues for Metaphysical Reflection

Complexity is perhaps the most essential characteristic of our present society.... We interact with ever more people, organisations, systems and objects. And as this network of interactions grows and spreads around the globe, the different economic, social, technological and ecological systems that we are part of become ever more interdependent.... Philosophy can help us to clarify the principles of thought that characterize complexity science and that distinguish it from its predecessors. Vice versa, complexity theory can help philosophy solve some of its perennial problems, such as the origins of mind, organisation or ethics.[20]

---

[20] Francis Heylighen, Paul Cilliers, and Carlos Gershenson, "Complexity and Philosophy," in *Complexity, Science and Society*, ed. Jan Bogg and Robert Geyer (London: CRC Press, 2007). These three authors have also published individually on complexity science. See, among others, Paul Cilliers, *Complexity and Postmodernism: Understanding Complex Systems* (London: Routledge, 1988); Carlos Gershenson, "How Can We Think the Complex?," in *Managing Organizational Complexity: Philosophy, Theory and Application*, ed. Kurt Richardson (Charlotte: Information Age, 2005); Francis Heylighen, "The Science of Self-Organization and Adaptivity," in *The Encyclopedia of Life Support Systems*, ed. Douglas Kiel (Oxford: Eolss Publishers, 2002); Francis Heylighen, "Cybernetics and Second Order Cybernetics," in *Encyclopedia of Physical Science & Technology*, ed. Robert Allen Meyers (San Diego: Academic Press, 2001).

Faced with the complexity of Reality that current science has shown us, some big questions arise: what is Reality *in reality*? Where does the domain of physics begin, and where does it end? Where does that of biology end? Where does that of consciousness, thought, culture, economics, and politics end? The main question may be how to describe ecology in this context, or rather an *ecosophy*, as Panikkar says.[21]

Reflection on the complexity of Reality involves a serious break with the conceptualization of modern metaphysics, sealed by the reductionist approach of Cartesianism. As we have just seen, the problems raised by complex systems are not only of a scientific speculative nature, but also confront us with some of the most pressing practical problems that human beings face today: ecology, information technology, markets, land use planning, etc. However, complexity also opens up avenues for metaphysical reflection, beyond the eternal modern and postmodern clichés of "overcoming metaphysics" or the "death of philosophy." It leads us to seek transversal readings and re-readings within the framework of current philosophy, for an intellectual project in line with today's issues. These avenues take us back to Spinoza (1632–1677) and then lead us to A. N. Whitehead's philosophy or Van R. Potter's bioethics; but also toward Henri Bergson—cited above—and Pierre Teilhard de Chardin, as well as Edgar Morin and Raimon Panikkar, to whom I will devote more space. The Jesuit Teilhard de Chardin will be discussed toward the end of the book. In this respect, a few words from the article I have just quoted ("Complexity and Philosophy") are significant: "The first challenges to reductionism and its denial of creative change appeared in the beginning of the twentieth century in the work of process philosophers, such as Bergson, Teilhard, Whitehead, and in particular Smuts, who coined the word *holism*, which he

---

[21] Raimon Panikkar, *Ecosofía. La sabiduría de la Tierra*, ed. Jordi Pigem (Barcelona: Fragmenta, 2021).

defined as the tendency of a whole to be greater than the sum of its parts."

Professor Keith Robinson writes about Whitehead in a complex article with the evocative title "Towards a Metaphysics of Complexity":

> Whitehead and Deleuze formulate a new kind of transcendental philosophy that allows us to think the self-actualizing structure *of the real*. Here is the key to *developing a realist ontology* that redefines the universal as individual, particular things, or actual entities produced by processes of individualization. These processes are driven by *intensive differences* (Deleuze) or *creative processes of concrescence and transition* (Whitehead), which, at certain critical or *balanced* thresholds, change mode and become self-organizing. . . .
>
> Whitehead and Deleuze give us something like *a nested ontology*, akin to the Chinese boxes that so fascinated Leibniz, and revealing what Whitehead would call the *connection of all the occasions* in which nature establishes relations with one another, and from which other entities arise spontaneously. This metaphysical picture correlates at a deep level with transformations in science, and especially the so-called *complex systems*.[22]

"To think *the structure of self-actualization of the real*" in order to develop a *realistic ontology* that knows how to relate the universal and the individual, the Whole and the part in the constant evolution of a dynamic Reality—this is the great challenge of a philosophy of complexity. This ontology that Robinson calls "nested"—like Chinese boxes or Russian dolls, where one contains a similar but smaller one, and within that another, even smaller, hinting at

---

[22] Keith Robinson, "Towards a Metaphysics of Complexity," *Interchange* 36, no. 1–2 (2005), 159; also Keith Robinson, ed., *Deleuze, Whitehead, Bergson: Rhizomatic Connections* (New York: Palgrave Macmillan, 2009).

infinity—represents *the connection of all Reality* in which each element contains the whole, which the science of complexity shows us with *complex systems*: nature establishes relationships of some entities with others, and from them other entities arise spontaneously.

Heylighen, Cilliers, and Gershenson, in the article cited above, believe that this philosophy of complexity is still in its infancy:

> *Uncertainty and subjectivity* should no longer be viewed negatively, as the loss of the absolute order of mechanicism, but positively, as factors of creativity, adaptation and evolution. Although several (mostly postmodern) philosophers have expressed similar sentiments, the complexity paradigm still needs to be assimilated by academic philosophy. This may not only help philosophy solve some of its perennial problems, but help complexity scientists become more aware of the foundations and implications of their models.[23]

Before approaching this contemporary philosophy of complexity, let us go much further back. The thought and wisdom of humanity have been answering the questions we asked at the beginning of this section for hundreds of years and through almost all cultures, from East to West, with something that for centuries has been called *philosophia perennis* in Latin, *perennial philosophy* in English.

The Millennial Challenge of "Perennial Philosophy": From Laozi, Shankara, Plotinus, Spinoza, and Meister Eckhart to Huxley, Jung, and Panikkar

Philosophia perennis has been describing the *seamless fabric* of Reality for centuries: Reality is One, total and undivided; in it, everything is interwoven. It is a very ancient concept, ranging from the *sanātana dharma* of Hinduism (the eternal truth

---

[23] Heylighen, Cilliers, and Gershenson, "Complexity and Philosophy" 131.

or order that governs the world) to the *eternal law* of the Holy Fathers of the Church (Clement of Alexandria, Origen, Gregory of Nyssa or Augustine of Hippo), to Muslim philosophy and that of the Renaissance (especially Pico della Mirandola). However, the Catholic Church transformed this concept of philosophia perennis into a synonym for Christian Scholasticism. Scholastic philosophy was seen as the culture of wisdom, and within it, Thomism as an expression of the *perennial* value of the doctrine of St. Thomas Aquinas. For this reason, it was recommended by popes and traditionalist Christian thinkers. The monk Agostino Steuco affirms this in his book *De perennis philosophia*, book X (1540), the first to use this term in modern times.

In a broader sense than that asserted by the Church, the idea was later taken up by Leibniz (1646–1716), who speaks of a *perennial philosophy* or *eternal philosophy* to designate the common and eternal philosophy that underlies the mystical currents of all religions; in particular, behind the mystical currents within them (*gnosis*).[24] Aldous Huxley later disseminated the concept in a work of the same title, in which he considers *perennial philosophy* to be "immemorial and universal."

Philosophia perennis is also a central concept of well-known contemporary authors from the East and West: the Hindus Ramakrishna (1834–1886) and his disciple Vivekananda, Coomaraswamy (1877–1947) and others; and the Westerners René Guénon (1886–1951), Alan Watts (1915–1973) and Ken Wilber, who speaks of a *neo-perennial philosophy*. Also, Raimon Panikkar (1918–2010), for whom "*perennis* does not indicate immobility, but regular appearance *per annos.*"[25]

---

[24] *Cf.* Charles B. Schmitt, "Perennial philosophy: From Agostino Steuco to Leibniz," *Journal of the History of Ideas* 27, no. 4 (1966).

[25] See Ken Wilber, *The Atman Project: A Transpersonal View of Human Development* (Wheaton, IL: Quest Books, 1996); Ken Wilber, *Los tres ojos del conocimiento* (Barcelona: Kairós, 1994); and Raimon Panikkar, *Paz e interculturalidad. Una reflexión filosófica* (Barcelona: Herder, 2002).

Aldous Huxley (1894–1963), English thinker and writer, dreamed of giving a new spiritual turn to the course of humanity. Despite his agnostic dalliances, he always kept the door to transcendence open and became deeply religious in full response to the vital yearning of his heart. He wrote novels, essays, short stories, poetry.... Particularly, books related to spiritual themes, such as *Eyeless in Gaza* (1936), which shows a growing interest in mysticism. He meets Swami Prabhavananda and the Vedanta Society of Los Angeles, and has a memorable meeting with Pope John XXIII. In one of his poems, he writes:

> Many are the doors of the spirit that lead
> Into the inmost shrine:
> And I count the gates of the temple divine,
> Since the god of the place is God indeed.
> And these are the gates that God decreed
> Should lead to his house: – kisses and wine,
> Cool depths of thought, youth without rest,
> And calm old age, prayer and desire,
> The lover's and mother's breast,
> The fire of sense and the poet's fire.
> But he that worships the gates alone,
> Forgetting the shrine beyond, shall see
> The great valves open suddenly,
> Revealing, not God's radiant throne,
> But the fires of wrath and agony.
> —*"Doors of the Temple"*

His readings and meditations led him to write a magnificent annotated anthology of mystical texts of all times: *The Perennial Philosophy*.[26] There we find philosophical and mystical texts of

---

[26] Aldous Huxley, *The Perennial Philosophy: An Interpretation of the Great Mystics, East and West* (New York: Harper Perennial Modern Classics, 2009).

masters from the East (*Bhagavad Gita* and the *Upanishads*, the *Dhammapada*, the *Diamond Sutra*, the *Lankavatara Sutra*, Laozi, Zhuangzi, Shankara, Rumi, Kabir, Ramakrishna, Tagore, Aurobindo, Coomaraswamy...) and the West (Dionysius the Areopagite, Augustine of Hippo, Bernard of Clairvaux, Meister Eckhart, Tauler, Ruysbroeck, Nicholas of Cusa, Böehme, the anonymous *Cloud of Unknowing*, *The Imitation of Christ* by Thomas à Kempis, John of the Cross, Teresa of Ávila, Catherine of Genoa, Catherine of Siena, Francis de Sales, Philip Neri, William Law, George Fox ...). Huxley maintains that the *perennial philosophy* is a search for truth that has some common elements in most cultures:

> a. The physical/phenomenal world—what we see with the empirical or *first eye*—*is not the only reality*; there is another non-physical reality that the senses cannot grasp, but to which the human intellect (*second eye*) and spirit (*third eye*) bear witness in its deepest essence.
>
> b. The human being reflects the nature of this reality, which is at the *core of the soul*.
>
> c. All human beings possess a capacity to see this reality, which they do not usually use, but this perception is their ultimate goal. The great religions seek to re-establish this *connection* between the *human soul* and the *ultimate and highest Reality*: the *God* of theistic religions and the *Absolute* of non-theistic religions.

What, then, is the *perennial philosophy*? A universal thought from East to West, from ancient civilizations to the present day. In the words of Huxley:

> The *perennial philosophy* is the metaphysic that recognizes a divine Reality substantial to the world of things and lives and minds; the psychology that finds in the soul something similar, or even identical with, divine Reality; the

ethics that places man's final end in the knowledge of the immanent and transcendent Ground of all being. . . . It is primarily concerned with the one, divine Reality substantial to the manifold world of things and lives and minds. But the nature of this one Reality is such that it *cannot be directly and immediately apprehended except by* those who have chosen to fulfil certain conditions, making themselves *loving, pure in heart, and poor in spirit*.[27]

Daily life offers no evidence that the human mind, *limited* as it is, possesses anything that resembles or is identical to the *unlimited* Divine Reality. However, when that mind enters meditation without words or concepts, the Divine Reality within it "becomes manifest, not only to the mind itself, but also, by its reflection in external behaviour, to other minds." And as Huxley explains: "Only by making physical experiments can we discover the intimate nature of matter. And only by making spiritual *experiments* can we discover the intimate nature of Spirit." Few people have met the conditions necessary for *direct* spiritual knowledge, but in every age, some have done so and have taught us that such immediate knowledge can be attained. These have been given the name of *saint, prophet, sage,* or *enlightened one.*" They knew what they were talking about. . . . For the Ultimate Reality cannot be directly and immediately apprehended except *by* those who made themselves *loving, pure in heart, and poor in spirit.*"[28] This *perennial philosophy* manifests a vision of the world as Unity in difference, a *non-dual* vision of Reality. It is neither monism nor dualism, but non-duality, which can see this unity with the difference that constitutes it.

The *perennial philosophy* in the East is present in the thought of Laozi (sixth century BC; the interrelationship of the *tao:*

---

[27] "Introducción," in Aldous Huxley, *La filosofía perenne* (Buenos Aires: Sudamericana, 1977), 7 and 9.

[28] *Ibid.*, 10–11.

"Oneness is simply the *direct and total truth*"), in the books of the Vedas ("In you dwells the world"), in Shankara's *advaita vedanta* (c. 788–820; the only reality is Brahman, the Absolute; the world is illusion, an apparent reality; the embodied soul is Brahman itself), and in the *visistadvaita* of Ramanuja (1017–1137) and the modern Hindu authors we have quoted, with rich Hindu, Buddhist and Taoist concepts. In Hinduism, in *advaita* (non-duality of Reality) and in the *rta principle* (interrelational harmony of the whole universe). In Buddhism, the *pratityasamutpada* (principle of relationship of all beings) stands out; two of its greatest masters are Nagarjuna (150–250) and Dogen (1200–1253), who says: "Great is the moon and wide is the radius of its rays of light, but it all fits in a drop of water." It is also present in Taoism—the interrelationship of the *tao*—and in tai chi, in which the relativity of everything shown is emphasized.

But this *philosophia perennis* is also found in Sufism—Islamic mysticism—with Al-Hallaj (857–922: "I became the One I love, and the One I love became me") or the Spanish Ibn'Arabi (1165–1240: "My heart is capable of accepting all forms"). The Iranian mystic Al-Jîlî (1366–1408) writes: "The perception of the Supreme Essence consists in coming to know, by way of divine intuition, that *you are He and that He is you, without there being any confusion between the two*, since the servant is servant and the Lord is Lord, and it is not a question of the servant becoming Lord, nor the Lord becoming servant" (*The Universal Man*). And in the Kabbalah—Jewish mysticism—with Ibn Gabirol (c. 1021-c. 1058) and the ten *sefirot* (enumerations or interconnected nodes of the Divinity expressed in the divine names that compose the "Tree of Life").

In the West, the vision of Reality as One and interrelated travels from Plotinus (204–270) to the pantheism of Jewish Spinoza (1632–1677). And, in the Christian tradition, we find it in the *unitive mysticism* of the Church Fathers, such as Clement of Alexandria (150–215; the first to use the word *mystikós*: "united with the Mystery"), Gregory of Nyssa (330–394) or Pseudo Dionysius Areopagite (6th century) who says that the world is a theophany and that "to be divinized is to let God be born in us"). Centuries later, we find it in Cistercian mysticism, from Bernard of Clairvaux (1090-1153, who sought to show the way of spiritual union with God through Christ in love) and his brother, the Cistercian and friend William of Saint-Thierry (1085–1148: "To will what God wills is to be like God . . . , to become what He is," *Golden Letter*) to Gertrude of Helfta (1256–1302) and her friend the Beguine mystic Mechthild of Magdeburg (1207–1282: "God awaits the soul beyond the human . . . and says to her: I will make you part of my nature; nothing at all will subsist between me and you," *The Shining Light of the Divine*), or the also Beguine Hadewijch of Antwerp (c. 1260).

In Franciscan mysticism, Bonaventure (1217–1274) proposes a compression of Reality from an integrating scheme of the different realities and speaks of recovering the harmony lost in paradise in order to attain a union and identification with God (*Itinerarium mentis in Deum*). The Dominican Meister Eckhart (1260-1328), the Christian mystic who best expressed the Unity and non-duality of Reality in texts such as the famous sermon "God and I are one"; Nicholas of Cusa (1401–1460), with his "learned ignorance" ("God contains all things, and is *omnia complicans*. . . . The world is a theophany, a *contractum maximum* of the divine being," *De docta ignorantia*); the German Lutheran mystic and poet Angelus Silesius (1624–1677), whose famous verses describe this union of everything ("When man is subtracted from multiplicity and returns to God, he attains unity"). And in recent times, Simone Weil (1909–1943: "Harmony is the unity of opposites") or Thomas Merton (1915–1968). For Christian mysticism, Unity resonates in the depths of Reality: a single truth, where *everything is part of the One*.

Finally, the vision of Reality as One and interrelated is in the contemporary philosophy and psychology of Jung ("He who looks outward, dreams, and he who looks inward, awakens"), William James, Raimon Panikkar, etc., and in the physics of Einstein, Eddington, Schrödinger, Heisenberg, etc.; or in the philosophy of Ken Wilber, for whom "seamless" does not mean without distinctive features; it does not mean that things and events do not exist, but that they subsist in a kind of balanced totality, . . . a *seamless totality*."[29] The physicist Fritjof Capra penned the words we read at the start of this book and which we expand on here:

> When I discovered the parallels between the worldviews of physicists and mystics… I had the strong feeling that I was merely uncovering something that was quite obvious and would be common knowledge in the future…
>
> The reluctance of modern scientists to accept the profound similarities between their concepts and those of mystics is not surprising… Fortunately, this attitude is now changing.
>
> The profound harmony between these concepts, as expressed in systems language, and the corresponding ideas in Eastern mysticism, is impressive evidence for my claim that the philosophy of mystical traditions, also known as the "perennial philosophy," provide the most consistent philosophical background to our modern scientific theories.[30]

---

[29] Ken Wilber, *Up from Eden: A Transpersonal View of Human Evolution* (Wheaton, IL: Quest Books, 2007) and Ken Wilber, *The Eye of Spirit: An Integral Vision for a World Gone Slightly Mad* (Boulder: Shambhala, 2001), for example. Also relevant here is Wilber, *Quantum Questions: Mystical Writings of the World's Great Physicists*, which contains texts by Einstein, Planck, Heisenberg, Schrödinger, Jeans, Pauli and Eddington.

[30] Capra, *El tao de la física*, 5. See also Fritjof Capra, *Sabiduría insólita* (Barcelona: Kairós, 2003).

Complexity in Contemporary Philosophy: Husserl, Zubiri, Amor Ruibal, Van Rensselaer Potter, and Alfred North Whitehead

As we have already said, the most important features that define *complexity* are the *global relational perspective* and the *entropic principle*; the *creation of order* in one part of the world occurs at the expense of the *destruction of order* in other parts of the world. This is vital for understanding the evolution in which matter has been immersed since the very beginning of the cosmos: *complicate life or die*. The universe seems to have an intrinsic tendency toward dynamism, fluctuation, and *complexification*. This is the basis of completeness. Italian professor Giuseppe Gembillo, editor of the journal *Complessità*, writes in one of his books:

> The philosophy of complexity is a rational and historical response to the theoretical reductionism of classical science and its philosophy. . . . Complexity has been considered the true symbol of the fragility of philosophical dialogue.[31]

He points out eight ways of meeting with complexity and a "meeting point of the paths: scientificity and knowledge today." We highlight four of them:

First. *From mechanism to organism*.[32] In contrast to the mechanistic reductionism of Descartes and Newton, everything that exists is articulated in organisms/systems; nothing exists in isolation. The pieces are "intertwined" and constitute an organized system. The system is and creates events. Each system, in its totality, is historical (*external historicity*); it is the human being who creates mathematics, physics, and philosophy. And each system is, internally, a connection-interaction of parts (*internal historicity*).

---

[31] Giuseppe Gembillo, *Filosofía de la complejidad* (Buenos Aires: Editora Latinoamericana, 2018), 13.

[32] *Cf. ibid.* 29–66.

Second. *From structure to history*.[33] Every system-organism is a *dissipative structure* because it is formed by self-organization from a state of disorder. Once formed, it consumes energy by dissipating it and contributing to the development of the entropy of the environment: there is no unilateral dependence, but a mutually conditioning interaction. This kind of unpredictable interaction establishes and guarantees the diversity that characterizes the real world. Prigogine gave a new meaning to the terms *stability* and *change*: everything has an intrinsic and specific structural stability, but is limited in time and subject to change. Everything that exists is complex and historical.

Third. *From object/subject-substance to event-subject*.[34] Turning from *reductionism to complexity* has radically changed the idea of the *object to know* and the *knowing subject*. Descartes maintained the Aristotelian intellect-sense contraposition: subject and object are "substantial" entities. The knowing subject (*res cogitans*) is a passive recorder of "objective" events. But Einstein pointed out that the scientific observer is not *outside* the universe. Heisenberg said that the experimenter is *a subject who affects the* observed *object*, changing the state prior to the observation. In life, we are both actors and spectators. The *object-substance* does not exist; Reality is *intersubjective*: no individual subject can claim to elevate their vision to a universal standard. And no object imposes itself by its clarity and evidence. *Everything that exists* is not simply situated in an external space, but *interacts with its environment* and is structured temporally.

Fourth. *From certainty to uncertainty*.[35] The classical idea that suffered the most radical defeat is that of "certainty." In a world in which everything changes and the pretension of rigorous predictability is gone, the "end of certainties" has become the

---

[33] *Cf. ibid.* 67–82.
[34] *Cf. ibid.* 83–98.
[35] *Cf. ibid.* 99–106.

only certainty (Prigogine). Heisenberg's *relations of uncertainty* and Prigogine's *historicization of nature* have closed the path. Everything that happens is unpredictable, the result of many causes. There are no certain "causes": knowledge and action are related.

Reflection on the complexity of Reality entails a serious break with the Cartesian reductionist approach not only of science, but also of modern metaphysics. The problems that complex systems raise are not only of a speculative scientific nature, but—as we have seen—confront us with some of the most pressing practical problems facing human beings today. And for years, complexity has been affecting the very conception of bioethics.

In contemporary philosophy, we can say that the father of phenomenology, Edmund Husserl (1850–1938)—who, among others, would influence Heidegger, Sartre, Ricœur, Max Scheler, Ortega y Gasset or Zubiri—speaks of the *intimate relationship of all the elements of Reality* as a "transcendental correlationism," starting from a "constituent consciousness." He speaks of the communion of bodies and spirits, of the intimate relationship between the cosmos, consciousness, and God himself.[36]

Xavier Zubiri (1898–1983) speaks of the relationship between the cosmos, consciousness, and the Divinity in *Nature, History, God*: Reality establishes my personal being from its intrinsic *fundamentality* by "taking hold of me"; this taking hold links us to the power of the real with *reconnection*.[37] I will say more about Raimon Panikkar's thought in this regard later on, but we cannot forget the contribution of the great Galician-Spanish thinker Ángel Amor Ruibal. Zubiri, Panikkar, and Amor Ruibal have something in common: a conception of Reality marked by *relation*, which reaches its culmination in the Catalan-Hindu thinker: the *ontological relativity* and *correlationism* of Amor Ruibal,

---

[36] *Cf.* Edmund Husserl, *Formal and Transcendental Logic: Essay on a Critique of Logical Reason* (Dordrecht: Springer Dordrecht, 1969).

[37] *Cf.* Xavier Zubiri, *Nature, History, God* (Lanham, MD: University Press of America, 1981).

the *respectivity* of Zubiri, and the *radical relativity/cosmotheandric perspective* of Raimon Panikkar.[38]

Amor Ruibal (1869–1930) speaks of the relationship between the universe, the human being and God from his concept of *ontological correlationism*: a profound sense of mutual communion and intimate correlation that links the beings of the universe with God; this correlation makes beings a whole that constitutes them and by which they are constituted. For him, the category of *relation/correlation* characterizes all reality. Knowledge itself is only a "peculiar mode of interrelation."[39] His central thesis lies in the theory of *universal relativity*, *universal correlationism* or *ontological correlationism*, which he also calls "universal synthetism": "A profound sense of mutual communion, of intimate correlation that links together, constitutively and dynamically, the beings of the universe, making of them a whole in a certain organic way, which they constitute and by which they are constituted."[40] The world appears as an organic system of elements in relation. This is how Amor Ruibal expresses it in his most important work:

> The works of Creation are pages of an immense book, where one adds to the others to give the totality of their meaning. . . . It is always the whole that gives formal being and intelligibility to the partial elements, which are there-

---

[38] *Cf.* Victorino Pérez Prieto, "Raimon Panikkar, Xabier Zubiri y Amor Ruibal. Un pensamiento marcado por la relación: del "correlacionismo ontológico" y la "respectividad" a la "perspectiva cosmoteándrica"," *Ilu. Revista de Ciencias de las Religiones*, no. 23 (October 2018); Victorino Pérez Prieto, "Raimon Panikkar y Xavier Zubiri en diálogo: realidad cosmoteándrica y respectividad," in *Panikkar hoy*, ed. Ignasi Moreta (Barcelona: Fragmenta, 2022).

[39] Andrés Torres Queiruga, "Amor Ruibal, pensador no cambio de século," in *O pensamento luso-galaico-brasileiro (1850–2000)* (Lisbon: Imprensa Nacional-Casa da Moeda, 2009), 280. *Cf.* also Xosé Luis Barreiro, *Mundo, hombre y conocimiento en Amor Ruibal* (Santiago de Compostela: Pico Sacro, 1978).

[40] Andrés Torres Queiruga, "Amor Ruibal," in *Dicionario enciclopedia do pensamento galego* (Vigo: Consello da Cultura Galega, 2008), 23.

fore related to it, as real and intrinsically as each being is intrinsic and real by virtue of the factors of which it consists. And inasmuch as each isolated being is only a relative whole which is organized with others, and on which others in turn depend, the same principle of relativity is then reproduced on the singular entities with respect to higher entities, and from which the whole in turn pours a new intelligibility upon the lower units.[41]

The "Bioethics" of Van Rensselaer Potter

Beyond the perspective of clinical or medical bioethics—whose main exponent today is the Spanish philosopher Diego Gracia—there is a *global bioethics* as a mode of thought and action for our era that forces us to confront the essential problems of life and death. This was developed by the American biochemist and oncologist Van Rensselaer Potter (1911–2001) and is a line of thought clearly and explicitly situated in the perspective of *complexity*. A great connoisseur of Potter's work writes:

> *Bioethics* is an activity of thought that emerges amid the crises of classical science and presents itself from many scientific and humanist spaces as an opportunity to contemplate together what we have so far contemplated in isolation; as the extraordinary possibility of reforming thought and building a social fabric not only from the anthropological, but also and at the same time from the biological and cosmological sphere. . . . We are in the best conditions to integrate what physics, biology, sociology, and philosophy have tried to say separately about the human being while

---

[41] Angel Amor Ruibal, *Los problemas fundamentales de la filosofía y el dogma*, 9 vols., vol. 7 (Santiago de Compostela: Seminario Conciliar, 1933), 212–213. New ed. incompl., 1995–1999, 5 vols.

discounting what is fundamental: the complexity that constitutes us.[42]

This is the perspective of the global and political bioethics coined by Van R. Potter, which aligns with the change in mentality of Morin's *complex thinking*. In 1962, Potter delivered the lecture "Bridge to the Future: The Concept of Human Progress," of which he himself says years later:

> What interested me then was questioning the progress towards which all the materialistic advances of science and technology were leading Western culture. In my view, it became the mission of bioethics: an attempt to answer the question: what kind of future is ahead of us? Do we have a choice? *Bioethics* became a vision that called for a discipline guiding humanity along the *bridge to the future*.[43]

Bioethically situated reflection on the planet's future and on the quality of life of the human species must be a reflection situated in every part of the planet, particularly amid the destructive mechanisms of neoliberal globalization. As Van Potter said, this *global bioethics* will be the name of a new discipline that will change knowledge and thought. Bioethics will have to be seen as a bioethical approach to the continuous search for wisdom, which I have defined as the knowledge of *how to use knowledge for human survival* and for the betterment of the human condition. I ask you to think of bioethics as a new scientific ethic that combines humility, responsibility and competence, is

---

[42] Sergio Néstor Osorio, *Bioética y pensamiento complejo, un puente en construcción* (Bogotá: Universidad Nueva Granada, 2008), 35.

[43] Van Rensselaer Potter, *Bioética puente, bioética global y bioética profunda*, Cuadernos del Programa Regional de Bioética (Bogotá: Organização Panamericana de la Salud, 1998), 25. *Cf.* Van Rensselaer Potter, *Bioethics: Bridge to the Future* (Saddle River, NJ: Prentice-Hall, 1971).

interdisciplinary and intercultural, and that intensifies the sense of humanity.[44]

As we shall see, this "knowledge of how to use knowledge for human survival" intimately unites Van R. Potter and Morin. This new knowledge is what he considers the foundation of bioethics, a new kind of interdisciplinary life science that integrates biology, human competence in accompanying human values and environmental problems, together with the improvement of the quality of life of human beings. Traditional ethics is about the interactions of people with each other; this bioethics is about the interaction between people and biological systems. Thus, says Potter, bioethics is essential for healthy decision-making and sound policy making. "We need an ethics of the Earth," says Potter, "an ethics of wildlife, an ethics of population, etc."[45] This is not only an applied ethics, but a true science of life, that affects "the entire universe and future generations," says Potter in the same place; an ethics with a truly holistic approach, related to "*deep ecology*."

In addition to this global and complex bioethics, the science of complexity opens up avenues for metaphysical reflection. The new perspectives of science lead us to seek readings and re-readings within the framework of current philosophy for an intellectual project in consonance with the demands of our time. As we have said, these paths take us back to Spinoza, jumping forward to Whitehead, Morin, and Panikkar.

The "Process Philosophy" of Alfred North Whitehead

Alfred North Whitehead (1861–1947) was an English mathematician and philosopher, a colleague of Bertrand Russell, creator

---

[44] Van Rensselaer Potter, *Global Bioethics, Building on the Leopol Legacy* (Michigan: Michigan State University Press, 1988).

[45] Potter, *Bioethics: Bridge to the Future*, 78.

of *process philosophy*. His philosophy later found application in a wide variety of disciplines: ecology, biology, physics, education, economics, psychology, and even theology.[46] This last was precisely the field in which I first encountered him. Henri Bergson went so far as to say that Whitehead was "the best philosopher writing in English."

For Whitehead, physics and metaphysics complement each other as two angles or ways of looking at the same Reality. His conception of Reality is organic/organizational: every fact is an organism, a "happening" or "*event*." His cosmology overcomes the old idea of substance and substantialist monism with a dynamic element and a perpetual dynamism. Moreover, his metaphysics seeks to surpass all the classical dualisms of metaphysics.[47] With a certain resemblance to what we will see later in Panikkar's *cosmotheandric perspective*, Whitehead establishes three intimately related orders of the real: physical energy, human experience, and divine experience; the latter is "conceived as an indefinite progress" and a "priority of God over existence."[48]

Whitehead argued that Reality consisted of *processes* rather than material objects, and that processes are best defined by their *relationships* to other processes. For Whitehead, scientists and philosophers always rely on assumptions about the way the universe operates, but these assumptions are not easy to perceive precisely because they are never challenged or questioned; thus, Whitehead questioned Western philosophy's assumptions about how the universe works. He says that even though they despise metaphysics, contemporary philosophers "long to formulate the

---

[46] *Cf.* Xavier Morales, *La relativité de Dieu. La contribution de la «Process Theology» à la théologie trinitaire* (Paris: CERF, 2017).

[47] *Cf.* entry in Josep Ferrater Mora, *Diccionario de filosofía* (Barcelona: Ariel-RBA, 2005), 3755–3756, with extensive bibliography on 3756–3758.

[48] *Ibid.*, 3756, second column.

first principles of metaphysics."⁴⁹ We must continually reimagine the basic assumptions that underpin our understanding of the universe if philosophy and science are to progress. For this reason, Whitehead regarded metaphysical investigations as essential for generating quality scientific and philosophical knowledge.⁵⁰ He pointed to the limits of language as one of the main culprits in maintaining a materialistic way of thinking, but acknowledged that it may be difficult to change it.

Whitehead aims to respond to Kant's philosophy, making an effort to *overcome the seemingly irreconcilable dualisms* of Kantian philosophy. He speaks of the "seamless fabric" of Reality, as opposed to the divisions, and as an offer of a *unitary description of the nature of things*. Reality consists of *processes* rather than independently existing *objects*; relations are not secondary, but *shape* the object. Processes are best defined by their *relationships* to other processes. Reality is a series of dynamic processes, never static and always forming more things; all objects change and evolve.

Even God himself enters into that relational Reality. Whitehead sees God and the world as complementary; the world's entities are fluid and changeable, longing for a permanence that only God can give. God Himself is in permanent change; He gives permanence to creatures, while they give Him material reality and change.

> It is as true to say that God is permanent and the World fluent, as that the World is permanent and God is fluent....

---

[49] Alfred North Whitehead, *Proceso y realidad* (Buenos Aires: Losada, 1956), 4. The English original, *Process and Reality,* was published in 1929. When the book appeared, someone said: "Not many people will read Whitehead's most recent book in this generation; in fact, not many people will read it regardless of generation. But its influence will radiate through the concentric circles of popularization until the commonest man will think and act in accordance with its ideas"; *cf.* Henry Nelson Wieman, "A Philosophy of Religion," *The Journal of Religion* 10, no. 1 (1930). In time, the book came to be regarded as the most impressive metaphysical text of the twentieth century.

[50] Whitehead, *Proceso y realidad*, 11.

> It is as true to say that the World is immanent in
> God, as that God is immanent in the World.
> It is as true to say that God transcends the
> World, as that the World transcends God. . . .
> What is done in the world is transformed
> into a reality in heaven, and the reality
> in heaven passes back into the world. . . .
> In this sense, God is the great companion—
> the fellow-sufferer who understands.[51]

Whitehead's originality and importance as a philosopher of the twentieth century lie in his effort to conceive of the nature of Reality independently of any *first principle*, identity, or metaphysical cause. This brings Whitehead closer to Nietzsche and Heidegger, but also to Bergson, to Bertrand Russell (who was a student and later a close collaborator of his) and, above all, to Deleuze, so different from him in other respects. The distinguishing feature of this tradition is "the effort to consider the conditions of *true experience* in terms of *self-organizing* or self-actualizing nature."[52] The main concepts of Whitehead's thinking are *creativity*, *process,* and *event.* His *search for harmony* ("harmony of harmony") and overcoming duality bring him closer to Morin and Panikkar.

COMPLEXITY AND INTERRELATEDNESS OF THE WHOLE OF REALITY IN EDGAR MORIN AND RAIMON PANIKKAR

Edgar Morin: Complexity and Aspiration to Totality

> *I recognized myself in the aspiration to totality . . . to connect dispersed truths and antagonistic truths. . . . Complex thinking is the exercise of a dialogue between the simple and the complex.*
>
> EDGAR MORIN, *Mes démons*

---

[51] *Ibid.*, 467 and 470–471.
[52] Robinson, "Towards a Metaphysics of Complexity" 162.

> *What beauty, what harmony, what profound unity, what complementarity and solidarity among the living! Yet life is gift and burden, it is marvelous and terrible. . . . So is the universe.*
>
> EDGAR MORIN, *Leçons d'un siècle de vie*

A "Planetary Thinker"

The physical theory of complexity and its global implications are the basis of the *complex thought* of the French thinker Edgar Morin (Paris, 1921), the "founding father" of complex thought and a true "planetary thinker," as Alain Touraine, one of today's most prestigious sociologists, described him. This thought is expressed above all in his seminal work *The Method*, but also in other books that we will cite here.

Morin—sociologist, scientist, thinker, and media figure—was a great reader from childhood, and had a strong lifelong critical mentality. From a young age, he was linked to Popular Front socialism and the Spanish Republican government; he actively participated in the French Resistance against Nazism during the Spanish Civil War, joining the French Communist Party in 1941. However, his relationship with the party deteriorated due to his critical positions, and he was expelled in 1952 following an article published in *France Observateur*. That same year he was admitted to the Centre National de la Recherche Scientifique-CNRS (National Center for Scientific Research), where he began his scientific and philosophical work based on the theses of *transdisciplinarity*, cybernetics, systems theory, and information theory. Despite his clashes with other academics, this work led him to develop the philosophy that made him known throughout the world, receiving numerous international awards: the French Legion d'Honneur, the Medal of the Italian Chamber of Deputies, the Orden del Mérito of the Spanish Government, the Gran Cruz da Orde de Santiago de la Espada of Portugal . . . as well as honorary doctorates from thirty-eight universities around the world. At the same time, he was well received by the youth of the 1960s and beyond; during the French student revolt of May 1968, he wrote articles for *Le Monde* in which he pondered the meaning and sense of that event.[53] Among his extensive oeuvre of more than fifty works, these titles deserve special mention:

First, the six volumes of *The Method. Towards a Study of Humankind* (1977–2004).[54] Other significant titles stand out, some of them in English: *L'esprit du temps* (1962); *Le paradigme perdu. La nature humaine* (1973); *Pour sortir du xxè siècle* (1981); *Science with Consciousness* (1982); *Introduction à la pensée complexe* (1990); *Mes démons* (1994); *La complexité humaine* (1994); *Homeland Earth: A Manifesto for the New Millennium* (1999); *Seven Complex Lessons in Education for the Future* (1999); *Civilisation et barbarie* (2005); *On Complexity (Advances in Systems Theory, Complexity, and the Human Sciences)* **(2008)**; *La voie. Pour l'avenir de l'humanite* (2011); *Penser global. L'humain et son univers* (2015); *The Challenge of Complexity: Essays by Edgar Morin* (2020); and finally *Leçons d'un siècle de vie* (2021), written on his hundredth birthday.

Sparsa Colligo, Dialogic and Transdisciplinarity

In one of his most personal books (*My Demons*), Morin magnificently describes the insights—the inner spirit (*daimon*, in Greek) that moved him—developed throughout an extensive life trajectory: aspiration to totality, complex and *dialogical* thinking.

> I recognized myself in the aspiration to totality . . . to connect dispersed truths and antagonistic truths. . . .

---

[53] *Cf.* Morin, Official International Web Site: https://edgarmorinmultiversidad.org/index.php/biografia-edgar-morin.html.

[54] Edgar Morin, *El método* (Madrid: Cátedra, 1981–2006), Vol. I-VI; Edgar Morin, *The Method: Towards a Study of Humankind* (New York: Peter Lang, 1992).

> *Complex thought* has the task, not of substituting the certain for the uncertain, the separable for the inseparable . . . but of effecting a *cognitive dialogic* between the certain and the uncertain, the separable and the inseparable, the logical and the meta-logica. . . . It is the exercise of an incessant dialogue between the simple and the complex.[55]

"Aspiration to totality" and "connecting truths": these are two fundamental keys to complex thought, which is the opposite of fragmentary thought: a *relational thinking*, which seeks to think Reality as a Whole; and therefore, a thinking that is not only interdisciplinary, but *transdisciplinary*. "We must recompose the whole," says the French anthropologist Marcel Mauss, quoted by Morin himself.[56] In the search for Reality as an interrelated whole, Morin's thought seeks the connection of dissimilar and apparently antagonistic truths. Thus, the other key to Edgar Morin is *the dialogic*: a *cognitive dialogic* between the certain and the uncertain, between the logical and the meta-logical, in the exercise of an *incessant dialogic*. The *dialogic* is the *dialogos*, the thought (*logos*) that walks (*dia*).

There is a Latin adage that describes this insight of Morin's: *sparsa colligo* (to link/unite the dispersed):

> My uniqueness lies in having wanted to link the diverse, *sparsa colligo*, and to have built my work on this principle. . . . My rejection of isolated truths gave rise to the principles of a *complex thought*, which relates what, from

---

[55] Edgar Morin, *Mis demonios* (Barcelona: Kairós, 1995), 203 and 213.
[56] Marcel Mauss is an anthropologist and sociologist considered one of the "fathers of French ethnology." The quotation is taken from Edgar Morin, *Les sept savoirs nécessaires pour une éducation du futur* (Paris: UNESCO, 1999); Edgar Morin, *Seven Complex Lessons in Education for the Future* (Paris: UNESCO, 1999).

diverse and multiple origins, forms a unique and inseparable fabric: *complexus*.[57]

In a critique of research and specialized, partialized and reduced contemporary knowledge, as opposed to the global humanist conception, Morin sees the need to know the world as it is: *an inseparable whole*. In Volume I of *The Method* ("The Nature of Nature"), he writes:

> Every neophyte who embarks on Research sees how the greatest renunciation of knowledge is imposed on him. He is convinced that it is impossible to construct a vision of man and the world. . . . He is integrated into a specialized team. . . . Specialist from now on, the researcher is offered the exclusive possession of *a fragment of the puzzle*, whose global vision must escape each and every one.[58]

For Morin, the choice is not between particular, precise, limited knowledge and the abstract general idea or unitary theory, which he rejects, but between *reductionism* and the *search for the whole* with a method "that can articulate what is known and reunite what is disunited." Morin is well aware of Adorno's well-known statement that "totality is non-truth"; but he interprets it in the sense that "Any system that pretends to close the world in its logic is an insane rationalization." Therefore, he proposes approaching the knowledge of Reality in a multidisciplinary and multi-referenced way for the construction of thought; approaching phenomena as an organic totality in a "relationship of *interdependence*," and breaking the "false clarities," in which "*uncertainty* becomes a viaticum" for the journey; because, as

---

[57] Morin, *Mis demonios*, 273.
[58] Morin, *El método*, Vol. I, 25.

Whitehead said, the same science "is even more changeable than theology."[59]

The French thinker developed a philosophical and scientific research marked by his thesis of *transdisciplinarity*. Morin not only seeks a way of thinking in which interdisciplinary exchanges between the physical, biological, and human sciences are embedded, but which favors and develops a truly transdisciplinary way of thinking. "We need to relearn how to learn," he repeats again and again; we need "a knowledge of knowledge, a theory of theory, a science of science." As Spanish poet Antonio Machado said in some well-known verses dear to Morin's heart: "Traveler, there is no path, but the path is made by walking." Or in the words of another of the greatest Spanish poets and mystics, St. John of the Cross, whom Morin himself quotes at the beginning of Volume I of *The Method*: "To reach the point you do not know, you must take the path you do not know."[60] In fact, the word *method* originally meant "to walk," to create the path as you walk in a constant search. All knowledge must be aware of its *provisionality*, of its burden of *uncertainty*. For this reason, complex thought must bring together elements from the sciences, philosophy, history, myths, religious symbols. . . . Edgar Morin constructs a method that attempts to meet the challenge of complexity. As he writes in one of his numerous works on *the method*,

> We need to address first the so-called *epistemological* point, which is where the critical examination of scientific

---

[59] *Ibid.*, 28, 29, 33; quoted in Whitehead, *Proceso y realidad*, 30.

[60] The literal text of St. John of the Cross says: "To come to what you do not know, you must go where you do not know." It belongs to a preparatory text for his work *Ascent of Mount Carmel*; a sketch in the form of a complex drawing that the author called "The Mount of Perfection." *Cf.* John of the Cross, *Vida y obras completas* (Madrid: Biblioteca de Autores Cristianos, 1973), 435 ; in English, *The Collected Works of St. John of the Cross* (Washington, DC: ICS Publications, 1991).

> theories takes place from the point of view of their value, their relevance, their coherence. This implies, of course, that experience (observation, experimentation, empirical control) is not enough to give validity to a theory; this is not a mere reflection of the data, but an organizing interpretation that integrates the data. This organizing interpretation of knowledge . . . must be examined as such from an obviously superior point of view. Superior means that epistemology must be a knowledge of knowledge, a theory of theory, a science of science. . . . Epistemology will here be relativized, open, complexified, and on this occasion between enclosing [*bouclante*] and open, knowledge and knowledge of knowledge. . . .
>
> Epistemology corresponds to a change of order in discourse. . . . It must be both a self-deepening of knowledge and a meta-surpassing of discourse.[61]

In one of his last interviews—in "coronavirus times"—Morin said, on the verge of turning one hundred years old:

> My philosophy is that life is a voyage in an ocean of uncertainties, and we can revitalize ourselves on some islets and archipelagos of certainties. We know this if we follow the lesson given to us by events; it is a flashing revelation. Everything is related! This is the philosophy of complexity.
>
> We see that from a small virus came an economic crisis, that this economic crisis is linked to the climate crisis. We see that our small person, our homes, our nation, Europe, everything is related. All this that seems separate to the spirits that catalog everything is in fact linked, and we

---

[61] Edgar Morin, "Il metodo del metodo," *Complessità* IV, no. 1–2 (2009), 6–7.

have a community of destiny that is obvious and must be seen.⁶²

In his latest book, he returns to his convictions from his centennial life experience, convinced that "everyone has a complex identity, that is to say, at once one and plural"⁶³; his is a "poly-identity," as French, Spanish, Italian, European, universal . . . and "above all humanist." His has been a life marked by "the unforeseen and the uncertain," which is the whole reality ("a chaosmos") with which he built his happiness, his harmony, between successes and mistakes:

> I am a Whole for me, being almost nothing for the Whole. I am one human being among eight billion, I am a singular individual and an individual different and similar to others. I am the product of improbable, random, ambivalent, surprising, unexpected events and encounters. And at the same time, I am me, a concrete individual, endowed with a hypercomplex self-organizing machine. . . . The brain gives each one the spirit and the soul, invisible to the neuroscientist, but emerging in each human being in their relationship with the other and with the world.⁶⁴

Edgar Morin constructs a method that attempts to rise to the challenge of complexity, convinced that we are in the prehistory

---

⁶² *Le monde d'Elodie*: "Edgar Morin: Tout ce qui semblait séparé est relié et nous avons une communauté de destinée," accessed on 04–05- 2020, https://www.francetvinfo.fr/replay-radio/le-monde-d-elodie/le-monde-d-elodie-edgar-morin-tout-ce-qui-semblait- separe-est-lie-et-nous-avons-une-communaute-de-destin_392qq61.html?-fbclid=IwAR0BfrAiGGnbDkqrVoRn6Ujupk7jP6xXEUZebXmdOI-dx- CdMsBb7vjueKoA-xtor=CS.

⁶³ Edgar Morin, *Leçons d'un siècle de vie* (Paris: Denöel, 2021), 9.

⁶⁴ *Ibid.*, 28.

Science and the Philosophy of Complexity

of the human spirit and that *only complex thought will allow us to civilize our knowledge*. From this, Morin draws the *three principles* on which he builds the paradigm of complexity, and from them he proposes seven "knowledges" for the education of the future. He is convinced that "human complexity leads to well-being" (*Leçons d'un siècle de vie*).

The Three Principles of the Complexity Paradigm

> We must understand that the revolution is played out today *not so much on the terrain of* good or truly opposed *ideas* in a life and death struggle against bad or false ideas, *but on the terrain of the complexity of the way ideas are organized.* The exit from the "planetary Iron Age" and the "prehistory of the human spirit" requires us to *think in a radically complex way*.[65]

We are in the prehistory of the human spirit, and "only complex thinking will allow us to civilize our knowledge," says Morin. The French thinker elaborated three principles to analyze Reality according *to the paradigm of complexity* and to give an answer to it.

1. *Principle of organizational recursion*

A *recursive* process, as opposed to a whirlpool, is one in which products and effects are both causes and producers of what produces them. The process of human reproduction is a continuum, in which we are reproduced and at the same time reproduce. This idea applies to society: it is produced by interactions between individuals, but once produced, it acts on individuals and reproduces them. This shows us a *recursive organization*, which breaks with the simple idea of cause-effect, product-producer, because everything produced is reintegrated into that which produced

---

[65] Morin, *El método*, Vol. IV, 25.

it in a cyclical process. The *principle of organizational recursion* is a self-constitutive model, which allows us to better understand the complex functioning of our current societies.

2. *Hologrammatic principle*

Like the hologram (from *holon*, all), which contains almost all the information of what is represented, the *hologrammatic principle* seeks to overcome the reductionism centered on the parts that make up the whole, to reach a vision of the whole, without being reduced to a holism that only sees that whole. Not only *is the part in the whole*, but *the whole is in each of its parts*. For example, in each cell is the totality of the genetic information of an organism; the same is true in the universe. Morin quotes Herbert A. Simon, who said that the human mind is a GPS[66]: the development of the general aptitudes of the mind allows a better development of the individual or specialized competencies.

The more powerful the general intelligence, writes Morin, the greater is its ability to deal with particular and special problems. Understanding particular elements requires the activation of a general intelligence that operates and organizes the mobilization of the knowledge of the whole in each case.[67]

---

[66] *General Problem Solver* (gps) is a computer program created in 1957 by Herbert Alexander Simon, John Clifford Shaw, and Allen Newell with the aim of building a machine capable of solving general problems. *Cf.* Allen Newell, *A Guide to the General Problem-Solver Program GPS* (Santa Monica: Rand Corporation, 1963). Herbert Simon (1919–2001) was an economist and social science theorist, winner of the Bank of Sweden Prize in Economic Sciences in memory of Alfred Nobel for "one of the most important researchers in the interdisciplinary field. The popular gps is an acronym for *Global Positioning System*, or "global positioning system," which makes it possible to determine the position of any object on Earth. The thinker Jordi Pigem makes a particular reading of these popular acronyms, which basically coincides with Morin, relating the personal with the global: Jordi Pigem, *GPS (Global Personal Social). Valores para un mundo en transformación* (Barcelona: Kairós, 2011). Pigem transforms it from a non-technocratic perspective, based on the idea, argued in his book, that what is really good in one of these spheres is also good in the other two.

[67] Morin, *Seven Complex Lessons in Education for the Future*.

3. Dialogic principle

The *dialogic principle* is "the complex association (complementary, concurrent, antagonistic) of instances necessary *together* for the existence, functioning, and development of an organized phenomenon." This principle is for Morin consciously distinct from the Hegelian *dialectic* and from the rationalization that strives to impose a "rational" truth. He goes so far as to say that "life is unintelligible if one does not appeal to the *dialogic*."[68] The *dialogic principle* is a principle of knowledge that unites or relates ideas or principles of two logics that may be antagonistic. Thus, the dialogic is a principle distinct from the Hegelian *dialectic*; it occupies the place of the dialectic in the relation "between antagonistic and complementary instances at the same time." And it goes beyond a *rationality* that wants to eliminate contradictions, recognizing their irreducibility.

From *self-eco-organization* the whole is inside the part, which is inside the whole—like the Russian dolls—which begins to include every aspect; the subject emerges in time with the world, and thus subject and object appear as two inseparable emergences of the self-organizing system-ecosystem relationship. On re-entering science, the elements that had been placed in parentheses (randomness, environment, and the creative subject), the tools are put in place to see these phenomena as less integrated; the emphasis is no longer on substances, but on emergences and interactions, to overcome the tragedy of thought.[69]

Complexity in the Education of the Future:
Seven Lessons for Education

Commissioned by UNESCO, Edgar Morin wrote a book[70] on what the education of the future should include, in line with

---

[68] Cf. Morin, *Mis demonios*, 208, 215, 267.
[69] Cf. Morin, *El método*, Vol. I.
[70] Cf. Morin, *Seven Complex Lessons in Education for the Future*.

his vision of *complex thought*. We will look at it in more detail because it will help us better understand his proposal. In the "Introduction," Federico Mayor Zaragoza, then Director General of UNESCO, says (italics mine):

> Tomorrow's world will have to be fundamentally different from the one we know today. . . . One of the most difficult challenges will be to modify our thinking to cope with increasing *complexity*. . . . We must *rethink the organization of knowledge*. To do this, we must break down the traditional barriers between disciplines and devise ways of *reuniting what has hitherto been separated*.

Morin himself says in the "Prologue" that this knowledge comprises "central or fundamental problems that *remain completely ignored or forgotten and that are necessary* for education in the next century" (italics mine):

> There are seven "fundamental" teachings that the education of the future should deal with in any society and in any culture without any exception or rejection, according to the uses and rules of each society and each culture. Moreover, *scientific knowledge*, on which this text is based in situating the human condition, *is not only provisional, but also uncovers deep mysteries* concerning the Universe, Life, the birth of the Human Being. *This opens up an undecidable question* in which philosophical options and religious beliefs intervene across cultures and civilizations.
>
> 1. *The blindnesses of knowledge: error and illusion*
> It says a lot that education, which is what tends to impart knowledge, remains blind to what human knowledge is . . . , to its difficulties and its tendencies both to error and

to illusion, and does not concern itself at all with making known what it is to know. . . .

The knowledge of knowledge must appear as a first necessity that would serve as a preparation to face *permanent risks of error and illusion* that never cease to parasitize the human mind. It is a matter of *arming each mind in the vital battle for lucidity*.

Error and illusion have been parasitizing the human mind since the emergence of *Homo sapiens*; we carry with us ideas that we believe to be immutable, when they are not, as history has shown us. Morin goes so far as to speak of the "determinism of convictions and beliefs," of a "cultural *imprinting*" that marks humans from birth. Moreover, our systems of ideas (theories, doctrines, ideologies) are not only subject to error, but also "protect the errors and illusions that are inscribed in them," particularly in "the invisible zone of paradigms," official beliefs or untouchable reigning doctrines. Consequently, "education must show that *there is no knowledge that is not, to some degree, threatened by error and by illusion.*"

We must be open to new ideas, as a whole, and not blindly cling to the old ones.

2. *The principles of relevant knowledge*

There is a major problem, which is the need to promote knowledge capable of addressing global and fundamental problems in order to include partial and local knowledge.

The supremacy of a fragmented knowledge according to disciplines often prevents the link between the parts and the totalities from operating, and must give way to a mode of knowledge capable of apprehending objects in their contexts, in their completeness. . . .

It is necessary to develop the natural aptitude of human intelligence to place all its information in a context and in a whole. It is necessary to teach the methods that allow to apprehend the mutual relations and the reciprocal influences between the parts and the whole in a complex world.

We must overcome fragmented knowledge and develop a general/global intelligence to solve problems, using knowledge in a multidimensional way and taking into account complexity, the relationship of the parts with the whole. For knowledge to be relevant, education must demonstrate:

- *Context*. Placing information and elements in their complex context.
- *The global* (the relationships between the whole and the parts). A society is more than a context, "it is a whole that is both organizing and disorganizing."
- *The multidimensional*. Complex units, such as the human being or society, are multidimensional; they include the biological, the psychic, the social, the affective, the rational, the spiritual, the historical, the economic, the religious. . . .
- *Complexity*. Relevant knowledge must face complexity; this occurs when the different elements that make up a whole are inseparable and there is an interdependent, interactive and inter-retroactive fabric.

For Morin, the gigantic progress of knowledge of the twentieth century has been diffused due to specialization that breaks up contexts; this poses enormous obstacles that impede the exercise of "relevant knowledge" in educational systems. These systems tend to oppose the humanities and sciences of the spirit with empirical sciences, and these are divided into hyper-specialized disciplines; thus, global/complex realities have been "dislocated." The biological dimension is enclosed in the biological departments; the psychic, social, religious and economic dimensions are separated in the departments of human sciences; "its subjective, existential, poetic characters are confined to the departments of literature and poetry; philosophy, which is by nature a reflection on all human problems, has in turn become a field enclosed within itself." This *hyper-specificity* prevents us from seeing both *the global* (fragmented into parcels) and the *essential* (which dissolves), and even prevents us from dealing correctly with particular problems, which need to be posed in a context.

3. *Teaching the human condition*

The complex unity of human nature is completely disintegrated in education through disciplines, which makes it impossible to learn what it means to be human. It is necessary to restore it in such a way that each one, wherever he or she is, becomes aware and conscious at the same time of his or her complex identity and of his or her identity common to all other humans. . . . From the disciplines, it is possible to recognize human unity and complexity by gathering and organizing knowledge dispersed in the natural sciences, human sciences, literature and philosophy, and to show the indissoluble union between unity and diversity of all that is human.

The education of the future must be a primary and universal teaching focused on the human condition; it must recognize its common humanity and, at the same time, acknowledge the cultural diversity of all that is human. Considering this, one might examine the project that seeks to incorporate empathy into the Quebec curriculum.[71]

---

[71] *Cf.* https://pedagogie.uquebec.ca/le-tableau/reduire-la-distance- par-la-pedagogie-de-lempathie; https://www.innovation-pedagogique.fr/articleq3q7.html.

Progress in the empirical and human sciences has modified ideas about the universe, the Earth, life, and the human being itself; but these contributions are still disjointed. Hence the need for a great *re-binding of knowledge* for the education of the future. The human being is a fully *biological* and *cultural* being, insists Morin. Although many of us prefer to speak of its dual *material* and *spiritual* dimension; a Reality that is neither dualistic nor monistic, but non-dual. To explain the human condition, Morin speaks of a ternary character in the human condition: the loop of brain ↔ mind ↔ culture; the loop of reason ↔ affect ↔ drive and the loop of individual ↔ society ↔ species:

> The human being is rational and irrational . . . subject to an intense and unstable affection . . . serious and calculating, but also anxious, anguished, joyful . . . a being of violence and tenderness, of love and hate . . . a being invaded by the imaginary who can recognize the real . . . who secretes myth and magic, but also science and philosophy; who is possessed by the Gods and Ideas, but who doubts the Gods and criticizes Ideas; who feeds on proven knowledge, but also on illusions and chimeras.

All truly human development means "the joint development of individual autonomy, community participation and a sense of belonging to the human species." This implies "ensuring that the idea of the unity of the human species does not erase the idea of its diversity, and that the idea of its diversity does not erase the idea of unity."

4. *Teaching earthly identity*

The planetary destiny of the human race is another fundamental reality ignored by education. It is relevant to teach the history of the planetary era that began with the communication of all the continents in the sixteenth century and to show how all parts of the world became interdependent, without hiding the oppressions and dominations that have plagued humanity and have not yet disappeared. The complexity of the planetary crisis must be highlighted by showing that all human beings . . . live in the same community of destiny.

Humans need to be aware that we are part of one planet, but indifference to our world has worsened over the years. Therefore: "We need to conceive of the unsustainable complexity of the world in the sense that we need to consider both the unity and the diversity of the planetary process. . . . The planet needs a polycentric thinking capable of aiming at a universalism that is not abstract, but conscious of the unity/diversity of the human condition."

However, the twentieth century "seemed to give reason to the atrocious formula according to which human evolution is a growth of the power of death." Death caused by the two most terrible wars in history, but also by the threat of two new powers of death: nuclear weapons, with their possibility of the global death of all humanity, the possibility of ecological death through the waste and emissions that degrade our biosphere due to an unbridled dominion of nature that leads humanity to suicide, and the latent self-destruction in each one of us through the growth of solitude and neurotic anxieties. "If modernity is defined as unconditional faith in progress, in technology, in science, in economic development, this modernity is dead," Morin wisely says. But we can glimpse the possibility of a new creation: *a terrestrial citizenship*, which seems to point to some countercurrents:

- The *ecological countercurrent*, which continues to grow.
- The *qualitative countercurrent*, in reaction to the invasion of the quantitative.

- The *countercurrent of resistance to the purely utilitarian life*, which manifests in the search for a life more dedicated to love and contemplation.
- The *countercurrent of resistance to the primacy of consumption*, the search for a lived intensity and the search for frugality.
- The *countercurrent of emancipation from the tyranny of money*. Money, today as in biblical times, is the great idol (Mammon) that threatens humanity.
- The *countercurrent that feeds the pacification ethics* of societies, souls, and minds.

This implies the emergence of an anthropological consciousness that recognizes our unity in our diversity:

- The *ecological consciousness* of inhabiting the same living sphere (biosphere) with all beings, recognizing our consubstantial bond with it and abandoning the meteoric dream of dominating the universe.
- *Earthly civic consciousness*, responsibility and solidarity with the Earth.
- The *spiritual awareness* of the human condition, which allows us to criticize each other, self-criticize, and understand each other.

5. *Facing uncertainties*

The sciences have made us acquire many certainties, but they have also revealed to us innumerable fields of uncertainty in the twentieth century. Education should include the teaching of uncertainties. . . . Learning to navigate an ocean of uncertainty through archipelagos of certainty is a necessity.

"Navigating in an ocean of uncertainties through archipelagos of certainty" is one of Morin's most brilliant phrases, in keeping with the essence of complexity (a *chaosmos*). "The future is called *uncertainty*," and we must learn to coexist with it, but in the hope of an evolution born of crises. "All evolution is the achievement of a deviation whose development transforms the system where it was itself born: *There is no evolution that is not disorganizing/reorganizing* in its process of transformation or metamorphosis." We will have to learn strategies to face the risks of these uncertainties.

6. *Teaching understanding*

Education for understanding is absent from our teachings. . . . Mutual understanding between humans, both near and far, is now vital for human relations to emerge from their barbaric state of misunderstanding.

Hence the need to study misunderstanding from its roots, its modalities, and its effects. This study would be as important, if not more so, if it focused not only on the symptoms but also on the causes of racism, xenophobia, and contempt.

Educating to understand mathematics or any other discipline is one thing, educating for human understanding is another; therein lies "the spiritual mission of education": to bring about understanding between people. For this, we need an "education for the obstacles to understanding": faced with the lack of understanding and with misunderstanding, with ignorance of the rites and customs of the other, with misunderstanding of the values of other traditional cultures (respect for elders, obedience of children, religious beliefs) and our contemporary democratic societies (worship of the individual and respect for freedoms), with the impossibility within one worldview to understand the arguments of another worldview, and, most importantly and most difficult, with the impossibility of understanding from one mental structure to another.

7. The ethics of the human race

Education must lead to an "anthropo-ethics," considering the ternary character of the human condition, individual-society-species. . . . We carry in each of us this triple reality. In the same way, any truly human development must include the joint development of individual autonomy, community participation, and the awareness of belonging to the human species.

This *anthropo-ethics* supposes the conscious and clear decision to:

- Assume the individual ↔ society ↔ species condition in complexity.
- Achieving humanity in ourselves, in our own personal awareness.
- Assuming human destiny in its antinomies and its fullness.

This *anthropo-ethics* asks us to work for the humanization of humanity, obey life and guide life, achieve planetary unity in diversity, and develop an ethics of solidarity and understanding.

This is the fascinating proposal of Edgar Morin's complex thought, with concrete proposals for social and educational application.

Raimon Panikkar: The Integration of the Whole of Reality in All Its Dimensions—Everything Is Related

> *Everything is integrated, assumed, transfigured . . .*
> *To contemplate all the fragments of our current world*
> *in order to gather them into a harmonic set.*
>
> R. PANIKKAR,
> *The Cosmotheandric Intuition*

> *Cosmotheandric intuition is the fully integrated intuition of the seamless fabric of the entire Reality . . . the undivided knowledge of all Reality.*
>
> R. PANIKKAR, *"La intuicion cosmoteándrica,"*
> *La nueva inocencia*

A *"prophet of the future."* Science, philosophy and theology, three 'modes' of knowledge of the one Reality that must be integrated. Panikkar and Morin

Raimon Panikkar (Barcelona, 1918—Tavertet, 2010) is one of the great Spanish thinkers along with Unamuno, Ortega y Gasset, Zubiri, and María Zambrano. A man of exceptional intellectual and human qualities, he had a broad, rich and unusual existential journey through the multiple realities that converged in him: the Eastern-Western human reality due to his Hindu-Christian origin (his father was Indian-Hindu, and his mother from a large Catholic family of Barcelona's bourgeoisie); the interdisciplinary academic and intellectual reality in philosophy, science and theology[72]; the intercultural and interreligious reality (which he himself defined as a *fourfold* Christian, Hindu, Buddhist and secular *identity*); and a life dedicated to thinking about the world, the human being and God, through more than seventy books and nearly 2000 articles, along with numerous courses and conferences around the world.[73] In this extensive oeuvre, significant

---

[72] He studied at various universities: science (Universidad de Barcelona), philosophy and literature (Universidad de Madrid) and theology (Universitá Laterana di Roma). He received his doctorates in philosophy (1946), chemistry (1958) in Madrid, and in theology in Rome (1961). His teaching career developed mainly in the US (1967–1987), but also in various universities in Europe and India.

[73] For Panikkar's vital and intellectual itinerary and the relation of his entire work, *cf.* "Introducción" and "La Obra completa de Panikkar," in Victorino Pérez Prieto and José Luis Meza Rueda, *Diccionario panikkariano* (Barcelona:

titles stand out: Volumes with their theses in philosophy (*El Concepto de naturaleza*, 1951), in science (*Ontonomia de la ciencia*, 1961) and in theology (*The Unknown Christ of Hinduism*, 1964).

> And other fundamental volumes for our subject: *Misterio y revelación* (1971); *The Trinity and World Religions* (1975); *Myth, Faith and Hermeneutics* (1979); *The Silence of God: The Answer of the Buddha* (1989); *A Dwelling Place for Wisdom* (1993); *La nueva inocencia* (1993, with some fundamental philosophical essays); *The Cosmotheandric Experience: Emerging Religious Consciousness* (1993); *Ecosofia* (1994); *Pensamiento científico y pensamiento cristiano* (1994); *Cultural Disarmament; The Way to Peace* (1995); *Invisible Harmony: Essays on Contemplation Responsibility* (1995); *The Experience of God: Icons of the Mystery* (2006); *Of Mysticism: Full Experience of Life* (2005); *La puerta estrecha del conocimiento* (2008); *The Rhythm of Being* (2010).

Panikkar himself recognized *existential risk* as a characteristic of his own existence, rooted as it was in more than one culture and developed on many fronts: "My personal circumstances made it possible for me to accept the risk of *conversion without alienation*, assumption without repudiation, synthesis and symbiosis without *falling into syncretism or eclecticism*."[74] Panikkar assumed throughout his life a *fourfold identity*: the Christianity in which he was born and educated, the Hinduism that was also part of him because of his paternal origin, the Buddhism that developed in him naturally, and finally a secular identity from living and

---

Herder, 2016). Most of Panikkar's work has been published in recent years as *Opera omnia* in Italian (Jaca, 2008–2021), Catalan (Fragmenta, 2009-), Spanish (Herder, 2015-), French (CERF, 2012–) and English (Orbis, 2014–2024).

[74] Raimon Panikkar, "Autobiografía intelectual. La filosofía como estilo de vida," *Anthropos*, no. 53–54 (1985), 24; in English, "Philosophy as Life-Style," *Philosophers on Their Own Work* (Bern 1978).

studying in the Western secular world. He became a "prophet of the future,"[75] a sage and mystic bearing a challenging message, unbound by any single institution. Panikkar has come to be described as "one of the paradigmatic thinkers of the Second Axial Age" for his interdisciplinarity, interculturality, and the originality of his thought.[76]

Raimon Panikkar had a strong friendship with Edgar Morin, with whom he agreed on fundamental perspectives, although he never used the word *completeness* in his writings. In an email that Morin sent me years ago, he told me that Panikkar was for him "a great spirit of the century," expressing his "full agreement with Panikkar." As we have seen, Morin seeks to reunite the scattered (*sparsa colligo*), aware that not only is the part in the whole, but that the whole is in the part. In the same way, Panikkar seeks the integration of the whole of Reality in all its dimensions, and repeats a similar Latin expression, very dear to him: *colligite fragmenta*, which we will examine below. At the level of language, there are original expressions used by both, although with a somewhat different meaning for each. Such is the case of *dialogic*; Morin speaks of the "dialogical principle," and Panikkar, of "dialogical thinking." For Morin, the *dialogic* occupies the place of dialectics in the relationship "between antagonistic and complementary instances at the same time" and goes beyond rationality. For Panikkar, *dialogue-dialogic* or *dialogic-dialogal*, as opposed to dialectical dialogue, is that which is "open to other philosophical visions and not only to *dialectical confrontation* and *rational dialogue*." Therefore, this dialogue takes place in the agora and not arena, as the dialectical one does; it does not pretend to win with the sword of reason, not even to convince, but to seek

---

[75] Raffaele Luise, *Raimon Panikkar. Profeta del dopodomani* (Milan: San Paolo Edizioni, 2014).

[76] Ewert Cousins, *Christ of the 21st Century* (New York: Element, 1992). Quote taken from the foreword by Joseph Prabhu in Raimon Panikkar, *The Rhythm of Being: The Gifford Lectures* (Maryknoll, NY: Orbis Books, 2010).

the truth together from different positions, in order to reach a mutual understanding and a more complete truth[77]: "The *dialogue-dialogal* . . . is the joint search for the common and the different, it is mutual fertilization, it is the implicit and explicit recognition that we are not self-sufficient."[78]

Science: The Hidden Unity of All Things

Raimon Panikkar's first university studies were in science, although it took him some time to obtain his doctorate in this discipline at the University of Madrid with the thesis *Algunos problemas limítrofes entre ciencia y filosofía: Sobre el sentido de la ciencia natural* (1958), which three years later would become one of his first books: *Ontonomía de la ciencia*. This was followed by numerous essays, published between the ages of twenty-five and thirty, that reflect his scientific training. Two of these stand out for their length and depth: "El indeteriminismo científico" and "La entropía y el fin del mundo: Un problema de cosmología." The first—over thirty pages long, including numerous mathematical formulas and their significance in physics—is on the inexactitude of relations and Heisenberg's indeterminacy principle. "Physics aspires to Metaphysics. . . . The whole process of any truth must necessarily end in Philosophy," Panikkar says here.[79] And in accordance with the new physics:

---

[77] Raimon Panikkar, "¿Dónde está el fulcro de la filosofía comparativa?," in *Sobre el diálogo intercultural* (Salamanca: San Esteban, 1990). *Cf*, on this and other Panikkarian concepts, the aforementioned *Diccionario panikkariano*.

[78] Raimon Panikkar, "Mística comparada?," in Various, *La mística en el siglo XXI* (Madrid: Trotta, 2002), 228.

[79] Raimon Panikkar, "El indeterminismo científico," *Anales de Física y Química*, no. 396 (1945), 603; the work is dated September 1944 and will later be collected in Raimon Panikkar, *Ontonomía de la Ciencia. Sobre el sentido de la ciencia y sus relaciones con la filosofía* (Madrid: Gredos, 1961). Heisenberg publicly stated the principle of indeterminacy or uncertainty in 1927 and received the Nobel Prize in 1932.

In nature there reigns a complex harmony resulting from the subordination of the orders of the various spheres of being. Every order does not destroy or suppress the lower organization, but is based on the possibilities that the latter leaves open. . . . The ultimate physical context of Reality is *indeterminable*, not *undetermined*.[80]

In "La entropía y el fin del mundo" ("Entropy and the End of the World") he uses fewer mathematical formulas, but again shows his solid scientific background. With a starting point in Clausius, he establishes the thermodynamic concept of *entropy* and studies the physical meaning of the first two principles of thermodynamics, in order to arrive at a possible symbiosis between science and philosophy in the face of the *ontological* structure of current physics. Over twenty years later, Panikkar published a long essay in *Arbor*: "Técnica y tiempo: La tecnocronía" (1966), which would also become a book under the same title.

Fifty years after his work on scientific indeterminism, he published a booklet with the evocative title *Scientific Thought and Christian Thought*.[81] For Panikkar, *scientific thought* is only "a very *particular and restricted* form of thought," due to the *active abstraction* it effects on a part of reality (*quantifiable parameters*) and the *passive abstraction* of that which does not fall within these parameters, excluding that which is not intrinsically objectifiable. *Christianity* is also "a particular and restricted form" of thought: *exegetical* (based on the Bible), *exclusive* (it claims to have the truth and does not want to deviate from it) and *existential* (a science of salvation). The scientific worldview is: (a) *mono-cultural* (European American), (b) *mono-rational*

---

[80] *Ibid.*, 599–600.
[81] Raimon Panikkar, *Pensamiento científico y pensamiento cristiano* (Santander: Sal Terræ, 1994).

(circumscribed to one type of rationality, mathematics), and (c) *self-sufficient* (it relies only on itself). Finally, the Christian worldview is: (a) *mono-theistic* (God is the cause of the world), (b) *anthropocentric* (man is the center of the universe), and (c) *a-critical* (it rejects science). Therefore, the conflict between modern science and Christian faith is "a *conflict between worldviews*," in which Christian thought was displaced by scientific thought. They are faced with a "worldview difference," and the only solution is to accept the relativization of all worldviews.

Philosophy: Integration of All Dimensions of Reality and "Wisdom of Love"

The main characteristic of Raimon Panikkar's thought is his *obsession with the Whole*, the search for harmony among the diverse aspects that make up Reality: "It is not a question of any part. It is not a question of partialities. . . . It is a question of the Whole."[82] It is the will to integrate all of Reality in all its dimensions, seeking its profound "invisible harmony." This is the reason for his studies in science, philosophy, and theology, because the three disciplines complement each other. He explains thus the reason for his itinerary, which relates to our aim here:

> I began by studying the subject. For years, physics and chemistry were my most serious intellectual occupations. At the same time, I began to study philosophy, not because I felt disenchanted with my scientific work. Rather, it was due to a continuity of my interests. . . . Then theology. . . . It was my pressing need for total immersion in full communion with Reality.[83]

---

[82] "Prologue" to Raimon Panikkar, *The Silence of God: The Answer of the Buddha* (Maryknoll, NY: Orbis Books, 1989).

[83] Panikkar, "Autobiografía intelectual. La filosofía como estilo de vida," 13.

For Panikkar, philosophy is bound to pose theological problems and theology is intrinsically permeated by philosophy. Theology and philosophy proceed together: "There is no 'philosophy' without a dose of faith, and there is no theology without reason. 'Philosophy' has faith in reason and theology must give some reason for its faith."[84] The conflict between philosophers and theologians must be overcome for the good of both. Theology and philosophy, with science and mysticism, are aspects or modes of knowledge of the one Reality, which has three inseparable dimensions: sensitive, rational, and mystical.[85] There cannot be a rupture between the sciences of nature and the sciences of the spirit; *integral*, total *thought* must consider both, for they are inseparable dimensions of Reality:

> We need both divine and human wisdom . . . but harmony has rarely been achieved. The balance has shifted towards dehumanizing theocentrism or degrading anthropocentrism. The philosopher is a lover of wisdom because he participates in the wisdom of love.[86]

If science is the first approach to Reality, reason is "the inner *eye*" that can see better than any other knowledge. Its range is short, however, because it's restricted by its own limits: the *rational* side of total Reality. Faith makes it possible to reach a higher degree of knowledge; this is the "inner *ear*" capable of perceiving Reality at a greater distance. Reason, faith, science,

---

[84] Raimon Panikkar, *Misterio y revelación. Hinduismo y cristianismo, encuentro entre dos culturas* (Madrid: Marova, 1971), 58–59. Panikkar is used to writing "philosophy" in quotation marks, because of his critical stance against a contemporary philosophy that disregards theology and metaphysics itself.

[85] *Cf.* Pérez Prieto, *Más allá de la fragmentación de la teología, el saber y la vida: Raimon Panikkar*, 171–180.

[86] Raimon Panikkar, *La experiencia filosófica de la India* (Madrid: Trotta, 1997), 15–16.

philosophy, and theology must walk together to search for true wisdom. It is a matter of returning to an *integral* knowledge and *wisdom* of Reality, a complete vision.[87] To arrive at this harmonic vision of Reality, Panikkar insists on the *relativity* of all the parts that make up Reality, as opposed to the predominant *absolutism* of one of them. But *relativity* is not the same as *relativism*, and each part of the whole has its own particular value: "The dilemma is not relativism or absolutism, but the recognition of the *radical relativity* of the whole of Reality."[88] Panikkar repeatedly insists on this *radical relativity*, which has an equivalent in the very rich Buddhist concept of *pratītyasamutpāda* (co-dependent relationality).

For Panikkar, philosophy is "wisdom of love" in a *cosmotheandric* perspective. The need to seek a harmonious vision of Reality is in the very concept of philosophy: rather than "love of wisdom," it is "wisdom of love": "It is the *sophia (jnana)* contained in primordial love . . . that emerges when the love of knowledge and the knowledge of love unite."[89] Elsewhere, he says: "The philosopher . . . has not split love from knowledge, nor has he subordinated the one to the other."[90] He had already written in one of his early works: "Love is the *unifying bond of the whole universe*."[91] It is love that unites all of Reality in its triple

---

[87] Panikkar, *Misterio y revelación. Hinduismo y cristianismo, encuentro entre dos culturas*, 60.

[88] Raimon Panikkar, *La Trinidad. Una experiencia humana primordial* (Madrid: Siruela, 1998), 18; in English, *The Trinity and the Religious Experience of Man: Icon, Person, Mystery* (Maryknoll, NY: Orbis Books, 1975).

[89] Panikkar, "Autobiografía intelectual. La filosofía como estilo de vida" 12. *Cf.* Victorino Pérez Prieto, "A filosofia como sabedoria do amor. Raimon Panikkar," *Humanística e Teologia* I, no. 34 (2013).

[90] Panikkar, *La experiencia filosófica de la India*, 16.

[91] Raimon Panikkar, *El concepto de naturaleza. Análisis histórico y metafísico de un concepto* (Madrid: Instituto de Filosofía Luis Vives, 1972), 257. *Cf.* also Raimon Panikkar and Hans Peter Dürr, *L'amore fonte originaria dell'universo. Un dialogo su scienza della natura e religione* (Rome: La Parola, 2011).

divine, human, and cosmic dimension; a relationship between matter and spirit.

"Ontonomy" of Science and Love of Matter: Critique of Science and Technology

The concept of *ontonomy* is fundamental in Raimon Panikkar's thought; it is profoundly related to complexity, although he does not name it. The thesis of his book *Ontonomía de la ciencia* is reflected in the title itself, as the author acknowledges in its introduction, where he contrasts this concept of *ontonomy* with the existing classical ones of *heteronomy* and *autonomy*, which had to be surpassed:

> After a first stage in which Science lived protected and sheltered, but also suffocated and bound by Philosophy, which *heteronomously* dictated its laws to all other knowledge, Science emancipated itself by claiming for itself complete *autonomy*, which led it to scientism... The autonomy that science regained . . . gradually gave rise to a harmonious *ontonomy* that allowed science to be integrated into human culture, without unilateral totalitarianism.
>
> I call *ontonomy* the recognition or development of the laws proper to each sphere of being or of human activity . . . without separation or unjustified interference. . . . Not all of reality is discovered by science, nor by philosophy, nor is scientific knowledge completely alien to or supplants philosophical knowledge. Science has its nature and its own peculiar sphere, with internal and constitutive relations, on the other hand, with Philosophy.[92]

---

[92] Panikkar, *Ontonomía de la Ciencia. Sobre el sentido de la ciencia y sus relaciones con la filosofía*, 110–111.

Ontonomy refers to the internal *nomos* of each being and expresses a concept that can be crucial both for scientific, philosophical, and theological thinking and for politics and economics. It is a matter of excluding both the separate or disconnected independence of the particular spheres of being (*autonomy*) and the domination of some spheres over others (*heteronomy*), in order to arrive at a harmonious integration of the different parts in the whole (*ontonomy*). A few years before *Ontonomía de la ciencia*, Panikkar published an interesting work, in which he gives us the most precise definition of *ontonomy*:

> *Ontonomy* describes this particular character of beings and uncovers the profound laws that derive from *ôn*, considered in its totality, as well as the *sui generis* relationship it has with the source and origin of all being. . . . *Ontonomy* discovers the mysterious and intrinsic laws that allow the harmonious development of a being, according to its intimate constitution, without doing violence to other beings. There is an *ontonomic* order that we have to discover, because only it discovers the structure of the world.[93]

In his pioneering book *Ontonomía de la ciencia*, Panikkar already highlights one of his most recurring themes, which falls squarely within the perspective we have just seen: the *critique of science and technology* because of the "blindness to the totality" of many scientists and their "lack of authentic and deep ontological concern." But Panikkar's critique of science is not *premodern;* it is not born of a prejudice against the scientific, but takes it into account and is a more radical critique than those of Husserl, Heidegger, Jaspers, Marcuse, or Habermas. For this reason, Raúl Fornet-Betancourt writes that

---

[93] Panikkar, *Misterio y revelación. Hinduismo y cristianismo, encuentro entre dos culturas*, 88–89, where "Le concept d'ontonomie" is collected.

Raimon Panikkar does not criticize or put us on our guard against science because of what science is, but rather because of what he *believes* it represents . . . , because of the *image* that has been created and that we ourselves cultivate. . . . It does not aim at condemnation, but at the *relativization of* the significance that science has in the history of humanity.[94]

Four fundamental concepts of Raimon Panikkar's thought are *colligite fragmenta, pars pro toto-totum in parte,* invisible harmony, and ecosophy.

1. *Colligite quæ superaverunt fragmenta, ne pereant.* These are the words of Jesus of Nazareth with which John ends the story of the multiplication of loaves and fishes (Jn 6:12). This phrase reveals something fundamental in Panikkar's thought: the need to collect all the scattered *fragments* of Reality, even the smallest ones. Let nothing be lost; everything matters for integrating the whole of Reality in all its dimensions in order to reconstruct the *harmonious whole*: "Nothing is despised. . . . Everything is integrated, assumed, transfigured. . . . Thinking all the fragments of our present world to gather them into a harmonious whole."[95]

As opposed to reductionism, the "habitual philosophical sin of the West," the main feature of Panikkar's philosophy is a preoccupation with the *Whole*, with a harmony between the various particular realities and the different cultural conceptions of the modern West and the East: "My great aspiration was and is to

---

[94] Raúl Fornet-Betancourt, "Ciencia, tecnología y política en la filosofía de Raimon Panikkar," in *La filosofía intercultural de Raimon Panikkar*, ed. Ignasi Boada (Barcelona: Pòrtic, 2004), 125–126.

[95] Raimon Panikkar, *La intuición cosmoteándrica. Las tres dimensiones de la realidad* (Madrid: Trotta, 1999), 19–20.

embrace, or rather to reach Reality in all its fullness."[96] The ultimate structure of Reality is that there is no *structure*, but *interrelationships* that constitute it, an interconnection of everything with everything. *Particularism* and *universality* are indissolubly united in Panikkar's reflection and life in the search for the interrelation of everything with everything. Reaching absolute Reality requires beginning with the particular, then turning back from this to the former.

> 2. *Pars pro toto* and *totum in parte*. My understanding of the whole of Reality (*totum*) is inevitably and rightfully shaped by my individual scientific, philosophical, cultural, and religious perspective (*pars*): we see the *whole in parts* (*per partem*) and *through* our *part* (*in parte*). "We see as much as we can see, but only *all* that *we* can see, our *totum*. . . . . Intentionally we turn to the *totum*, but . . . we know the *totum* only *in parte* and *per partem*."[97] The *pars pro toto* effect, by which we take a part for the whole, must be superseded by the experience of the *totum in parte*: the discovery of the *whole* in our respective *parts* knowing that they are *parts* of that whole, *not the whole*. There is no authentic knowledge if it is not of the whole; but we always know partially: we know a part as *part of the whole*, not as something self-consistent. That is true knowledge.
>
> 3. *Invisible harmony*. "The thirst for unity and harmony, innate in man, can in no way be quenched at the source that is apparently reserved for contemporary thought," scientistic and rationalist.[98] *Invisible harmony* is that which

---

[96] Panikkar, "Autobiografía intelectual. La filosofía como estilo de vida" 13.

[97] Panikkar, *La experiencia filosófica de la India*, 109. *Cf. Diccionario panikkariano*, 25–27.

[98] Panikkar, *La intuición cosmoteándrica. Las tres dimensiones de la realidad*, 23.

exists in all of Reality, and must exist between all sciences, cultures, and religions. It is opposed both to a dualism that pits some against others and to a monism, an "ecumenical Esperanto" that makes differences, their richness, disappear. It is a matter of trusting in the harmony of humans and the cosmos; difficult but possible.

Reality is not monolithic; it cannot be reduced to a single vision, which would be unilateral. "The streetlight of the West is not the only streetlight we have"; there are other streetlights in the city and in humanity.[99] The West does not have the exclusive right to reason and intelligibility, nor are Western philosophy, science, and theology the only lights we have to discover the truth. For this reason, Panikkar speaks of what he considers the "Descartes fallacy" (all that I see "with clarity and distinction" is truth); the evidence may be our criterion of truth, but *my* evidence may not be so for *you*. Furthermore, "the truth may be broader, deeper or even different from what I, even "we," see with *clarity and distinction*."

4. *Ecosophy*. This is a "wisdom-spirituality of the Earth," rather than a simple *ecology* or "Earth science." It is a "new balance," not so much between man and Earth, but "between *matter and spirit, space-time* and *consciousness*. A wisdom that manifests a cosmic trust and faith."[100] Panikkar insists that in recent years, we have not changed the dominant mentality of modernity: the Earth as a simple

---

[99] Raimon Panikkar, *Sobre el diálogo intercultural* (Salamanca: San Esteban, 1990), 103.

[100] Raimon Panikkar, *Ecosofía. Para una espiritualidad de la tierra* (Madrid: San Pablo, 1994), 114–115. In this regard, in addition to the corresponding entry in the *Diccionario panikkariano, cf.* José Luis Meza Rueda, "Ecosofía: otra manera de comprender y vivir la relación hombre-mundo," *Cuestiones Teológicas* 37, no. 87 (2010).

object. Ecology speaks of the "rational use of resources" or "soft exploitation," but this is nothing more than prolonging the agony to which humans have subjected the Earth, seeking the benefit of a few. If it is true that ecology has awakened us to this problem, it must be confronted in a much more convincing way: "It is our *attitude* towards the Earth that must change radically."[101]

Panikkar coined the term *ecosophy* to counter an ecology that does not want to unmask the Western belief in progress, the myth of history and the idol of modern science. In the early 1970s, Panikkar and the Norwegian philosopher Arne Naess—who did not know each other, but were both concerned about the relationship between humanity and the world—coined the same term but with different meanings, although there are similarities in the transition from *ecological* science to *ecosophical* wisdom.

Arne Naess (1912–2009) has been called "the father of *deep ecology*." For him, interconnectedness or interdependence is the essential factor of ecology: an ecosystem is an interdependent system, a network of relationships. *Ecosophy* is a "deep ecology" capable of recognizing the vital nature of the world and leads to a radical revision of the relationships between communities of living beings, where the human community is only one of these communities.[102] Other prominent European thinkers, such as Edgar Morin and Félix Guattari, have thought along the same lines for years. Guattari's book *The Three Ecologies* deserves special mention, since it uses the word *ecosophy* in relation to an understanding of ecology: natural, social, and mental;[103] Félix Guattari considers ecological disturbances to be the visible

---

[101] Ibid.

[102] Arne Naess, "Self-Realization in Mixed Communities of Humans, Bears, Sheep, and Wolves," *Inquiry*, no. 22 (1979), 231–241.

[103] *Cf.* Félix Guattari, *Las tres ecologías* (Valencia: Pre-textos, 1996); in English, *The Three Ecologies* (New Jersey: The Athlone Press, 2000).

part of a deeper evil, related to our way of organizing life, and proposes an ethical-political articulation between environment, social relations, and subjectivity.

For Raimon Panikkar, *ecosophy* goes beyond the Gaia theory (the Earth as a living entity),[104] because it reveals matter to be a factor of Reality as essential as human consciousness or the divine: *cosmotheandrical* reality. Ecosophy reintegrates the three dimensions within a wisdom of human living; it entails a change of attitude on the part of the human being, a new level of consciousness on which the survival of humanity and the Earth depends. This implies that Panikkarian *ecosophy* entails a decentering of man; in other words, it tones down the *anthropocentrism* that has done so much damage to both the Earth and humans.

The 'Cosmotheandric' or 'Theoanthropocosmic' Reality: God-Human Being-World

Raimon Panikkar developed a very enticing formulation of what Reality is, which he called the *cosmo-the-andric* intuition or—using a more inclusive term—*theo-anthropo-cosmic*. A totalizing vision in which God-Human Being-Cosmos are completely related. It is perhaps the best elaboration on the relationality of the whole of Reality manifested by complex thinking.

> *Cosmotheandric intuition* is the fully integrated intuition of the seamless fabric of the whole of reality... the undivided knowledge of the whole of Reality.
> What counts is the whole reality, matter as much as spirit, good as much as evil, science as much as mysticism, soul as much as body... Without denying the differences and even

---

[104] *Cf.* James Lovelock, *Gaia: A New Look at Life on Earth* (Oxford: Oxford University Press, 2000).

recognizing a hierarchical order within the three dimensions, the *cosmotheandric principle* emphasizes their intrinsic relationship.[105]

There are not three realities, God, Human, and World; but neither is there one, either God or Human or World. Reality is *cosmotheandric*.

> Our way of looking makes Reality appear to us sometimes under one aspect and sometimes under another. God, Man, and the World are, so to speak, in an intimate and constitutive collaboration to build Reality, to advance history, to continue creation.... God, Man, and World are on a single adventure, and this commitment constitutes the true Reality.[106]

This concept of Panikkar's expresses the indissoluble and totalizing union that makes up all of Reality; the triple dimension of Reality (to *others*, to the *world*, and to *God*), that we may attain harmonious communion: *cosmotheandric reconciliation*. Cosmotheandric knowledge is "the primordial form of consciousness," which "has appeared since the dawn of humanity as the undivided knowledge of the whole." It is a constant in human culture, for "man has never been satisfied with partial truths and now suspects that many traditional convictions may only be partial."[107] Today, this intuition is the holistic vision of Reality. The *theo-anthropo-cosmic reality* manifests as a *relationship* that constitutes divine, human, and cosmic reality. This perspective discovers the Trinitarian structure of the Whole:

---

[105] Panikkar, *La intuición cosmoteándrica. Las tres dimensiones de la realidad*, 53.
[106] *Ibid.*
[107] *Ibid.*, 53–54.

Theos-Anthropos-Cosmos. God/Divinity, Human Being/Consciousness, Cosmos/Nature:

a. *Theos.* The divine dimension, the Divinity. It is "the abyssal dimension" of Reality. At once transcendent and immanent, unfathomable and inexhaustible. It is the fons et origo totius realitatis." God is that dimension of more and better for both the world and the human being. Because the cosmos is not "an isolated fragment of matter and energy," but is something living, it participates in the divine dynamism.[108]

b. *Anthropos.* The human being, the "factor of Consciousness" and will. This is not an individual, but a person: "a knot in a network of relationships that can reach to the very antipodes of the real." The isolated individual is non-viable: "the human being is only human with the firmament above him, the earth below him, and his companions around him."[109] But, in addition, every real being is related to consciousness; it is something thinkable, which is related to the knowledge of the human being. This "dimension of consciousness" is the human dimension, which manifests itself *in* and *through* the human being.

c. *Cosmos.* This is the material element of Reality, energy. Every being "is found in the World, and there partakes of its uniqueness." This is not to say that God is "worldly," but that "a God without the World is not a *real* God, such an abstraction does not exist."[110] "To isolate man from God and the world is to strangle him." In the intrinsic relationship between the divine, the human and the cosmic, Panikkar recognizes that modern languages are more incapable of

---

[108] Panikkar, *La intuición cosmoteándrica. Las tres dimensiones de la realidad*, 96–97.

[109] *Ibid.*, 97–98.

[110] Raimon Panikkar, *La nueva inocencia* (Estella: Verbo Divino, 1993), 59–60.

expressing Reality than the ancient ones, in which myth played a fundamental role.

Man is no less a man when he discovers his divine vocation, nor do the Gods lose their divinity when they are humanized, nor does the World become less mundane when it bursts into life and consciousness.... The cosmotheandric vision of Reality is equivalent to a totalizing and integral vision of all that exists.[111]

Complexity Theory and Raimon Panikkar

The Rhythm of Being: The Gifford Lectures is Raimon Panikkar's philosophical-scientific testament. It collects and expands on his presentations at the prestigious Gifford Lectures (Edinburgh, 1888–2020), which featured leading physicists (Bohr, Eddington, Heisenberg, Peacocke, Polkinghorne...), philosophers (Whitehead, James, Dewey, Bergson, Schweitzer, Arendt, Taylor, Ricœur, Marcel...), theologians (Barth, Brunner, Tillich, Moltmann...), and specialists in other fields of research and knowledge. The thesis that Panikkar repeats here is that *cosmic rhythm* is the *universal condition of being*, an expression of the harmony of the universe:[112]

> Life is rhythm.... Life is a dance.... This choral dance is a combination of harmony and rhythm... We all participate in rhythm because rhythm is another name of Being (p. 37).

> Rhythm is more than the interconnection of things or events; it is their *intraconnection*, the indwelling of all in all (p. 45).

---

[111] *Ibid.*, 61.

[112] The following pages are based on the original lectures in Panikkar, *The Rhythm of Being: The Gifford Lectures*.

> Rhythm is always perceived as a Whole. It has no real parts. Any partition would destroy the rhythm, which is not the sum of its components... If you do not perceive the Whole, there is no rhythm.... Rhythm manifests the peculiar relation between rupture and continuity, between the old and the new (p. 47).

The holistic perspective of Reality in which everything is inter-related—in Panikkar's vocabulary, *intra-related*—and a conception of matter and the universe opposed to the reductionist-mechanistic one permeate this book and all of Panikkar's thought. He constantly repeats in his work his opposition to the modern tendency to compartmentalize everything, separating the pieces of the puzzle, because this makes the holistic perspective and that "experience of the rhythm" of the universe and the Self impossible: "The experience of Rhythm is a holistic experience" (p. 78). This puts it very close to the conception of the world that marks the theory of complexity, although, as I have already said, Panikkar never specifically uses that expression. For Panikkar and Morin, the whole is not the sum of the parts. For both of them, as for the quantum perspective, it is clearly impossible to apply to Reality the Cartesian method of decomposing the complex problem into smaller problems that are easier to solve, and then successively recomposing the totality as the sum of the partial solutions.

Heisenberg stated that "a sharp distinction between animate and inanimate matter can certainly not be made" (*Physics and Philosophy*). José Luis Sampedro writes beautifully: "Of course, the stone also lives, with the life of the whole universe."[113] Similarly, for Panikkar, everything around us is in continuity with nature: "Every natural entity is *a living cell*, part of a whole and a *reflection*

---

[113] José Luis Sampedro, *El río que nos lleva* (Havana: Arte y Literatura, 1989), 130.

of the whole at the same time. Not only plants and animals are living, but also mountains and rocks."[114] Inert matter, like plant and animal life, participates like human beings in the *cosmotheandric* reality. There is a continuity in the ontonomic difference of the different dimensions.

Georges Charpak, 1992 Nobel Prize in Physics, writes: "Matter is free!"; "Freedom, or the multitude of possibilities that radical form represents to us, is deeply rooted in the very heart of quantum mechanics and its laws."[115] And Ilya Prigogine speaks of the "creativity of nature."[116] Similarly, in consonance with the perspective of Reality provided by the theory of complexity, Panikkar thinks that "reality is a constant novelty," it is in constant process, and even that "matter also has a degree of freedom."[117] The freedom of matter is certainly not that of humans, of consciousness, but insofar as it is immersed in cosmic reality, it participates in the same dimension.

In the "Introduction" to a book by the young Italian philosopher Paolo Calabrò, we read:

> Matter is free. The world has a consciousness. Thought modifies thought. The whole is greater than the sum of its parts.... Some scientific intuitions, from quantum mechanics to chaos theory, show a surprising affinity with Panikkar's thought and the same sensitivity to the themes of unity and continuity of the real. In Panikkar's vision, cultures meet in the common task of moving toward the knowledge of things, to a greater awareness of themselves, to harmony

---

[114] Panikkar, *Ecosofía. Para una espiritualidad de la tierra*, 58.

[115] *Cf.* George Charpak, *Siate saggi, diventate profeti* (Milan: Codice, 2004).

[116] *Cf.* Prigogine and Stengers, *La nueva alianza. Metamorfosis de la ciencia* ; in English, *Order Out of Chaos: Man's New Dialogue with Nature* (London: Verso, 2018).

[117] Raimon Panikkar, *La puerta estrecha del conocimiento. Sentido, razón y fe* (Barcelona: Herder, 2008), 78.

with the cosmos.... The truth is that reality is the web of relationships that bind all things to all other things. There are no caesuras. Things touch each other.[118]

In conclusion, we see that Panikkar, although he never used the word *complexity*, has a similar qualitative-complex, not quantitative-reductionist, discourse. The interrelation of everything with everything marks total Reality, with its complexity between order and disorder, as we saw in the first chapter, and this is related to the thermodynamic structure of Reality, which we have discussed here. Particularly to the principle of entropy, which we call *the motor of evolution and complexity*, because it represents the need for an ever more complex organization; entropy demands at every instant a greater organization, an ever more complex self-organization.

For Panikkar, Reality is complex and apparently contradictory, but harmonious: In it, the human-consciousness dimension is intimately united with the cosmic-material and the spiritual-divine; temporal things, historical human realities, and ideal and spiritual entities are also intimately united. For Panikkar, then, *Reality is a harmonious whole*, in which the human-cosmic-divine dimensions are united in the dynamism and *rhythm of Being*.

---

[118] Pablo Calabrò, *Le cose si toccano. Raimon Panikkar e le scienze moderne* (Milan: Diabasis, 2011).

3

Environmentalism and Interrelationality in the Bible and in Other Religions and Cultures[1]

> *To produce and nurture, to create without possessing,*
> *to multiply without submitting, that is the mystery of life.*
> LAOZI, *Book of Tao (Daodejing)*

> *There is an infinite net of threads throughout the universe.*
> *. . . In each intertwining of threads there is a person, and*
> *in each person there is a jewel. And each jewel reflects not*
> *only the light of every other jewel in the net, but also all the*
> *other reflections that manifest throughout the entire universe.*
> RIG-VEDA, *"Indra's Net"*

> *Creation lives in the hope that it, too, will be set free from*
> *its bondage to decay and obtain the glorious liberty of the*
> *children of God. We know that the whole creation has been*
> *groaning in travail together until now.*
> PAUL OF TARSUS, *Letter to the Romans 8:20–22*

---

[1] Much of the contents of this chapter appear in my publications on the subject, updated and reworked here with new approaches. These publications can be found in the Bibliography.

> *I realized that my own poor trifling existence was one with the immensity of all that is and all that is still in process of becoming.*
>
> PIERRE TEILHARD DE CHARDIN,
Writings in Time of War

THE UNITY AND HARMONY OF REALITY IN EASTERN AND PRIMITIVE CULTURES

In Hinduism and Buddhism

Like many other texts from the East, the words of Laozi quoted above reflect the wisdom of Eastern and other ancient religions: the human being is totally immersed in nature, is part of it, and must therefore live in total harmony with it. *The salvation of every human being is inseparably linked to the salvation of the whole universe.* A Hindu dictum wisely states: "The person who has seen God in the temple of his soul, will see him in the temple of the universe." And Valmiki, the poet to whom the most popular version of the *Ramayana* is attributed, says: "What the waves are to water, the world is to Brahman. Those who have not yet known the Truth see everything as separate. Those who know, see God everywhere; the ignorant, on the other hand, see the world in its diversity."

In Hinduism, *everything is related to everything*, as the words of the *Rig-veda,* one of the fundamental texts of the Hindu tradition, also proclaim. In "Indra's Net" (Avatamsaka), Reality is "an infinite net of threads throughout the universe," or an infinite web of jewels reflecting each other. Each is reflected in all the others, and itself reflected in each of the reflections and in the reflections of the reflections. The human being is not an *individual* who can exist separately, he is a *person* who exists only in a *knot of relationships*; there is nothing that can exist in isolation.

The human being is part of nature, and there is no insurmountable distance from other beings, especially living beings. Even the belief in reincarnation leads to a particular attitude of respect for other living beings, since they are part of the same chain of reincarnations in which each person is involved. For this reason, human beings are recognized as having the same rights as other animals: they are all part of an "inseparable community of destiny." Mahatma Gandhi summed up this spirituality magnificently: "To one day see face-to-face the Spirit of truth that pervades the whole universe, we need to come to love as our own all that is most insignificant in creation."[2]

Thus, in the Hindu conception of Reality, *everything is intimately united*. This total and harmonious vision of Reality is expressed in the very rich Hindu concepts of *advaita* and the *rta* principle.[3] *Advaita* is "non-duality" or "a-duality": the "a-duality" of all beings that make up Reality—the world, humans, and the Divinity itself included. Non-duality expresses unity in difference; an integral state that embraces all the different spheres of existence in unity. According to this, consciousness feels and knows itself to be part of the ultimate Reality. This implies a unified experience between body, mind, and spirit; between the self and others, between the self and the world. The *advaita* experience is that of one who "knows the universal unity of the Self" without ceasing to see "beings," according to the *Bhagavad Gita* (6, 32).

The other rich concept of Vedic Hinduism intimately linked to this is the *rta* principle; the principle of harmony of all beings, order, rule, and truth. No being is identified with another, but neither is it separated from the others; everything is intimately united; it is the principle that governs the cosmic and sacred

---

[2] Mahatma Gandhi, *An Autobiography: The Story of My Experiments with Truth* (Ahmedabad, India: Navajivan Publishing House, 1993).

[3] *Cf.*, for *advaita* and the *rta* principle, Pérez Prieto and Rueda, *Diccionario panikkariano*, 31–40 and 246–247.

order. Through the *rta* the sun rises and moves, rivers flow, trees grow, and animals are born and develop. For humans, it is the path one must follow toward one's goal; therefore, a righteous and honorable person will always try to preserve the *rta*. Collectively, this principle refers to *dharma*, the action of each person in relation to those norms that refer to one's karma.

Similarly, Buddhism offers a vision of the individual deeply rooted in the cosmos; in its radical environmentalism, the salvation of every human being is inseparable from nature. In Buddhist cosmology, the evolution of the world is closely related to the ethical conduct of individuals (*digna nikaya*). Only by mastering our mind and reducing the uncontrolled force of our passions can we restore peaceful equilibrium. For the Buddha, "from speaking or acting with a tainted mind comes suffering," while "from speaking or acting with an undefiled mind comes happiness" (*Dhammapada*).[4] The taintless is "that which refused to kill the living, is full of compassion, and gives all beings love"; for compassion does not refer only to the relationship with other human beings, but with all that exists.[5]

For Buddhism, such fundamental concepts as compassion (*karuna*) and interdependence (*pratityasamutpada*) are intimately linked. The latter is the concept that best represents in Buddhism the relationship of everything to everything in Reality.

---

[4] The full text of this fundamental Buddhist scripture, meaning "The Path of Righteousness," traditionally attributed to Gautama Buddha and part of the *Pali Canon*, is available online at https://www.gutenberg.org/files/2017/2017-h/2017-h.htm.

[5] *Cf.* Juan Manzanera, "Ecología y espiritualidad," in *Ecología y cristianismo. XV Congreso de Teología* (Madrid: Evangelio y Liberación, 1995), a work focused almost exclusively on Buddhism; also Martine Batchelor and Kerry Brown, eds., *Buddhism and Ecology* (New Delhi: Motilal Banarsidass, 1995), which includes studies by Buddhists from Japan, Thailand, Sri Lanka, Vietnam, Tibet and the West.

Pratityasamutpada is the Buddhist doctrine by which all physical and psychic phenomena are mutually conditioned in a precise order, constituted by the chaining of the twelve *nidana* ('sources', 'origins').[6]

The basis of Buddhism as a religion and philosophy is the idea that there is no self-sustaining reality: "no permanent substance, no 'subject' in the metaphysical sense of the term," neither individual nor universal.[7] The Buddhist notion of *pratityasamutpada* expresses the idea of the *relativity of all Reality*: everything is deeply interrelated and nothing exists in isolation.[8] Gautama Buddha explains it in a few simple sentences: "This is because that is"; "This is so because that is so"; "If there is no this, there is no that"; "Nothing can exist by itself, nothing can exist alone." The great Buddhist master Thich Nhâ't Hanh says, "Touching yourself, you touch the whole," and "One thing is made up of all other things. One thing contains the whole cosmos."[9] Raimon Panikkar adds that the concept of *pratityasamutpada* is the central point of all Buddhism; he describes it as: "The *radical* and constitutive *relativity* of everything; the universal concatenation of all things."[10] The Buddhist doctrine of *pratityasamutpada* is thus meant to manifest that all the elements of Reality and all material or spiritual processes are relative and conditioned; they are indissolubly interrelated.

---

[6] Paul Massein, "Pratityasamutpada," in *Diccionario de las religiones*, ed. Paul Poupard (Barcelona: Herder, 1987), 1431.

[7] "Anatta," *ibid*. 65.

[8] *Cf.* Pérez Prieto and Rueda, *Diccionario panikkariano*, 233–235.

[9] Nhâ't Hanh, *Bouddha et Jésus sont des frères*, 9 and 10; in English, Nhâ't Hanh, *Going Home: Buddha and Jesus as Brothers*.

[10] Raimon Panikkar, *El silencio del Buddha. Una introducción al ateísmo religioso* (Madrid: Siruela, 1999), 119–120; in English, Panikkar, *The Silence of God: The Answer of the Buddha*.

Buddhist environmentalism seeks a *deep ecology* in the most valuable sense of the expression. As Thich Nhâ't Hanh also writes:

> Ecology in Buddhism has to be a deep ecology. And not only deep, but universal, because there is also pollution in consciousness. . . . That is, we have to practice an ecology of consciousness. Otherwise, our internal pollution will spill over into the lives of others.[11]

In Primitive Religions and in Current Religions of Indigenous Peoples

For primitive religions, the human being is totally immersed in nature, which is considered sacred, marked by the numinous and the divine. According to *animism*, a common element of all these religions, everything created has a soul, a vital force. Mother Earth is a living organism, full of sacred mystery in which all existence is interwoven. The salvation of the human being is inseparable from nature, which humans must care for and repair with rites of atonement: music, dance, meditation, ceremonies, and sacrifices affirm this union with the earth.

In the West, the Celtic peoples left the deepest imprint of the intimate relationship between humans and nature due to their close relationship with it and the knowledge they extracted from it. The Celts based their beliefs on nature, since it was the environment in which they were immersed and which gave them shelter, warmth, and food. In observing its behavior and evolution, they associated it with the other phenomena of life, which were given a sacred character. The worship of each form of natural life was intended to obtain the benefits of the qualities linked to it. The Roman historian Tacitus writes of them:

---

[11] Thich Nhâ't Hanh, *Buddhism and Ecology* (London: Cassell, 1992), 102.

"This common nature interwoven with the gods fuses men into a community."[12]

In the Celtic world, trees signified the pure essence of the nature of which they are a part. Trees and forests were symbols of life and protection; forests were their temples, where they held their festivals, rituals, and ceremonies; their culture developed around them and became the central axis of their mythology and rites. The power of the gods was found mystically in each of the trees of the forest, and each tree was consecrated to a god. The trees were a source of energy and established the physical-divine nexus on three planes: (1) the trunk of the tree was the material world, from which they extracted firewood and food; (2) the roots that went deep into the subterranean soil were the world of dreams, through which one entered the underworld and the very secret of the wisdom of the earth; and (3) the crown and branches that rose into the sky and were moved by the wind were the part of the tree that signified the divine plane of consciousness. The tree was so important to the Celtic peoples that the male and female Druids lived in them and studied them in depth.[13]

The Indigenous cosmovision of the peoples that survive today in America and Africa, far from being an outdated refuge of the past, can be a valuable contribution to an ecological alternative, recovering values that should not have been lost because of the reductionist vision of modernity. They themselves, who do not always ignore the contributions and values together with the dangers of modern technology, know that the modern powers, proud of their development, "deepened inequality, ambition, crisis, ecological destruction, and seriously endangered the

---

[12] Quote taken from Gustavo Fernández, "La mirada ecológica del culto celta," Mystery Planet, https://mysteryplanet.com.ar/site/la-mirada-ecologica-del-culto-celta/.

[13] *Cf.* https://www.efeverde.com/noticias/arboles-sagrados-celtas-dioses/. Also Jean Markale, *Druidas. Tradiciones y dioses de los celtas* (Madrid: Taurus, 1989).

planet's equilibrium; the alternative position of the Indian people emerges vigorous with its historical responsibility, the product of its cosmic vision and its harmonious coexistence with nature."[14]

The *Pachamama,* or Mother Earth,[15] totemic goddess of the Incas to whom gifts were offered in agricultural and livestock ceremonies in the Andean world, is a widespread image among most pre-Columbian peoples. She is not only a goddess, but a worldview, a system of religious beliefs and ecological-social actions among the Indigenous peoples of South America—especially the Quechua, Aymara, and other ethnic groups of the Andean region—that survive to this day.

The cosmic vision of these peoples is summarized in an Indigenous document:

> From community we understand the meaning of what is human and the possibility for each and every one of us to achieve a harmonious life. Likewise, this fraternal coexistence is also with all beings, that is, with nature.
>
> We do not feel we *own it*; it is our *mother*, it is not a commodity, it *is an integral part of our life*. It is our past, present, and future. We believe that this sense of the human and of the environment is not only valid for our communities or for the Indo-American peoples. We believe that it is an option, an alternative, a light for the peoples of the world, oppressed by a system based on domination among men, among peoples, in the domination of nature.[16]

---

[14] From the Quito indigenous document "Nuestra visión cósmica," in Giulio Girardi, Jesús Espeja, and Enrique Dussel, *Cristianismo, justicia y ecología* (Madrid: Utopía, 1994), 37. Also several articles in *Concilium*, no. 261, 1995, particularly Sylvia Marcos, "La sacralidad de la tierra. Perspectivas mesoamericanas," *Concilium*, no. 261 (1995).

[15] Pachamama comes from *pacha*, an Aymara and Quechua term meaning 'earth', 'world', 'universe', 'time', and from *mama*, 'mother.'

[16] Girardi, Espeja, and Dussel, *Cristianismo, justicia y ecología*, 37–38.

In 1856, Chief Seattle of the Suquamish tribe expressed the Indigenous perspective in a famous speech to Governor Isaac Stevens of Washington, a white man who sought to purchase their land. The speech attributed to him is considered one of the most beautiful and profound manifestos on the relationship between human beings and nature:

> How can you buy or sell the sky, the warmth of the land? The idea is strange to us. If we do not own the freshness of the air and the sparkle of the water, how can you buy them? Every part of this earth is sacred to my people. Every shining pine needle, every sandy shore, every mist in the dark woods, every clearing and humming insect is holy in the memory and experience of my people.... The sap which courses through the trees carries the memories of the red man.
>
> *We are part of the earth and it is part of us.* The scented flowers are our sisters; the deer, the horse, the great eagle, these are our brothers. The rocky crests, the juices in the meadows, the body heat of the pony, and man, all belong to the same family....
>
> This shining water that moves in the streams and rivers is not just water but the blood of our ancestors. If we sell you the land, you must remember that it is sacred, and you must teach your children that it is sacred and that each ghostly reflection in the clear water of the lakes tells of events and memories in the life of my people....
>
> This we know: *the Earth does not belong to man; man belongs to the earth.* All things are connected like the blood which unites one family. All things are connected.[17]

---

[17] This version of Chief Seattle's speech has been widely circulated, though it is the product of a modern writer, inspired by Seattle's words.

One of the best-known mystical experiences of the North American Indians is that of Black Elk (1863–1950), a Sioux holy man[18] who had to witness the extermination and degradation of his people (including the 1890 massacre of Wounded Knee). We know the experience from his beautiful story of the "Great Vision," narrated at the end of his life, but which speaks of an experience during his adolescence. This story describes the communion/union between matter and spirit, the human being, nature and the cosmos.

> I was standing on the highest mountain of them all, and round about beneath me was the whole hoop of the world. And while I stood there I saw more than I can tell and I understood more than I saw; for I was seeing in a sacred manner the shapes of all things in the spirit, and *the shape of all shapes as must live together like one being.*[19]

In contrast to this harmony with nature in primitive and Eastern religions, the Judeo-Christian tradition has been accused of being at the ideological forefront of the human assault on nature. Certainly, we need to learn from these cultures today, and a true interreligious dialogue is necessary to achieve a wiser ecological spirituality, in which Christians become aware of their limitations: the Christian West is the most predatory culture in history. But first, we cannot fall into a vision that is overly naive; the old primitive innocence was accompanied by oppressive violence in human relations, even to the point of human sacrifice, especially among the Aztecs; moreover, today we cannot pretend to return to a supposed *lost paradise.* Second, we must see to what extent

---

[18] Black Elk eventually converted to Catholicism and was baptized, but continued as the spiritual leader of the tribe, as he saw no contradiction between tribal traditions and Christianity.

[19] John G. Neihardt, *Black Elk Speaks: Being the Life Story of a Holy Man of the Oglala Sioux* (Lincoln: University of Nebraska Press, 1961), 43.

the harsh accusation of ecologists against Christianity—accused of having created in Western man the attitudes that led to the current ecological disaster, of having favored anthropocentrism, i.e., the lordship of man, which would give him a free hand to do with creation as he pleased, as Lynn White denounced and we shall examine later—are true, false, or at least reductionistic. Moreover, Christianity is accused of despising matter in favor of the spirit. . . . It is asserted that "Christian pride" would ultimately trigger ecological tragedy, as human beings no longer feel connected to nature and its future. We will see later that, although these accusations are partly true, Judeo-Christian roots are profoundly ecological.

THE CURRENT CHALLENGE OF ENVIRONMENTALISM AND HOLISTIC SENSITIVITY. ECOLOGISTS, PROPHETS OF OUR TIMES

> *The human beings who inhabit the Earth today and who are approximately over forty years old, carry on their shoulders the enormous responsibility of having degraded our planet, more so than any other generation or generations before them, or than any of the other millions of species that exist or have existed.*
>
> JOSÉ MANUEL SÁNCHEZ RON, *La ciencia, su estructura y su futuro*

An ecological and ecopacifist conscience has grown in the last forty years. We have come to realize that today's human beings bear on our shoulders the grave historical responsibility of having degraded life on Earth in the last hundred years more than in the previous twenty centuries. That knowledge alone, however, is not enough; this awareness obliges us to act, renewing the respect and love for life shown by ancestral cultures and demanded by present times. The modern Western world has forgotten the wisdom of Laozi or Chief Seattle and other wise men and women from before Christianity.

The global militancy of ecologism has been forgotten amid simplistic, idyllic depictions that frequently try to paint it as merely "beautiful flowers and small bushes." But ecology is not pure environmentalism, *naturalism,* or *utopian ideology,* as it has been accused of being. For this reason, it is necessary to clarify the terms *ecology, ecologism,* and *ecologists.* Most ecologists do not seek to stop growth, but to *redefine it*; progress must go beyond the pragmatic to reorient its path. In the words of one of its theoreticians:

> Ecologism is *a critical analysis of industrial society,* its economy, its technology, its institutions.... It is *an ethical sensibility that seeks to place the person at the center* of the movement of society. It calls for *a true revolution of the spirit* to reconcile the need for culture with nature.... *Ecologism is the humanism of tomorrow.*[20]

"Ecology," "Environmentalism," and "Environmentalists"

Ecology was not born with the ecological struggles, but in the work of *ecologists.* It is a science, a branch of biology that studies the interaction between living beings and their environment; it is "the science of the house." It appeared at the beginning of the twentieth century, although its name had already been coined by the German biologist Ernst Haeckel in 1866. *Ecologists* are the scientists who study it and the teachers who teach it; heirs of the old naturalists, from Linnaeus to Darwin. But true ecology is not a neutral subject; it implies taking sides in the great conflicts of our time: the relationship with the Earth and the North-South conflict. This leads us to *ecologism.*

---

[20] Dominique Simonnet, *L'Écologisme* (Paris: PUF, 1994), 4.

Although it learns from ecological science, *environmentalism* wants to be much more than that. It emerged years later, in the 1960s, following the ecological crisis of the fifties, which represented a first awareness of dangerous technologies and models of development with irreversible effects. Environmentalism is a social movement that, out of concern for the house and its people, fights peacefully against the degradation of living conditions in order to achieve harmony between human beings and nature, and among human beings themselves. This is why environmentalism is a new humanism. The contemporary ecological concern is heir to the old naturalism—sharpened by the nuclear threat—which soon gained a much broader awareness of the problem and the objectives it wanted to achieve, to reach a critique of society as a whole: technological development, and socioeconomic, political, and cultural structures. The environmental movement is neither pure *naturalism* nor pure *utopian ideology*, but is nourished by a scientific analysis and takes into account the political economy in its alternative proposals for an ecological society. It could not be otherwise if it wants to give an answer that considers the reality of the oppression of great masses of the world's population. It is more: a spirit, a conception of life.

And the *environmentalists* are the active members of the environmental movement, who take the bio-ecological paradigm very seriously to point toward a new humanism that answers the serious problems of humanity and the ecosystem. Like the old prophets, environmentalists are irreducibly critical of the unjust system imposed by liberal capitalism, which, in addition to destroying the Earth's habitat, condemns large swaths of the population to a misery that plunges them ever deeper into an ever-growing abyss.

The *environmentalists* are dangerous for the *establishment* because they want to change this unjust and predatory system from the root, from its foundation in a rapacious economy, whose god is the maximum economic return in the exploitation of Sister Earth. Environmentalists are the most critical of the alleged "end of history" proclaimed by neo-capitalism in its apotheosis at the end of the twentieth century and the beginning of the twenty-first. "Ecology provokes noise, fury, and violent reactions, proof that it threatens capitalist political and economic interests, particularly those of multinational corporations."[21] They are ridiculed and mercilessly attacked by this intolerant liberalism, accused of being fanatics, crazy, and opposed to progress, killjoys and generators of unemployment because of their criticism of a type of industrial development. Ecopacifism is today the greatest critical conscience of Western society, and its members are the immutable prophets of our time. Some have paid with their lives for their commitment to the Earth, in the face of economic and political powers. The penultimate in a long list was the Honduran indigenous leader Berta Cáceres, assassinated in 2016 in La Esperanza (Honduras), after years of receiving threats against her life.

Ecopacifism and Ecofeminism: Alter-Globalism, Environmentalism, and the Third World

Today, environmentalism is closely linked to the peace movement (*ecopacifism*), to the feminist movement (*ecofeminism*), and to *alter-globalization*.

Ecopacifism is a movement that simultaneously embraces environmentalism and pacifism. It intimately unites the peaceful

---

[21] Susan George, "La ecología, principal apuesta para el siglo XXI," *Le Monde diplomatique*, November 16, 1996. The author, director of the Transnational Institute of Amsterdam and alternative writer (with works such as *The Debt Trap: Third World and Dependency*, and *The Religion of Credit: The World Bank and Its Secular Empire*), explains how ecologism is "the number one public enemy" of the American right wing, which is why it has given rise to more than fifty anti-ecology organizations in the United States.

struggle for the rights of the Earth with the struggle for peace: it seeks harmony between human beings and the whole of nature, of which they are a part. Pacifism is opposed to war and all forms of violence, both as an ideology and as a political and religious movement.[22] *Ecopacifism* is at the heart of the green political movement, which defined pacifism as the first and most important of its ideological pillars.[23] Its tactics include active nonviolence, civil disobedience, conscientious objection, outreach campaigns, and peace education. From the beginning, one of its most important objectives has been the anti-nuclear and anti-militarist movement, which characterized the German ecopacifist party (The Greens) after the Second World War. *Ecopacifism* is today the greatest critical consciousness of Western society; it is one of the greatest challenges of our time.

Ecofeminism arises from the evident link between the feminist and environmentalist movements. To opt for a harmonious life means taking into account all aspects of life and, consequently, everything that threatens that harmonious life. It challenges everything that threatens life and unites all the movements that fight against this threat of domination as an oppressive power. For this reason, it was not long before *ecological* and *feminist* sensibilities were united; feminism as a movement that, in a patriarchal society in which man holds the power and imposes his mental schemes, struggles for the full participation of women in economic, political, social, and religious life, for the same rights as men. From the relationship between ecology and feminism was born the term *ecofeminism*,

---

[22] In its contemporary origin, standing out for its radicalism is the pacifism of Leo Tolstoy, whose book *The Kingdom of God Is Within You* converted another of the great leaders of contemporary pacifism: Mahatma Gandhi, as he himself acknowledged. Gandhi and Tolstoy exchanged several letters as well.

[23] *Cf.* Jorge Riechmann, *Redes que dan libertad: introducción a los nuevos movimientos sociales* (Barcelona: Paidós, 1994), 301.

coined in 1974 by the French writer and feminist Françoise d'Eaubonne (1920–2005). *Ecofeminism* was born, above all, from the encounter between radical environmentalism ("deep ecology") and feminism.[24] *Deep ecology* examines the symbolic, psychological, and ethical patterns, the destructive relationships of human beings with nature, and seeks, above all, to replace them with a life-affirming culture.[25]

> *Ecofeminism* is at once a spiritual movement, a philosophy of life, a political resistance. It is radically opposed to neoliberal globalization. . . .
> Still today considered too extremist by certain feminist groups, this utopian and ethical thinking is nevertheless very reasonable, since it places the sacred value of life above all else.[26]

In Eastern thought, the work of Vandana Shiva stands out.[27] A Hindu feminist, physicist, and philosopher, she mobilized millions of Indian peasant women in the struggle against deforestation, pesticides, and transgenics through the Chipko Movement,

---

[24] *Cf.* the work of the feminist theologian Denise Peeters: Denise Peeters, "Pour une théologie à l'école de l'écologie," *Lumen vitæ* 48, no. 1 (1993), 51–65; it contains an extensive bibliography.

[25] There is no complete overlap between ecofeminist positions and the rest of ecological feminism. *Ecofeminism* argues that women have a different, "natural" relationship with the environment and politics. *Ecological feminism* criticizes them for not getting the analysis of "gender relations" right, being unable to generate a policy adequate to the great environmental threat and not addressing the political problem. *Cf.* Teresa Agustín, "Feminismo y ecologia," in Various, *Ecología y cristianismo. XV Congreso de Teología* (Madrid: Evangelio y Liberación, 1995).

[26] Marina Galimberti, "Écoféminisme: Utopie ou nécessité?," http://www.penelopes.org:80/archives/pages/beijing/. *Cf.*, in Spanish, María Luisa Cavana, Alicia Puleo, and Cristina Segura, *Mujeres y ecología. Historia, pensamiento, sociedad* (Madrid: Al-Mudayna, 2004).

[27] *Cf.* Vandana Shiva, *Staying Alive: Women, Ecology, and Development* (Berkeley: North Atlantic Books, 2016).

one of the most symbolic struggles in the relationship between women and the environment. She is called "the *grande dame* of ecofeminism." For her, ecofeminism is a movement as old as life itself and consists of putting life at the center of social, political, and economic organization. The three principles of ecofeminism are:[28] (1) The Earth is alive, sacred, and connects all living beings; people who take more than they need from the Earth are plundering it. (2) Nature has been replaced by patriarchy, and women, who are part of nature, are subordinated to men and production; creativity has been displaced by capitalism and its bio-piracy; creation becomes destruction, and creation disappears. (3) Respect for all living beings in their diversity.

Finally, an important aspect of ecologism is its *relationship with the poor and the Third World*, an ecologism that is part of a militant alternative and liberating culture: *alter-globalization*. The struggle for the oppressed Earth is also the struggle for the most oppressed human beings, for the victims of the same unjust and predatory system that oppresses this Earth. When we go beyond a bucolic environmentalism, we find the great mass of the impoverished, the greatest victims of the predatory capitalist system—the reality of the Third World. Defending nature and attacking the causes that degrade and pollute it must be inextricably linked to the cause of the poorest, who suffer most from ecological degradation: ecologism means betting on the defense of the weakest in this humanity of offensive inequality. We will explore this further in Pope Francis's revolutionary encyclical *Laudato si'*.

In a world that has never had so many means to solve its vital problems (food, housing, health, etc.), the poverty in which most humanity is immersed is even more scandalous. Giulio Girardi

---

[28] *Cf.* Vandana Shiva, "Ecofeminismo, derechos de la naturaleza, suma kawsay. Diálogo con mujeres ecuatorianas y conferencia," Seminario de Feminismo Nuestroamericano, 2010, http://seminariodefeminismonuestroamericano. blogspot.com/2013/04/vandana-shiva-ecofeminismo-derechos-de.html.

speaks of *ecological racism*, referring to a new concept emerging in the thought of Indigenous peoples and which was coined in 1992 by Rigoberta Menchú: *the crime of ecocide*. Girardi even speaks of *ecogenocide* against Indigenous peoples.

> The destruction of the environment causes the physical and cultural destruction of peoples in the first place; because it violates their right to political, economic, ecological and cultural self-determination, destroys their food sources, provokes violent displacements, etc.
>
> The root of ecocide and genocide is the logic of big capital or the total market, which reduces the Earth to a commodity.[29]

Holistic Sensitivity, the New Paradigm; An Interrelational Worldview

To lay the foundations for a consistent *environmentalism*—which is what interests us here in relation to complexity and relational thinking—we need a *holistic sensibility*. The word *holism* was coined by the South African statesman Jan Smuts in a 1926 book,[30] where he defines holism as "the fundamental factor of everything in the universe." Holism is a paradigm inherited from the sensibility that seeks to include all forms of life (*hólos*, 'totality'), recognizing the *interdependence of all of* them, and seeking to attenuate the *absolute divisions* between human beings, between human beings and all other beings, between the organic and the inorganic, or the old dualisms of spirit-flesh, mind-body, subject-object. For this reason, Leonardo Boff writes:

---

[29] Girardi, "Capitalismo, ecocidio, genocidio: el clamor de los pueblos indígenas," in Girardi, Espeja, and Dussel, *Cristianismo, justicia y ecología*, 30.

[30] *Cf.* Jan Smuts, *Holism and Evolution* (New York: MacMillan Company, 1926); a more recent edition is from Gestalt Journal Press, 2013.

> Ecology implies a basic attitude: to *think always holistically*, continuously see *the totality* . . . , the *organic interdependence of all elements*. . . . Ecology *is either holistic or it is not ecology*.[31]

The holistic vision of the cosmos places environmentalism at a higher and deeper level than the biological and sociopolitical. It aims to attain the concern for an interrelational worldview that encompasses all existing Reality, ranging from the environmental and biological aspects to the cosmological, philosophical, theological, ethical, and spiritual. Thus, we must speak of an eco-technology, an eco-politics, a social ecology, and a mental ecology, for the illness of our world is the symptom revealing that our mind is ill. But we must also speak of an ecological ethics and even of a spiritual eco-logic.

A radical ecological attitude proposes a paradigm shift, where we are not *above* natural reality but *within* it, allowing us to once again *feel* the Earth and the cosmos, the way our ancestors felt and loved them. We are "children of Adam," as the biblical story says, or what is the same: "children of the earth" (*adamâ*).

THE BIBLE AND ECOLOGY: BETWEEN CONTEMPLATION OF THE HARMONY OF THE UNIVERSE AND THE DENUNCIATION OF DESTRUCTIVE SIN

The Bible Is Inherently Green

Biblical Cosmovision and the Conflict of Cosmovisions

The Bible is not a book of science, not even of history in the strict sense of faithfully narrating events, but a book of faith and

---

[31] Leonardo Boff, *Cry of the Earth, Cry of the Poor* (Maryknoll, NY: Orbis Books, 2002).

theology. Its authors are fundamentally interested in transmitting the religious experience, the encounter and relationship with God on the part of exceptionally religious persons and people, with all their contradictions and inconsistencies, which they are not in the habit of hiding.

The biblical authors had a cosmological and historical vision different from ours, but quite precise in its historical and cultural context, which they shared with the neighboring peoples, especially the Babylonians. They accepted this consensually, without conflict. The biblical worldview was based on a universe—the *cosmos,* from the entrance of Hellenic culture into Semitic culture—conceived as a *cosmic house.* In it, the center was the Earth, flat and seated on the columns of Hades, with its peaks (mountains), its chasms (seas), and its valleys. Above it was the celestial vault, a dome supported on each side by columns from which hung luminaries: the Sun, which illuminated the day and moved every day from east to west, and the Moon and stars to illuminate the night. This vault had floodgates that contained the upper waters. This is how this worldview is reflected at the beginning of the Bible:

> In the beginning God created the heaven and the earth.... And God said, Let there be a dome between the waters, to separate the waters from the waters.... God made *the dome,* and separated the waters under it and the waters above it. God called the vault *sky.*... And God said, Let the waters which are under the heavens be gathered together into one place, and let the dry land appear.... God called the dry ground *land,* and the gathered waters he called the *seas....* And God said: Let there be *lights* in the vault of the skies to separate the day from the night, and let them serve as signs to distinguish the seasons, the days and the years.... And to give light to the earth ... he made two great lights. (Genesis 1, 1–15)

The Bible does not invent this conception; it neither defends nor attacks it, it accepts it without further ado. The only thing it defends is the idea of God as Creator and Lord of all. With regard to the texts that interest us here—the biblical accounts of creation—it is necessary to state at the outset something that Galileo Galilei said centuries ago: "The Bible does not speak of *how* heaven *goes*, but of *how one goes* to heaven,"[32] an obvious play on words that uses the word *heaven* with a double meaning, one physical and the other religious. As is well known, the biblical and Greek-Ptolemaic cosmologies maintained for centuries and the modern-contemporary cosmology arising from the Copernican revolution and its defense by Galileo are very different. Following the perspective of the ancient Greek philosophers—slightly different from the biblical conception, claiming that the Earth was curved and perhaps spherical, but in any case without inhabitants at the antipodes—the cosmology of the Greek astronomer Ptolemy (AD 100–170) was *geocentric*, stating that the Earth was immobile and was the center of the universe and that the Sun, the Moon, the planets and the stars of the celestial vault revolved around it. The cosmology of the cleric Copernicus (1473–1543) was *heliocentric*: the center of the universe is near the Sun; orbiting around the Sun are the planets of the solar system; the stars are distant objects that remain fixed and therefore do not orbit around the Sun. Copernicus did not publish his work on heliocentrism until 1543, the year of his death; it was Galileo (1564–1642) who took it up years later and defended Copernicus's revolutionary ideas, condemned in his time. Thus, a *conflict of worldviews*[33] has

---

[32] Galileo Galilei, *Carta a Cristina de Lorena y otros escritos* (Madrid: Alianza, 1987), 65. *Cf.* Polkinghorne's approach in John Polkinghorne, *Ciencia y teología* (Santander: Sal Terræ, 2000); in English, John Polkinghorne, *Science and Theology: An Introduction* (Minneapolis: Fortress Press, 1998).

[33] For Raimon Panikkar, a *kosmology* is a cosmovision, a vision of the world; that is why he speaks of a "worldview conflict," which sets the worldview

prevented the modern world from gathering the wealth that both worldviews contribute.

There are currently three fundamental attitudes toward the biblical accounts of creation. A very common one today is to *scorn them* as antiquated narratives and incompatible with current scientific data; narratives that, in addition, had harmful consequences concerning the scientific and evolutionist conception. An opposing attitude is the traditional one: these chapters are the Word of God, and it is necessary to *interpret them literally*. A third position, accepting the new scientific conception, tries to correctly interpret what the biblical texts say, but place their *understanding in the* cultural *context* of their time; not as scientific affirmations, but with the religious intent to describe the relationship of God with nature and humans, of the relationship between humans and God, and of human beings with each other (sin as confrontation).[34]

If the second attitude—*creationism* in its most rigid and radical position—is fundamentalist, impossible to support with what we know today through science about the origin and evolution of the world and its species (including humans), the first is reductionist and its prejudices prevent us from discovering the real message of the texts. Only the third one, which the best and most serious biblical scholars have been studying for years, is acceptable. Knowledge of the Mesopotamian creation stories has helped us find the cultural matrix of the biblical stories, understand their symbols, and pinpoint their motivations. This motivation is not, as is usually said, *intellectual* (to explain the existence of the world),

---

of the "*mythos* kosmos in which we believe we are living" against the "*logos* kosmos on which we reflect," which implies a necessary "relativization of all worldviews." *Cf.* "Pensamiento científico y pensamiento cristiano," in Panikkar, *La puerta estrecha del conocimiento. Sentido, razón y fe,* 64–65.

[34] *Cf.* José Luis Sicre, "La creación, don de Dios," in *Ecología y cristianismo. XV Congreso de Teología,* ed. Various (Madrid: Evangelio y Liberación, 1995), 77–78.

but vital: God creates for the Covenant, and the Covenant of Sinai is the biblical presupposition of creation, not the other way around, which indissolubly links creation and history.[35] The biblical authors want to show the fascination for creation as the loving work of God and the care he takes of it. God's concern at seeing his world plunged into self-destructive chaos, despite the original harmony of creation; the story of Noah is an ecological parable about God's concern for creatures and the role of humans ("The flood results from the perversity and corruption of men; the earth pays the price for their violence and depravity")[36]. The fate of the Earth and the fate of humans are intimately linked. Hence, the prophetic denunciations against violence toward the poor and creation, and the ecological wisdom manifested in its books of laws. Thus, the encyclical *Laudato si'* rightly speaks of "the wisdom of the biblical stories" (65–83).

The fundamental biblical statements about the relationship between humans and the Earth—some very pertinent to the subject of this book—include:

- The biblical perspective is not anthropocentrism, but *theocentrism*: it is God who is at the center; the human being is *also* a creature.
- A God who is *transcendent and immanent* at the same time. He *is* in the world, but *is not reduced* to the material world.
- Not dualism, but *a unitary vision* of the human being: matter and spirit are *intimately linked* in him and walk together toward a final fulfillment.
- Humans were not directed by God to dominate-plunder the Earth, but were tasked with *living* in harmony with it and *caring for it*, like good gardeners.

---

[35] *Cf.* Juan Luis Ruiz de la Peña, *Teología de la creación* (Santander: Sal Terræ, 1986).

[36] Catherine Charlier, "L'Alliance avec la nature selon la tradition hébraïque," in *Religion et écologie*, ed. Danièle Hervieu-Léger (Paris: CERF, 1993), 25.

- An invitation to *contemplate* the world and what is in it; creation *is a whole*, a reflection of God's beauty and goodness; the human being is immersed in it.

Fundamental Ecological Texts of the Tanakh[37]

The Two Accounts of Creation in Genesis: The Human Being in Creation

Eden is not a historical description of a human past that *was not*. Rather than the *lost paradise* of the beginning, it is the anticipated image of future fulfillment to which human beings and all creation are called. The garden is not a gift from God for the selfish pleasure of humans, but the environment in which they may develop their co-creative activity. Adam and Eve are part of the whole of all living beings; they are there as gardeners, to take care of it, as the Lord does over the world: peacefully and gently.

There are two accounts of creation in the Bible, in chapters 1 and 2 of the book of Genesis. The first (1:1–2, 4a) was called *priestly* (P, after the German *Priestercodex*). The second (2:4b-3:24) was called *yahwist* (Y, for the first letter of the name Yahweh, God in this account). Although this theory of the two sources separated by several centuries—between the seventh and ninth BCE—has come to be questioned in recent years by numerous scholars who affirm the possible contemporaneity of the two accounts, it is still the hypothesis that has the most weight today in the study of the book of Genesis.

---

[37] The *Tanakh* is the Hebrew Bible, the canon of the twenty-four canonical sacred books of Judaism organized in three parts: Torah (Law), Nevi'im (Prophets) and Ketuvim (Writings). Although we use the Christian Bible here (which contains seven deuterocanonical books not included in the Tanakh), we prefer this nomenclature to the classic *Old Testament*. We use the Spanish version of the Bible from La Casa de la Biblia.

Genesis 1:1–2, 4a. In the first story, the sacred author wants to tell the story of the people and the realization of God's promises; but to place the characters in the story, he first needs the setting: a world that is not only the people of the Covenant (Israel), but the whole of humanity. This is a magnificent poem, which echoes the Babylonian *Enuma Elish*, but is clearly distinct from the consequences of its mythology: God appears to organize (*cosmos*) the disorder of the world (*chaos*), in order to make, in a progressive process, a harmonious creation.

The creation of the universe culminates in the creation of the human being (*Adam*). The human being becomes the masterpiece of creation, made "in the image of God" in order to enter into a relationship of interpersonal dialogue with him. The human being receives from God the mission to *dominate* (v. 26 and 28) all created beings, and to fill and *subdue* the earth (v. 28) so that creation may progress and perfect itself according to God's plan. But this dominion is not meant to turn the human being into a despot, but into the *caretaker* of this created world. The author even goes so far as to make Adam and Eve vegetarians (v. 29); in the harmony of paradise, it is a shocking mentality that a living being should be killed for food. If the Creator *dominates* creation by taking care of it, respecting the laws of each being (v. 11 and others), the human being cannot act otherwise. This is what the most serious exegesis of these biblical texts teaches us. The word *subdue* (*kabas*) has the usual meaning of "to set foot on an object or living being"; a gesture that, far from being something necessarily violent, simply symbolizes care and protection: "Since man, following the mission of the peace-loving Creator, has to set foot on the earth, this nuance suggests something very different from that violent meaning, to which could be added arbitrary exploitation." The same is true of the word *dominate* (*radah*): "It must be beyond the intention of the text a kind of tyrannical domination, in keeping with the ancient Eastern ruler's ideal of the good and just shepherd. . . . *Radah* means the shepherd's walk with his sheep, leading them to good pasture, caring for them and defending them."[38]

Genesis 2:4b-3:24. The second story, emphasizing the influence of wisdom, aimed to explain the beginning of the human race. As it is written by sages, the human being appears as a sage who knows all the botanical and animal species. The author's perspective is different from the previous one: he is not interested in the creation of the universe; what interests him is to reflect on the human being and the way to find the meaning of his life, specifically, the problem of evil. The fate of humans and the Earth will always be closely linked. The very play on words between *adam* (human being) and *adamâ* (earth) insists on this strong link between the human being and the Earth; an earth in which his life is rooted and which he must care for with tenderness.

Human comes from *humus* (earth, mud); therefore, he is intimately joined to it: he is a "son of the earth" in whom the divine spirit (*ruah*) exceptionally breathes. He is in Eden as a gardener, to tend the garden and to grow and develop as a person through this work, walking with it toward cosmic fullness. For this reason, it is necessary to de-reify nature in order to turn it into a subject of rights. In the biblical conception, the human being belongs to the same category as all other living beings (*nefesh hayya*), even if he is superior in the hierarchy. To break human harmony and the harmony with creation (*sin*)[39]

---

[38] Alexandre Ganoczy, "Ecological Perspectives of the Christian Doctrine of the Creation," *Concilium*, no. 236 (1991), specifically "The Double Meaning of *Subdue* and *Dominate*," 62–64.

[39] To speak of the *sin* of Eden, we must first keep in mind that it is not a historical account, but a prophetic-sapiential reflection on the drama of human existence and a call for human beings to overcome this situation, since it is contrary to the will of the Creator. *Original sin* is the fruit of the state of imperfection and immaturity of the human being, and the *fall* of the natural order, the expression of the necessary situation of an evolving cosmos. While the *order* of paradise is the image of the harmony to which the human being

is to initiate a process of self-destruction. Everything was good, but nature, from the beginning, suffered the consequences of man's *anti-ecological sin*.

Two Accounts from Leviticus And Deuteronomy: Living in Harmony with the Cosmos

Leviticus and Deuteronomy are two books of the Pentateuch (the Hebrew Torah), full of laws that feel distant for Christians and today's secular world, but which provide us with some interesting pages on the concern of God and humans toward all of nature.

Leviticus 25:1–12. "The seventh year shall be a year of absolute rest for the land," or with another translation: "so that the land may have a Sabbath." It is a text that speaks of the rest of the land: a *sabbatical year* (25:2–7) every seven years -the Sabbath is the seventh day, of rest and praise to God—and a *jubilee year* (25:8–12), which takes place every fifty years (seven weeks of years: 7 x 7 = 49 + 1 = 50). The *sabbatical* and the *jubilee* year are both years of ecological rest for the earth, so that it is not exhausted by unbridled exploitation, and humans may live in harmony with it. Moltmann rightly says: "The biblical creation ethic is essentially a *Sabbath ethic*, because the Sabbath is the law of creation.[40]

According to this concept of the sabbatical year, the *land is not given to the people* of Israel, but rather it seems that it is *the people*

---

and all creation are called, the *disorder* caused by the fall would be the current reality and that of all of human history from the beginning (irrationality, violence . . .); the unfinished process of the human being, the Kingdom of God that suffers violence, as Jesus of Nazareth said.

[40] Jürgen Moltmann, *La justicia crea futuro. Política de la paz y ética de la creación en un mundo amenazado* (Santander: Sal Terræ, 1992) 91; in English, Jürgen Moltmann, *Creating a Just Future: The Politics of Peace and the Ethics of Creation in a Threatened World* (London: SCM Press, 1989).

who are given the land to care for it; thus, this sabbatical year is the secret of human harmony with creation.

Deuteronomy 30:15–20. In a similar vein, Deuteronomy has some impressive words in the third oration of the book:

> Behold, today I set before you life and happiness, death and misfortune. If you listen to the commandments of the Lord your God . . . , following his ways . . . , you will live and be fruitful... But if your heart turns away, if you do not listen, if you allow yourself to be carried away and bow down to other gods and worship them, I declare today that you will perish without remedy; you will not live long on earth.
>
> *Before you are life and death, blessing and curse. Choose life and* you and your offspring *will live.*

These words are charged with a clearly prophetic tone, and place the people before a double path, "life and death, blessing and curse"; a crossroads where they must necessarily choose to either live in harmony with nature or in struggle against it, prostrating themselves before the depredatory idol of productivity. Their future depends on it: "choose life and you will live."

The Psalms: The Songs of Harmonious Creation

It is in the Psalms where the biblical *greenery* is most explicitly and widely manifested; where *communion and cosmic harmony* are sung with the most strength and beauty. These marvelous literary creations know how to find words that not only express, but sing in our ears the Reality of God, Lord of the Earth, who has a passion for his sons and daughters and for all creation, both living beings and inanimate matter. Creation is not seen as a function of human utility, as an illusory anthropocentrism might claim, but as a value in itself.

The spirituality of the Psalms is, in this sense, a *contemplative spirituality*; it invites us to contemplatively admire the whole of creation as the marvelous work of God and, through it and in it, to admire God's constant presence and action. A labor that continues each day, with the loving care of its Creator. Creation is inhabited by God, which invites us to live in it as in a sacred temple and to constant thanksgiving and *praise*.

Psalm 8. "O Lord our God, how wonderful is your name in all the earth!" An invitation to the contemplation of creation; to feel immersed in it, to know God in it, and to know humans themselves.

Psalm 19. "The heavens proclaim the glory of God, the firmament proclaims the work of his hands, the day to the day gives the proclamation, the night to the night gives the tidings." The psalm describes a magnificent communication of all the elements of creation, an interconnection of everything.

Psalm 96. "Let the heavens rejoice, and let the earth be glad. | . . . the sea and all that fills it." Again, a song of praise to all creation in harmony.

Psalm 104. "Thou hast settled the earth upon its foundations. . . . | How many are thy works, O Lord! Thou hast made them all in wisdom." A poetic gloss on the Genesis 1 account, another invitation to contemplation.

Psalm 114. "When Israel came out of Egypt . . . The sea when it saw them fled. . . . What aileth thee, O sea, that thou fleest? And ye mountains, that ye leap like rams? . . . In the presence of the Lord the earth dances." It is the *dance of creation*. The human being appears in it as one more element in the context of nature.

Psalm 147. "How good it is to sing to our God: count the number of the stars, and call each one by name." Another invitation to the praise of God, to the confidence and respect of creation, and to the contemplation of a nature that renews itself every day with the power of the Spirit, which acts from within matter, as Teilhard de Chardin will write.

Psalm 148. "Praise the Lord from the heavens! | . . . Praise the Lord from the earth, you sea monsters and all the oceans, you mountains and all the hills!" Another song of praise to the Creator God in which all of creation is seen by the psalmist as a cosmic instrument, where God's glory resounds harmonically as in a beautiful symphony.

The Utopian Cry and the Denunciation of the Prophets

The Prophets denounce the mistreatment and injustice suffered by the poor, linking them to the mistreatment of the earth, and cry out for the recovery of the broken harmony, which will come especially in the messianic era.

Amos 4:7–9. "I withheld rain from you the three months before the harvest. . . . I smote you with blight and blight, I dried up your gardens and vineyards." The most ancient of the prophets who left us written work raises his tragic voice, announcing an ecological catastrophe caused by sin, manifested in the predatory spirit of the powerful who oppress people and lands.

Hosea 4:1–3. "There is neither faithfulness nor love. . . . Therefore the land is destroyed and all that lives in it dies of thirst, the wild animals as well as the birds of the sky." An impressive plea by the prophet Hosea against "those who rule the land" and oppress the weak, the people, and the earth. The source of the death that chokes the country is the wickedness of the heart of the powerful: lying, perjury, theft, murder, idol worship. The prophets repeat again and again that the *idol* par excellence is Mammon, money; a voracious and insatiable idol that kills the life of the poor and indeed all life.

Isaiah 14:7–8. "How the tyrant is ended! . . . The earth rests quietly, . . . even the cypresses celebrate your ruin, and the cedars say: 'Since you succumbed the woodcutter does not come up to cut us down.'" Isaiah is the great prophet of Israel. His lengthy book is the labor of a school that continued its work for over two hundred years (740 BC–485 BC), and which biblical scholars divide into at least three parts: I Isaiah, II, and III; a brilliant text of great creative capacity. In Isaiah II, above all, the harmony of creation is a recurring theological theme; the death of the people and the death of the earth are intimately linked. Chapter 24 evokes an ecological disaster due to sin, injustice, and ongoing war: "The earth will be devastated, completely plundered. . . . The land languishes and withers . . . , it has been profaned by its inhabitants, because they have transgressed the law by violating the perpetual covenant." In spite of everything, the prophetic word always ends with hopeful tones: "The Lord God . . . will destroy death forever, wipe away tears from all faces and wipe away reproach from the earth" (Is 25:6–8). The restoration of the people is a new creation; the messianic times are like a return to the harmony of paradise (Is 11:1–10). Justice and the harmony of creation are intimately linked: there can be no true ecological peace without economic and political justice. The eschatological dream is to rediscover complete harmony between humans, all other living beings, and all of Reality.

This text is a satire against the king of Babylon. The kings of Assyria and Babylon, besides cutting off heads, indiscriminately cut down the cedars of Lebanon and the cypresses of Amanus, both as an expression of their proud power and for military reasons. But God breaks the tyrant's rod. Therefore, nature exultantly joins in the people's song for the fall of the tyrant with these beautiful and ecologic views. The coming of peace brings harmony to the earth.

Jeremiah 12:10–11. "Numerous shepherds have devastated my vineyard . . . , they make my favorite field a wilderness. . . . The whole land is desolate." Jeremiah is the second of the great prophets of Israel. His sensitivity protests the idolatry and social injustice that turn the fertile land into a desert and wasteland

(Jer 12:10–13). The prophet cries out against the plunderers who ravage and destroy the land.

Daniel 3:56–88. "All ye works of the Lord, bless the Lord. . . . Sun and moon, bless the Lord. . . . Cold and heat, bless the Lord. . . . Let the earth bless the Lord." This is the beautiful song of praise of Daniel and his young companions, thrown into the fire by the tyrant. The author invites us to bless the Lord with the sun, the moon, and the stars, the plants and the animals, because God is great and all of creation is the work of his love. It is another antecedent of the Franciscan *Canticle of the Creatures*; or, more recently, of Ernesto Cardinal's *Cosmic Canticle*.

The Wisdom of Israel: Books of Wisdom, Job, and Ecclesiastes

The sapiential literature of Israel constantly calls for a contemplation of creation; in it, the divine reality is manifested, and the mystery of the world and the human condition are illuminated.

Wisdom 11:24–26. "Thou lovest all that exists and dost not abhor anything that Thou hast made. . . . How would it subsist if Thou didst not will it? . . . Lord, friend of life." It is in the book of Wisdom that the word *cosmos* appears most often in the entire Tanakh (19 times). This is no doubt because of its Hellenistic origin, but here the world is not handled capriciously by the divinity as with the Greek gods, but is cared for with tenderness. The book of Wisdom constantly insists on the loving presence of God in creation; for its author, the order of the cosmos leads us to the knowledge of the Creator.

Job 38:4–7, 16–18, 25–27, 34–36; 39:5–8. "Where were you when I formed the Earth?. . . . Do you know who set his seal? . . . Who enclosed the sea with a double door . . . ?" The book of Job is a tremendous plea against an illusory anthropocentrism. The universe does not revolve around human beings; all natural reality has a value in itself, which comes from being also a creature of God, like the human being himself. That is why, when

Job "overwhelms" God with questions about his suffering, the answer of the Lord comes in the form of questions that cannot find an easy answer among the wise.

Ecclesiastes 3:19–20. "One and the same is the fate of men and animals: the death of the one is like the death of the other, both have the same vital breath.... All come from dust and return to dust." Qoheleth bluntly expresses the unity of destiny of human beings with all creation.

Jesus of Nazareth, an "Ecologist": The Cosmic Christ

Jesus of Nazareth, the most vivid portrait of God, was an "ecologist" *avant la lettre*, who loved nature, who felt intimately united to it through deep bonds, who lived in harmony with it and who invited his followers to admire it, respect it, work it, and enjoy it justly. As the Gospels show, he always valued positively the radical goodness and dignity of matter and of all creation: "Nothing that is outside a man can defile him. It is what comes from within that defiles a man" (Mk 7:15). His creative and authoritative word (Mk 1:22) is even independent of the authority of the Prophets. Paul's texts show, as we shall see, that Christ came to bring about the unity of the universe, heaven and earth.

The Gospels: Jesus, Nature and the Cosmos

The whole of Jesus's life is completely framed in the natural environment of a fundamentally rural world, in direct and constant relationship with nature.[41] His family is from the village of Nazareth, his mother a young farmer and his father a craftsman. He spent thirty years in that humble village: the school, the daily chores, the natural cycles of the seasons with their

---

[41] *Cf.* John Dominic Crossan, *The Historical Jesus: The Life of a Mediterranean Jewish Peasant* (Edinburgh: T&T Clark, 1992).

sowing, pruning, reaping and harvesting. . . . The wisdom that Jesus learned living in the village, in contact with nature, with his roots, is then evident in the way he speaks and presents his message.

Jesus of Nazareth is not an academic philosopher who speaks in abstract discourse; he starts from life, from concrete realities, from real daily events, from the work of the people and the observation of nature. This Galilean makes a profound observation of natural and social life without remaining superficial (Mark 13:28 and Matthew 6:26–30); he is able to grasp the greatness of the small and the harmonious unity of all Reality. For this reason, the people who listened to him were amazed, because "he spoke with authority" (Mk 1:22), not with hollow words or simply glossing over the Law, like the rabbis, but *with revealing* words. In this way, the good news (*Euangélion*) is a natural wisdom framed in the reality of nature, with the freedom of the birds and animals of the mountain.

Even his birth is framed in a space of harmony with nature. The stable in Bethlehem—the symbolic place where the Gospel situates his birth—is a magnificent setting that places Jesus squarely in natural reality: he is born in the silence of the night, with the stars in the sky as the background filtering through the cracks in the stable, at the feet of animals, with the common smell of manure and straw. The *ecological* and humble shepherds—always immersed in the wildness of nature—are the first worshippers and messengers of the birth of the Savior, an announcement in which the firmament also participates (Luke 2). Ian Bradley values the wisdom that this beautiful account of Luke, more theological than historical, conveys to us about Jesus's relationship with nature:

> In picturing the infant Jesus as lying on a bed of straw surrounded by cows and sheep and oxen children's Christmas story-books may well embody a deep truth about Our

Lord's relationship with nature that we tend to overlook in the adult church. Previous generations have been more ready to make the connection that this imagery suggests. In 1655 the diarist Ralph Josselin dreamed that Christ was born in a stable "because he was the redeemer of man and beast out of their bondage by the Fall."[42]

Even the choice of the day of birth, which the Church fixed centuries later on December 25, seems to have a strong relationship with nature. On that day, the Romans celebrated *Natalis Solis Invicti*, the Feast of the Birth of the Sun on the winter solstice; a natural pagan feast that was Christianized, emphasizing that there was no greater star than Jesus Christ, as Zechariah had already prophesied: "By the tender mercy of our God, the sun will visit, that is born from above, to enlighten those who sit in darkness and the shadow of death, to direct our steps to the way of peace" (Lk 1:78).

After the years spent in the village, Jesus left the family home and went to immerse himself in the Jordan River to receive John's baptism, with Heaven and Earth in intimate connection: "As he came up out of the water, the heavens were opened and he saw the Spirit of God" (Mt 3:15–17). The public life of Jesus is prefaced by a time of discernment, reflection, and prayer in the harshness and solitude of the Judean desert, where he "lived among the wild beasts," but in harmony with them and with the whole cosmos (Mk 1:13); an account that manifests the messianic harmony announced by the prophet Isaiah. This full harmony of Jesus with creation will also be seen by those who follow him in amazement: "Who is this man, that even the wind and the sea obey him?" (Mt 8:27)

---

[42] Ian Bradley, *Dios es verde. Cristianismo y medio ambiente* (Santander: Sal Terræ, 1993), 110–111; in English, Ian Bradley, *God Is Green: Christianity and the Environment* (London: Darton, Longman & Todd, 1990).

Finally, Jesus chooses a group of friends—fishermen, not scholars!—and goes off to announce the Kingdom of God along the roads of Palestine, in contact with nature, walking the land for hours and hours, day after day, the dusty roads and the sown fields, sleeping many nights in the open or in the villages he entered. The Gospels tell how, in the midst of the hard and intense days with the people, Jesus liked to withdraw and retire to the mountains, to the solitude of the countryside or to the silence of the night, to better find himself and his Father God, in the harmony of the cosmos; there, he prayed more at ease and found it easier to communicate with the Father (Mk 1:35; Lk 6:12 . . .).

In his preaching, Jesus habitually used images of nature that showed a profound knowledge of it; both in his *parables*—impregnated with a wisdom developed in contact with nature—as in the examples for any occasion: the wheat and the weeds (Mt 13:24–30), the vine and the branches (Jn 15:1–6), the mustard seed (Mt 13:31–32), the lost sheep (Lk 15:4–6). . . . A great biblical scholar comments: "These images come from the conviction that what there is between the *natural order of the world* and the *spiritual order* is not pure analogy, but an *intimate affinity*; the Kingdom of God is similar to the processes of nature."[43]

> Look at the birds of the air; they neither sow nor reap nor gather into their barns, and yet your heavenly Father feeds them. . . . And why do you worry about clothing? See how the lilies of the field grow; they toil not, neither do they spin; and yet I tell you that not even Solomon in all his splendor was clothed like any of them. (Mt 6:26–29)

But Jesus, like the old prophets, also denounces the situation of oppression, injustice and death, as well as its consequences, in

---

[43] Charles Harold Dodd, *Las parábolas del Reino* (Madrid: Cristiandad, 1974), 21; in English, Charles Harold Dodd, *The Parables of the Kingdom* (Glasgow: Fontana Books, 1961).

which the destiny of the people and of the earth are intimately linked: "Peoples will rise up against peoples and kingdom against kingdom, and there will be famines and earthquakes in various places" (Mt 24:7).

Finally, the Nazarene, victim of the oppression of the powerful, dies on a hill, naked, with a crown of thorns as an ornament, nailed to a piece of wood. The evangelists sing sonorous words of how the whole of creation identifies with and is in solidarity with that innocent man who was executed; nature mourns his death with the cry of a new world that sounds like childbirth:

> From noon on, the whole region was in darkness until three o'clock.... And Jesus gave up his spirit with a loud cry. Then the veil of the temple was torn in two from top to bottom; the earth shook and the stones cracked. (Mt 27:45, 52).

John and Paul: The Cosmic Christ and the Fullness of Reality

The Christ proclaimed by the Christian faith goes beyond the historical reality of Jesus of Nazareth to become Christ the Savior of humanity and of the entire cosmos: the *cosmic Christ*. The Christian faith goes so far as to state that in that Man the presence of God was so exceptional that it can only be expressed in such an extreme affirmation as to say that he is "the only-begotten Son of God made flesh." This is what theology calls the *incarnation*: that Jesus of Nazareth is the Kyrios, the cosmic Christ, the Lord of Heaven and Earth and the principle of harmony for all Reality.[44]

---

[44] In the cosmology that underlies these texts of John and Paul, the biblical reference is undoubtedly predominant, but also the apocalyptic references and the Greco-Roman cosmologies, among which the Stoic example should be highlighted as one that invites us to conform to the order of Reality in which we find ourselves and which transcends us. Also the Gnostic conceptions, with their struggle between good and evil, light and darkness.

The Evangelist John expresses it grandly in the Prologue of his Gospel, calling Jesus Christ the Word (*Logos*) of God made flesh (Jn 1:1–3; 14). It is the profound union between Divinity and humanity; a union *without division,* but a union *without confusion*; a *hypostatic union,* as the Councils of Chalcedon (451) and Constantinople II (533) said of Jesus the Christ.[45] This total God-human, spirit-matter communion (*theandrism*, which Panikkar later expanded into *cosmotheandrism*, uniting the cosmic dimension to the divine and human) is the best expression of the non-duality of Reality:

> At the beginning
> the Word already existed . . .
> and the Word was God. . . .
> All things were made by it,
> and without it nothing was made
> of all that came into existence. . . .
> *And the Word was made flesh
> and dwelt among us.*

The idea of a Christ who is not only the *savior* of humanity, but also the *creator* and *consummator*, who maintains and *evolves the cosmos*, was developed above all by Paul of Tarsus. In a special way, the Pauline cosmic hymns affirm that Christ is the *firstborn* of every creature, of the new creation, through whom everything *comes into being*. He is the principle of *reconciliation* of all, of the intimate union of all Reality, both human and non-human; reconciliation of human beings and of the whole cosmos with

---

[45] The Chalcedonian Creed states: "We confess one and the same Son and Lord Jesus Christ . . . truly God and truly man . . . *without confusion, without change, without division, without separation.*" DS 301–302; Heinrich Denzinger and Peter Hünerman, *El Magisterio de la Iglesia* (Barcelona: Herder, 2000), aka Enchiridion Symbolorum.

God. Christ is *the pleroma*, the fullness of all, the cosmic totality. This is manifested in the hymn with which the Letter to the Colossians begins, a true cosmic hymn:

> Christ is the image of the invisible God,
> the firstborn of every creature.
> In him all things were created,
> things in heaven and on earth. . . .
> Christ exists before all things
> and they all have their consistency in him.
> . . .
> God was pleased to make *fullness* dwell in him,
> and through him to reconcile to himself all things,
> both things in heaven and things on earth,
> bringing peace through his blood
> shed on the cross. (Col 1:15–20)

It is a text in which the *cosmic Christ* is clearly manifested, in direct connection with the historical Jesus who died on the cross, who unites what was divided.

Another beautiful hymn along these lines is the one at the beginning of the Letter to the Ephesians (Eph 1:3–14): Christ is "the head of all things, things in heaven and things on earth"; he is called to "bring history to its *fullness*," "to bring about the *unity of the universe*." In this way, the whole universe, heavenly and earthly, will attain its unity in Christ, the principle of unity, the fullness of all Reality.

And in the Letter to the Romans, the longest and most theologically dense of the Pauline letters, Paul says that creation lives in the hope that it *too* will be freed from the bondage of corruption.

> For creation it is anxiously awaiting the manifestation of what the children of God will be.... *Creation lives in the hope that it too will be freed from the bondage of corruption and thus participate in the glorious salvation of the children of God.* We know that the whole of creation is groaning with birth pangs to this day. But not only it, we too, who already possess the first fruits of the Spirit, groan within ourselves, sighing for God to make us his children and free our bodies. (Rom 8:19–23)

All Reality, animate and inanimate, participates in the redemption of Christ. His resurrection represents the triumph of life over death, the total liberation from finitude. Using the Jewish apocalyptic tradition, which spoke of the convulsion of the whole earth in the judgment of God, Paul sees the human being and all creation indissolubly united in salvation and in the dawn of the new creation. It could not be more strongly stated that the universe and humanity walk together on the same path to their fullness.

Finally, we find this cosmic Christ in the Apocalypse. At the beginning of the book: "I am the Alpha and the Omega, who is, who was and who is to come, the Almighty" (Rev 1:8). And at the end: "I am the Alpha and the Omega, the First and the Last, the Beginning and the End" (Rev 22:13).

This Alpha and Omega Christ of all Reality is at the basis of Teilhard de Chardin's anthropological-cosmological-theological conception: Christ is the beginning (A) and the end (Ω), the Omega Point that attracts humanity and the cosmos in the constant ascent of matter toward its consummation.[46] *Christogenesis* is the process by which the Christ "prepared by cosmic evolution"

---

[46] In the evolutionary process, Teilhard speaks of *the geosphere* (geological evolution), the *biosphere* (biological evolution) and the *noosphere* (the evolution of universal consciousness in the human being). Thanks to this last phase, humankind evolves toward the *christosphere*, the process in which the entire universe evolves toward Christ. This evolution can be summarized as:

is consummated at the Parousia "when the Mystical Body is totally finished."⁴⁷ Then, humanity and the universe will form the *Total Christ*; "the Universal Christ presented by the Gospels and more especially by St. Paul and St. John," Teilhard himself states.⁴⁸ *Matter and spirit will be* one when evolution converges at the Omega Point. The *Omega Point* is the *cosmic Christ*, the maximum point of synthesis of the spiritual and the material, integrated in the space-time of the universe. Teilhard explains that space and time are organically united, forming the "fabric of the universe," the *seamless fabric* of which we spoke in the first part.

"I believe that Evolution is directed toward Spirit. I believe that the Universe is an Evolution. I believe that the Spirit flows into the Personal. I believe that the supreme Personal is the Christ-Universal," writes Teilhard.⁴⁹ This conception expresses the "*Christic diaphany* of matter"; it is "a new mysticism" that unites Heaven and Earth, an eternal human aspiration, in the words of one of Teilhard's greatest connoisseurs, the biologist and thinker Claude Cuénot.⁵⁰

Leonardo Boff writes regarding Teilhard's conception:

Cosmogenesis-Biogenesis-Noogenesis / Anthropogenesis-Christogenesis, from the Alpha of the origin to the final Omega Point.

⁴⁷ Claude Cuénot, *Nuevo léxico de Teilhard de Chardin* (Madrid: Taurus, 1968), 90; *cf.* 89–92.

⁴⁸ Pierre Teilhard de Chardin, *Ciencia y Cristo* (Madrid: Taurus, 1968), specifically "Sobre el Cristo-Universal," 37–44.

⁴⁹ Pierre Teilhard de Chardin, *Como yo creo* (Madrid: Taurus, 1970), 105; in English, *How I Believe* (Perennial Library, 1969).

⁵⁰ "Through *cosmogenesis* a conciliation between the abscissa OX (below) and the coordinate OY (above) appears possible through a *via tertia*, OR, forward. Through... the ascent of cosmogenesis to the encounter with divine grace, the ancient passion for the divine can be synthesized with the ancient passion for the Earth." Claude Cuénot, *Ciencia y fe en Teilhard de Chardin* (Barcelona: Plaza & Janés, 1972), 100–101; in English, Claude Cuénot, *Science and Faith in Teilhard de Chardin* (London: Garnstone Press, 1967). For this Christological conception of Teilhard's as a paradigm for a new Christology, see also Ilia Delio, *Christ in Evolution* (Maryknoll, NY: Orbis Books, 2008).

Everything is being gestated within the cosmogenic process to the extent that more complex orders emerge, more and more internalized and interconnected with all beings. When there is a certain level of accumulation of this background energy, then the emergence of historical facts and of each singular person occurs.

The one who saw this gestation of Christ in the cosmos was the paleontologist and mystic Teilhard de Chardin, the one who reconciled the Christian faith with the idea of extended evolution and with the new cosmology. He distinguishes the *Christic* from the *Christian*. The Christic is presented as an objective datum within the process of evolution. It would be that link that unites everything with everything. Because it was within it, it could one day burst into history in the figure of Jesus of Nazareth, the one through whom all things have their existence and consistency, in the words of St. Paul.[51]

The *cosmic Christ* is very present in the ecological conception of the Brazilian liberation theologian. Already in one of his first books, he writes:

> Jesus-man is the result of a long process of cosmic evolution. As a body-spirit, Jesus of Nazareth was also a knot of relationships with the human and cosmic totality that surrounded him. He experienced this in a limited way in his historical situation in the Palestine of his time. But the resurrection realized the total openness of the man-Jesus to the proportions of the God-Jesus. . . . His capacity for communion and communication with the matter of the world was fully realized, so that he is not present only in Palestinian space and time, but in the totality of space and

---

[51] Boff, "El Cristo Cósmico: Una espiritualidad del universo."

time. The resurrection revealed the cosmic dimension of Christ, filling the world and human history from the beginning.... The cosmic Christ, resurrected, penetrated the heart of matter and of all creation.[52]

In another of his early writings, recently updated, Boff writes:

In the Christian sphere, an ancient tradition has been revived: that of the cosmic Christ. Texts dating back to the beginnings of Christianity, especially the reflections of St. Paul, present Christ as the head of the cosmos, affirming that everything was made by him, in him and for him. This conception has led to the birth of a true cosmic mysticism. Christ is not found only in the Scriptures, in the Church or in the consecrated host; his natural place is the cosmos. And since the cosmos is the result of an immense evolutionary process, Christ is also part and fruit of that process. There must be signs of him imprinted in the convolutions of this already long journey of our universe.

But cosmic Christology does not only seek to understand the dimensions of Christ's reality that reach out to the universe; it also seeks to respond to an ever-present quest of the human spirit: what is the factor, the energy, the link that makes the universe a cosmos and not chaos? This interest is not only historiographical but mainly existential: How can the Unity of the Whole be conceived, how can it be revealed, how does Christianity elaborate its answer?[53]

---

[52] Leonardo Boff, *Jesucristo el Liberador* (Colombia: Indo-American Press, 1977), 217–219; in English, Leonardo Boff, *Jesus Christ Liberator: A Critical Christology for Our Time* (Maryknoll, NY: Orbis Books, 1978).

[53] "Introduction," in Leonardo Boff, *Evangelio del Cristo cósmico. Hacia una nueva conciencia planetaria* (Madrid: Trotta, 2009). His groundbreaking book was published as Leonardo Boff, *O Evangelho do Cristo Cósmico* (Petrópolis: Editora Vozes, 1971).

Boff will return to the theme on numerous occasions, especially in his book *Ecología: Grito de la Tierra, grito de los pobres*.[54] He assumes Teilhard's perspectives as the path of evolution from cosmogenesis to *Christogenesis*: "The Word gradually ascended the ladder of energies and beings to the point of taking on a specific face in . . . Jesus of Nazareth, who was then called the Christ . . . at work in it was the Christic principle." With the new scientific conception applied to theology, he says: "Christology becomes Christogenesis." With *Christogenesis*, "the entire universe, through Jesus, takes a leap forward and upward and offers the human mind a datum that it bore within itself but that had not yet emerged to this extent: that God is Father and that we are all sons and daughters." When Christians call Jesus "the Christ," they state that in the man of Nazareth the mystery of God was manifested to the highest, unsurpassable degree: he is *God-man*, the self-revelation of God. In this way, "the Christian faith becomes the spearhead of cosmic consciousness": the *cosmic Christ*.

A text from the Coptic Gospel of Thomas (*logion* 77), one of the apocryphal Gospels discovered in 1955 in the Gnostic library of Nag Hammadi, highlighted by the biblical scholar Joachim Jeremias, is a magnificent expression of this cosmic Christology:

> I am the light that is above all.
> *I am the all*: the all has gone out of me, and
>   the all has returned to me.
> Cut the wood, I am there,
> lift the stone and you will find me there.[55]

---

[54] Quotes from Leonardo Boff, *Ecología. Grito de la tierra, grito de los pobres*, (Madrid: Trotta, 1996), Chapter 9: "El Cristo cósmico" (221–234); in English, Boff, *Cry of the Earth, Cry of the Poor*.

[55] Joachim Jeremias, *Unknown Sayings of Jesus* (Eugene, OR: Wipf and Stock, 2008).

4

Green Christian Faith Betrayed. Theology and the Churches in the Face of Ecological Challenge. Pope Francis and *Laudato Si'*

Christianity is the most anthropocentric religion the world has seen. . . . It made it possible to exploit nature in a mood of indifference to the feelings of natural objects.

LYNN WHITE, "The Historical Roots of Our Ecological Crises"

Christian faith is intrinsically Green; the good news of the Gospel promises liberation and fulfilment for the whole of creation.

IAN BRADLEY, *God Is Green: Christianity and the Environment*

Our common home is like a sister with whom we share our life and a beautiful mother who opens her arms to embrace us. . . . We have come to see ourselves as her lords and masters, entitled to plunder her at will.

POPE FRANCIS, *Laudato si'*

> *All creatures are connected. . . . All beings need each other.*
> *. . . Everything is connected.*
>
> POPE FRANCIS, *Laudato si'*

GREEN CHRISTIAN FAITH BETRAYED: CHRISTIAN THEOLOGY AND THE CHURCHES IN THE FACE OF ECOLOGICAL CHALLENGE

Christians and Their Share of the Blame for the Assault on the Environment

Throughout their two thousand years of history, Christians have forgotten the ecological wisdom and harmony of Jesus of Nazareth and the biblical texts. Or that of Francis, the mystic and poet of Assisi, with his motto Deus meus et omnia ("My God and all things"); a true cosmic slogan, a call to recover the broken harmony with oneself, with God and with all of nature.

The Judeo-Christian religion, like Islam,[1] was strongly criticized by *environmentalists* for having created in Western man the attitudes that led to the current ecological disaster. The cause lay in favoring anthropocentrism, which led him to do whatever he wanted with creation. Lynn White (1907–1987) was the first to launch this accusation against Christianity in an article published in *Science* magazine, quoted hundreds of times until it became a classic text: "The Historical Roots of Our Ecological Crisis." Like him, many others saw in what was called the "Judeo-Christian concept of conquest of nature" one of the elements that originated the ecological problem:

---

[1] *Cf.* Antonio Lucena, "La ecología y las grandes religiones," in *Ecología y cristianismo. XV Congreso de Teología*, ed. Various (Madrid: Evangelio y Liberación, 1995).

> *Christianity is* the most anthropocentric religion the world has seen. Christianity, in absolute contrast to ancient paganism and Asia's religions (except, perhaps, Zorastrianism), not only established a dualism of man and nature but also insisted that it is God's will that man exploit nature for his proper ends. (. . .) Christianity made it possible to exploit nature in a mood of indifference to the feelings of natural objects. (. . .) Man's effective monopoly on spirit in this world was confirmed, and the old inhibitions to the exploitation of nature crumbled.[2]

White made a harsh accusation against Christians. In addition to having favored anthropocentrism, Christianity would despise matter in favor of spirit. This "Christian pride" would ultimately trigger the ecological tragedy, because human beings would no longer feel connected to nature and its future.

But as we have seen above, although we must acknowledge that the texts of Genesis emphasize the superiority of human beings over nature and that the Christian tradition was imbued with the conviction of human domination/exploitation of nature rather than love and respect for it, it is also true that in the Bible nature appears as a reflection of its Creator and as something that the believer must respect and care for; the human being forms a single reality with all that exists. Moreover, in the most authentic current of the Judeo-Christian faith there is no negative conception of the world, since its starting point is God's salvation embedded in the reality of matter: an *incarnationist* dynamic. The biblical God is not at all *spiritualistic*, but rather *materialistic*: he is more concerned with material reality than with "spiritual" reality. The Christian conception of reality is not *dualistic*, but *unitary*: matter and spirit are intimately linked and walk together

---

[2] Lynn White, "The Historical Roots of Our Ecological Crises," *Science*, no. 155 (1967), 1203–1207.

toward the final fullness; the *cosmic Christ* realizes the unity of the universe (Eph 1:3–4; Col 1:15–20; Rev 21 . . .).

But we Christians must accept our share of the blame for the assault on the environment: we must accept our sin, which, like all sin, is also the fruit of selfishness and waste. Thus stated Anglican theologian Ian Bradley:

> Christian faith is *intrinsically Green*; the good news of the Gospel promises liberation and fulfilment for the whole of creation. (. . .) But to find this green Gospel . . . we need to clear away centuries of anthropocentric thinking which has put man rather than God at the centre of the universe and which has made the Church in the western world at least one of the prime aiders and abetters of the exploitation and pollution of the earth's resources.[3]

To give just a few examples of important Christian thinkers, we can cite Thomas Aquinas, the great medieval philosopher and theologian, who wrote: "If any text of Scripture seems to forbid us to be cruel to animals, it is only because either being cruel to animals makes us cruel to human beings, or because the harm caused produces a material injury to mankind." In the sixteenth century, the reformer Calvin stated: "The end for which all things were created was that men should lack none of the comforts and necessities of life." Also in the twentieth century, Professor John Dickie, theologian of the Church of Scotland, said: "The world exists for us and not for itself." And Cardinal John Henry Newman, the great Anglican-born thinker who converted to Catholicism, went so far as to write in the *Catholic Encyclopaedia*, "We can use [animals], we can destroy them at pleasure . . . for our own ends, for our own benefit and satisfaction."[4]

---

[3] Bradley, *Dios es verde. Cristianismo y medio ambiente*, 15.

[4] *Cf.* the bibliographical references in Bradley, *ibid.* 29–31.

However, Jews, Christians, and Muslims are not the only ones responsible for this lack of harmony in the relationship between human beings and nature. Throughout the centuries, the plundering of nature by humans, especially in the West, has been commonplace, although without much awareness of having prepared the current disaster. Above all, enlightened and secular ideology gave rise to mechanistic and technicist thinking born of an Enlightenment that wanted to shake off the "yoke" of the Church and religious mystery. An ideology that gave the human being a free hand over all creation so that he could believe himself to be the leader, lord, and omphalos of the world. Descartes said in his *Discourse on Method* that the human being is "master and possessor" of nature (*maître et possesseur de la nature*).[5] As we have seen, the Cartesian discourse is mechanistic and objectifies nature. If Francis Bacon put forward the idea that the modern human must *conquer and control* nature, Descartes, the first modern philosopher of technology, was the one who developed the idea of human dominion over nature through technology: we are the *possessors* of nature, and we can use it as we please.

Contemporary Christian Theology in the Face of Ecological Challenge

Environmentalism is a real challenge for religions, and calls for "solidarity and a pact between generations," as the Galician-Spanish theologian Xosé Chao Rego wrote. However, theology has neglected its reflection on nature in favor of history, so it is necessary to return to a cosmological vision and a theology not only of history, but also of nature.[6]

---

[5] René Descartes, *Discourse on Method* (London: Penguin Classics, 1964), part VI.

[6] Xosé Chao Rego, "Creación," in *10 palabras claves en religión*, ed. Andrés Torres Queiruga (Verbo Divino, 1992), 146–151.

We must recognize that even the most innovative modern Christian theology was too tied to an anthropocentrism that took little account of nature; it was centered on individual or social salvation, referring only to the present or the future of human beings in their history. In Europe, this was the case of liberal theology and the theology of secularization, particularly the existential theology of Rudolf Bultmann. Or in the Catholic sphere, the anthropocentric theology of Karl Rahner or Edward Schillebeeckx, centered on the drama of the human being and his personal relationship with God. Or even in the political theology of Johann Baptist Metz. Despite everything, Schillebeeckx and Metz are the authors of the ecological introduction to a magnificent monograph in the international theological journal *Concilium*.[7]

Fortunately, this is not the whole reality. We also have great contemporary theologians such as Albert Schweitzer (1875–1965), who said from the perspective of ancient Eastern wisdom: "I am the life that wants to live in the midst of the life that wants to live."[8] And with him, more theologians, such as Wolfhart Pannenberg (1928–2014), whose *Anthropology* touches the theme of creation in ecological perspective, or A. R. Peacocke[9]. And above all, Jürgen Moltmann: his work includes books with evocative titles like *God in Creation* and *Justice Creates the Future: The Politics of Peace and the Ethics of Creation in a World under Threat*. In the latter volume, the German theologian devotes the third chapter, half of the book, to our perspective: "The Ecological Situation; Theory and Ethics of Creation" (pp. 77–140). There, among other things, he says:

---

[7] *Cf.* Various, "No hay cielo sin tierra," *Concilium*, no. 236 (1991).

[8] Albert Schweitzer, *Civilization and Ethics* (London: Unwin Books, 1961).

[9] Wolfhart Pannenberg, *Anthropology in Theological Perspective* (Edinburgh: T&T Clark, 1999); Arthur Peacocke, *Creation and the World of Science* (Oxford: Oxford University Press, 1979).

The change we must make in order to experience that in the nature of the earth and together with all living beings we "form one family" must *begin with the image of God that guides us.* . . . For the earth is more than just the property of its Creator. . . . All we need is to return to the original wisdom of our own religious tradition and discover what was repressed by that absolutist and masculine image of God proper to Modernity. It is a question, concretely, of rediscovering the *one and triune God*.[10]

At the end of the twentieth century, Rosino Gibellini made a simple but quite complete assessment of the ecological reflection of Christian theology, from the first works to the paths that were opened later on. Gibellini sees that the ecological debate started in the 1970s engaged with theology in an effort to liberate Christianity from the unilaterally anthropocentric process of Modernity. In view of this, he rightly points out that today "we are already far from the theological interpretations of the biblical mandate of *dominium terræ*, which took place in Modernity."[11] But I believe that many theologians are still reticent about the importance of ecology in theology.

In Spanish theology, great theologians such as González Faus, González de Cardedal, José María Castillo, or Xabier Pikaza have not shown special sensitivity to the subject, although it should be noted that Pikaza has published some work with a clear ecological attitude.[12] Torres Queiruga published a book

---

[10] Moltmann, *La justicia crea futuro. Política de la paz y ética de la creación en un mundo amenazado*, 83; in English, Moltmann, *Creating a Just Future: The Politics of Peace and the Ethics of Creation in a Threatened World*.

[11] Rosino Gibellini, "El debate teológico sobre la ecología," *Concilium*, no. 261 (1995).

[12] Xabier Pikaza, *El desafío ecológico. Creación bíblica y bomba atómica* (Madrid: PPC, 2004), 200. He had already collaborated with other authors years earlier in Various, *El desafío ecológico. Ecología y humanismo* (Salamanca: Universidad Pontificia, 1989).

with the eloquent title *Recuperar la creación*; good theology, but it does not address the ecological question, nor does it reflect this vision of the human being in the cosmos, as the subtitle itself points out: "Toward a *humanizing* religion." In spite of everything, he recognizes that "the new ecological sensibility is taking on a truly epochal importance."[13] The topic does appear explicitly in a substantial volume by another Galician theologian: Xosé Chao Rego, who has expressed concern about the issue and an ecological sensitivity on other occasions.[14] Other theologians, such as the prematurely deceased J. L. Ruiz de la Peña or Raimon Panikkar—whose very rich thinking in this regard we have already seen—have approached ecologism. Ruiz de la Peña has worked extensively on Christian anthropology, and it is not surprising that he approaches the subject when dealing with creation, although he does not devote much space to ecologism itself.[15] More space is devoted to it in collective volumes such as *Cristianismo, justicia y ecología*.[16]

Two Theologies in Relation to Environmentalism: Feminist and Liberation Theology

I would like to highlight here two theological lines that have been converging with environmentalism in recent years: feminist theology and liberation theology.

Feminist theology has long been trying to break the *androcentric* and even *anthropocentric* circle of theology on behalf of women. Its contribution to eco-theology is fundamental, especially for two reasons. First, because of the greater development of the

---

[13] Andrés Torres Queiruga, *Recuperar la creación* (Vigo: SEPT, 1996), 99.

[14] Xosé Chao Rego, *Na fronteira do misterio. Credo para xente non credula* (Vigo: SEPT, 1995), especially the section "O desafío ecolóxico," (146–151). Also Xosé Chao Rego, *Camiño verde. Ecoloxía e creación* (Santiago: Irimia, 1996).

[15] Ruiz de la Peña, *Teología de la creación*.

[16] Girardi, Espeja, and Dussel, *Cristianismo, justicia y ecología*.

human dimension of *anima* (the capacity for tenderness and compassion, care, sensitivity, receptivity, availability, intuition, capacity to relate to the concrete . . .) as opposed to the hyperdeveloped *animus* of men (control, force, power, dominion, reason, drive . . . which often lead to violent animosity), although both must be integrated in women and men; the harmonious and non-dominant collaborative relationship of women with Nature—Mother Earth—and the cosmos. Second, because of their capacity to carry out actions in common, without hierarchical struggle, as opposed to the "cock of the henhouse" spirit that men suffer from. To bet on life in harmony will mean considering all aspects of life and, consequently, everything that threatens it.[17]

There are significant works that expound on this theological labor. First, those of the pioneering feminist theologian Rosemary Radford Ruether, which include *Gaia and God: An Ecofeminist Theology of Earth Healing*.[18] From Sallie McFague, *Models of God: Theology for an Ecological and Nuclear Age* (to which I will refer later) and Anne Primavesi's *From Apocalypse to Genesis: Ecology, Feminism and Christianity*; two excellent works, from which I have learned a great deal on the subject. Particularly, the latter is one of the best books on environmentalism and Christianity.

For Anne Primavesi, the term *ecofeminism* is born precisely from the juxtaposition of ecologism, feminism, and Christianity, considering that she wants to keep in mind not only women

---

[17] *Cf.* Victorino Pérez Prieto, "Ecoloxismo, feminismo e cristianismo. Unha relación indispensable," *Encrucillada*, no. 163 (2009), 302–312.

[18] Rosemary Radford Ruether, *Gaia and God: An Ecofeminist Theology of Earth Healing* (San Francisco: HarperOne, 1994). Also *New Woman, New Earth: Sexist Ideologies and Human Liberation* (New York: Seabury Press, 1975); *Ecotheology: Voices from South and North* (Geneva: World Council of Churches, 1994); and, with other authors, *Women Healing Earth: Third World Women on Ecology, Feminism, and Religion* (Maryknoll, NY: Orbis Books, 1996).

and Nature, but also man, integrating the three aspects from a holistic and inclusive perspective, from the ecological paradigm and from the critique of the hierarchical paradigm. All this by rereading chapters 1–3 of the book of Genesis in the light of the ecological paradigm. A rereading that contrasts with the dominant hierarchical-patriarchal view of women and Nature, so that Christians can contribute to participating in the integrating vision of the human being in Nature proposed by the ecological movement, seeing the need for a new creation and the regeneration of life proposed in the book of Revelation. The Apocalypse is not set at the end of time, but here and now, because of the force of death and destruction generated by today's humanity. Therefore, the book is intended to be "a theological act of faith in the future, faith that the world and Christianity can be regenerated by the power of the spirit acting from within living matter."[19]

Finally, ecofeminism gradually attained the cosmic spirituality that is ardently sought today. Sometimes through esotericism and witchcraft—so reviled in history written by men—that speak of the alternative wisdom of women, who had to seek their own paths, often at the cost of their lives. This cosmic spirituality seeks to overcome the dualism that confronts spirit and matter, the cosmos, humans, and God.[20]

Today's *liberation theology* is very present in ecological reflection. It knows that the countries it reflects upon are the first victims of the destruction of the planet at the hands of the rich of the North, who have always oppressed them. Leonardo Boff is the one who has stood out the most, with numerous

---

[19] Anne Primavesi, *Del Apocalipsis al Génesis. Ecología, feminismo y cristianismo* (Barcelona: Herder, 1995), 11f., 17f., and 20; in English, *From Apocalypse to Genesis: Ecology, Feminism and Christianity* (Minneapolis: Fortress Press, 1991).

[20] *Cf.* Joseph R. DesJardins, *Éthique de l'environnement. Une introduction à la philosophie environnementale* (Quebec: Presses de l'Université du Québec, 1995).

eco-theological publications.[21] In *Ecology* he dedicates a section to the relationship between the two, which start out from the same bleeding wounds: misery and the systematic aggression against the Earth. Boff clearly criticizes the anthropocentrism of the Catholic Church, derived from androcentrism, because "it breaks the fundamental law of the universe, which is that of solidarity, the interdependence of all beings."[22] In a recent interview, he said something that I fully agree with and that the reader can see reflected throughout my book:

> It is not possible to do an updated theology without a profound dialogue with the new vision of the world coming from the sciences of life, of the Earth, of the cosmos. . . . Few theologians have accepted this challenge. . . . It forces us to study different sciences: quantum physics, the new biology, astrophysics, chaos and complexity theory. . . . The dialogue of theology with ecology and with the new cosmology forces us to change the paradigm. The paradigm of Western philosophy and theology is essentialist, based on *nature, substance, essence*. . . . It is necessary to change the way of thinking about God, history, the Church. God is the dynamism of three divine persons in communication

---

[21] In addition to Boff's aforementioned *Cry of the Earth, Cry of the Poor*, see also the following: *Ecology and Liberation: A New Paradigm* (Maryknoll, NY: Orbis Books, 1995); *The Tao of Liberation: Exploring the Ecology of Transformation*; *La dignidad de la Tierra. Ecología, mundialización, espiritualidad*, vol. 2000 (Madrid: Trotta, 2000); *El despertar del águila* (Madrid: Trotta, 2000); *Una ética de la Madre Tierra. Cómo cuidar la Casa Común* (Madrid: Trotta, 2017); *Liberar la Tierra. Una ecología para un mañana posible* (Madrid: San Pablo, 2018). And with Anselm Grün, *Becoming New: Finding God within Us and in Creation* (Maryknoll, NY: Orbis Books, 2019); *Lo divino en el ser humano y en el universo. Camino hacia la unificación* (Madrid: Trotta, 2019).

[22] Leonardo Boff, "Teología de la liberación y ecología: alternativa, confrontación o complementariedad?," *Revista internacional de teologia*, no. 261 (1995).

with each other and with creation. . . . The same that Francis indicates in the encyclical *Laudato si'*: everything is relationship.[23]

Churches in the Face of the Ecological Challenge

In the response that the Christian Churches have given to the ecological problem, without overlooking the justice of the criticisms mentioned above, it must be acknowledged that as early as the 1970s, with the first beginnings of environmentalism, documents appeared that progressively showed awareness of the ecological problems of the Earth, adopting the environmentalist proposals.[24]

The Protestant and Orthodox Churches

A pioneer in the churches' response to the ecological problem was a commission of inquiry established in 1975 by the Church of England. It spoke of the need for a "religious representation of the world that reflects the common order in which man and other living creatures live together; an order in which man, his work and organic and inorganic nature can relate to each other."[25] In 1986, the Religion, Science and Technology group of the Church of Scotland published a documented environmental report entitled "As Long as the Earth Lasts."

---

[23] Annachiara Sacchi, "Entrevista a Leonardo Boff, exponente destacado de la teologia de la liberación. El ecoceno como alternativa al Antropoceno," Rebelión, 2020, https://rebelion.org/el-ecoceno-como- alternative-to-anthropocene/.

[24] *Cf.*, although it is now twenty years old, Danièle Hervieu-Léger, ed., *Religion et écologie* (Paris: CERF, 1993) for an approach to different Christian perspectives on ecology, from Benedictine and Orthodox to new religious movements. Specifically, "Initiatives œcuméniques pour la sauvagarde de la création," by Françoise Lautwan (220–238).

[25] Taken from Bradley, *Dios es verde. Cristianismo y medio ambiente*, 22.

The World Council of Churches, created in 1948, has been promoting a reflection on environmentalism for decades, always linked to justice and peace.[26] It does so through working groups, conferences, and major world meetings. Since the Vancouver Conference (Canada) in 1983, the meeting has been called Justice, Peace and the Integrity of Creation, which will remain a generic title in perpetuity. Apart from this Canadian ecumenical conference, the work of the Basel (Switzerland) conference in 1989, with a large Catholic participation, and that of Seoul (South Korea) in 1990, with its document "Towards an Alliance for Justice, Peace and the Integrity of Creation," stand out.[27] In the latter, Cardinal Kim (1922–2009), a Catholic archbishop of Seoul known for his commitment to human rights, said: "If only all these Churches would unite in the pursuit of justice and peace in our society and in the world, if we would put as much energy into promoting respect for nature as we put into running our church organizations, I believe that the Kingdom of God would not be far away." The Seoul document contains a decalogue of fundamental affirmations:

---

[26] To date, there have been the following major meetings of the World Council of Churches: Amsterdam (Netherlands), 1948; Evanston (Illinois, USA), 1954; New Delhi (India), 1961; Upsala (Sweden), 1968; Nairobi (Kenya), 1975; Vancouver (Canada), 1983; Canberra (Australia), 1992; Harare (Zimbabwe), 1998; Porto Alegre (Brazil), 2006; Busan (South Korea), 2013. The conference on Ecological Theology and Environmental Ethics of the World Council of Churches continued in subsequent years until the present day (2025). The 2022 conference in Kolympari (Crete) dealt with the issue of life changing ecological theology and environmental ethics to avert a climate crisis.

[27] *Cf.* an extensive reference up to the beginning of the 1990s in René Coste, "Justicia, paz, salvaguardia de la creación," *Concilium*, no. 236 (1991). Also in Jacques Briard, "Bâle et Seoul: générosités, limites et enjeux d'Églises," *Lumen vitæ* 4, no. 1 (1993). The final document of Seoul is intended to be, in its own words, "an ecumenical affirmation of faith and hope in the face of the crisis of our time," recognizing the interdependence of the issues of justice, peace and the relationship with nature, and calling on all Christians to engage in this unique struggle: "let its point of impact be justice, peace and the protection of the environment," *ibid.* 43.

1. We affirm that every exercise of power must be accountable to God.
2. We affirm God's option in favor of the poorest.
3. We affirm the equal value of all races and all peoples.
4. We affirm that men and women are the image of God.
5. We affirm that truth is the foundation of a community of free beings.
6. We affirm the peace of Jesus Christ.
7. We affirm that all creation is willed by God.
8. We affirm that the Earth belongs to the Lord God.
9. We affirm the dignity and commitment of the new generation.
10. We affirm that people's rights are a gift from God.

In that spirit, Patriarch Bartholomew, the Orthodox Patriarch of Constantinople, declared in the 1990s: "That human beings degrade the integrity of the earth and contribute to climate change, stripping the earth of its natural forests, pollute the waters, the soil, the air.... All this is sin. All this *is sin*."[28] He later spoke of the need for everyone to repent of their own ways of damaging the planet, because "to the extent that we all generate small ecological damage," we are called to recognize "our contribution—small or large—to the disfigurement and destruction of creation" (Message for the Day of Prayer for the Protection of Creation, 2012). Patriarch Bartholomew proposed "moving from consumption to sacrifice, from greed to generosity, from waste to the ability to share, in an asceticism that means learning to give, and not simply to renounce. It is a way of loving, of moving little by little from what I want to what God's world needs. It is liberation from fear, from greed, from dependence" (Conference

---

[28] Address at Santa Barbara in California (November 8, 1997); *cf.* Bartholomew I, *On Earth as in Heaven. Ecological Vision and Initiatives of Ecumenical Patriarch Bartholomew*, ed. John Chryssavgis (New York: Fordham University Press, 2012).

at the Utstein Monastery-Norway, 2003). Moreover, Christians are called to "accept the world as a sacrament of communion," with the conviction that "the divine and the human are found in the smallest detail contained in the seamless garments of God's creation."[29]

In 1993, the Parliament of Religions in Chicago issued a Declaration on the ecological issue, with a clear holistic perspective:

> The *human person* is infinitely precious and must be protected unconditionally. But *the lives of the animals and plants* that populate the planet with us also deserve protection, conservation and care. The uncontrolled exploitation of the natural principles of life, the ruthless destruction of the biosphere and the militarization of the cosmos are a crime.
>
> *All of us* in this cosmos *are reciprocally interrelated* and dependent on each other. Each of us depends on the good of the collective. Therefore, it makes no sense to claim human dominion over nature and the cosmos, but rather we must devote ourselves to fostering human community with nature and the cosmos.

The Catholic Church

In the specific Catholic field, there were small papal declarations by Paul VI in the 1970s, by John Paul II in the 1980s and 1990s, and Benedict XVI starting in 2000. But the Catholic Church's official commitment to ecology emerged with Pope Francis and the encyclical *Laudato si'* in 2015.

One of the first official Catholic documents on ecology was that of the German Bishops' Conference, *Future of Creation-Future of Humanity*, in the early 1990s. Other documents followed:

---

[29] *Cf.* Patriarch Bartolomé, "Global responsibility and ecological sustainability. Closing remarks," I Halki Vertex, Istanbul (June 20, 2012).

the allusions to the theme in the document of the Latin American Bishops' Conference in Aparecida, Brazil (2008), and so on. Finally, the allusions in some encyclicals of Paul VI and John Paul II.

In 1971, Paul VI referred to the ecological problem, presenting it as a "dramatic consequence" of the uncontrolled activity of human beings: "Because of an unconsidered exploitation of nature, human beings run the risk of destroying it and of becoming victims of this degradation, . . . pollution and waste, new diseases, absolute destructive power, . . . creating for tomorrow an intolerable environment" (*Octogesima adveniens*, 21). In his speech at the FAO (UN Food and Agriculture Organization) in 1970, he spoke of the possibility of an "ecological catastrophe under the effect of the explosion of industrial civilization," underlining the "urgency and necessity of a radical change in the behavior of humanity."

John Paul II named Francis of Assisi "heavenly patron of ecologists" in 1979, and alluded to ecology in his encyclicals *Laborem exercens* (1981), *Sollicitudo rei socialis* (1987), *Centesimus annus* (1991) and *Evangelium vitae* (1995).

> We make too little effort to *safeguard the modal conditions of a genuine human ecology*. Not only has the earth been given by God to man, who must use it with respect for the original idea that it is a good, according to which it has been given to him; even man is for himself a gift of God and must therefore respect the natural and moral structure with which he has been endowed. (*Centesimus annus*, n. 38.)

More specifically, he dealt with ecology in other public statements. The most important was on the twenty-third World Day of Peace in 1990 (*Peace with God the Creator, Peace with All Creation*).

> When man departs from the plan of God the Creator, he causes disorder that has repercussions on the rest of creation. . . . If man is not at peace with God, the earth will not be at peace either. (n. 5)
>
> A global vision of the problem is necessary, seeing the whole universe as a true cosmos with a balance that must be respected. (n. 7–8)

In a General Audience on January 17, 2001, Pope John Paul II reiterated that "God made man the steward of creation":

> We must therefore encourage and support the "ecological conversion" which in recent decades has made humanity more sensitive to the catastrophe to which it has been heading. Man is no longer the Creator's "steward," but an autonomous despot, who is finally beginning to understand that he must stop at the edge of the abyss. . . . At stake, then, is not only a "physical" ecology that is concerned to safeguard the habitat of the various living beings, but also a "human" ecology which makes the existence of creatures more dignified, by protecting the fundamental good of life in all its manifestations and by preparing for future generations an environment more in conformity with the Creator's plan. (n. 4)

For his part, Benedict XVI renewed the invitation to "eliminate the structural causes of the dysfunctions of the world economy and correct the growth models that seem incapable of guaranteeing respect for the environment" (Address to the Diplomatic Corps at the Holy See, 2007). And in his encyclical *Caritas in veritate* (2009), he stated that "the degradation of nature is closely linked to the culture that shapes human coexistence" (51).

We can highlight other documents of the Church, especially in Latin America: the allusions to the theme in the *Aparecida*

Document of the V Conference of the Latin American Episcopate (2008), and ten years later, another specific document on ecology: "Missionary Disciples Custodians of the Common Home. Discernment in the Light of *Laudato si'*" (2018). The *Aparecida Document*, drawn up at the Shrine of Our Lady of Aparecida in Brazil, says that in Latin America and the Caribbean an ecological consciousness is increasingly growing: "The natural wealth of Latin America and the Caribbean is today experiencing an irrational exploitation that is leaving a trail of dilapidation, and even death, throughout our region" (n. 473). Nature is a free inheritance that we have received; it is a gift, but a gift that demands responsibility and care. More elaborate and committed has been the Pastoral Letter of the CELAM on Integral Ecology, *Missionary Disciples Custodians of the Common Home, Discernment in the Light of Laudato si'* (2018). The text was linked to the reflection of the Churches and Mining Network. In it, the Latin American bishops want to "enter into a dialogue with everyone about our common home" and especially "about how we are building the future of the planet."

POPE FRANCIS AND *LAUDATO SI'*: ENVIRONMENTALISM AND COMPLEXITY

Pope Francis's ecological encyclical is an event of planetary importance, religiously, ethically, socially and politically. Considering the enormous influence of the Catholic Church, it is a crucial contribution to the development of a critical ecological consciousness. It is a document of great richness, proposing a new interpretation of the Judeo-Christian tradition, in rupture with its "Promethean dream of world domination," and a profoundly radical reflection on the causes of the ecological crisis.

MICHAEL LÖWY, *"Considerações sobre o Papa Francisco."*

> The divine and the human meet in the slightest detail in the seamless garment of God's creation, in the last speck of dust of our planet.
>
> POPE FRANCIS, *Laudato si'*

> We have forgotten who we are; creatures in the image of God called to live in the same common home. We were not created to be pillagers; we were intended and desired to be at the center of a web of life composed of millions of species lovingly united. . . . It is time to rediscover our vocation as children of God, brothers and sisters . . . and custodians of creation. It is time to repent, to return to the roots . . . connected to creation.
>
> POPE FRANCIS, *A great hope, the guardianship of the creation*

Pope Francis and His Challenge to Thought and to a World in the Midst of Destruction

Pope Francis has brought about a real revolution in the Church. He was welcomed as "the pope of springtime," after the long "ecclesial winter" that the Church had with John Paul II and Benedict XVI.[30] Frédéric Lenoir, sociologist, phenomenologist of religions and thinker, currently one of the most popular French writers on religious matters, wrote at the beginning of his book on the pope:

> In less than a year, Pope Francis has been able to touch people's hearts. Every day I meet believers and non-believers, Catholics, Protestants, Jews, agnostics and atheists

---

[30] *Cf.* Victorino Pérez Prieto, *La búsqueda de la armonía en la diversidad. El diálogo ecuménico e interreligioso desde el Concilio Vaticano I* (Estella: Verbo Divino, 2014), 44–54.

who tell me that the new pope has moved them . . . by his simplicity, his warmth, . . . his freedom of speech, his condemnation of the arrogance, immorality and hypocrisy of some clerics, . . . his irrevocable condemnation of the financial logic that destroys human beings and the planet.[31]

But among the many aspects of this multifaceted pope, the one that interests us here is his search for harmony with all of creation and his relational conception of Reality: everything is interconnected. Francis has courageously denounced a situation on our planet that oppresses the poorest and nature itself, the result of seeking and prioritizing economic profitability above all else. In his speech at the World Meeting of Social Movements in Santa Cruz de la Sierra (Bolivia, July 9, 2015) he said some words that he has repeated on many occasions:

> The earth, peoples and people are being savagely punished. And behind so much suffering, so much death and destruction, one can feel the stench of what Basil of Caesarea—one of the first theologians of the Church—called "the dung of the devil": unbridled ambition for money reigns. This is the *devil's dung*.
>
> [. . .] When capital becomes an idol and directs the choices of human beings, when the greed for money

---

[31] Frédéric Lenoir, *Francisco, la primavera del Evangelio* (Madrid: PPC, 2014), 7. Many other books have been published on Pope Francis, including Austen Ivereigh, *The Great Reformer: Francis and the Making of a Radical Pope* (New York: Henry Holt, 2014); Marco Politi, *Francisco entre lobos. El secreto de una revolución* (Mexico: Fondo de Cultura Económica, Mexico, 2015); Javier Martínez-Brocal, *El Papa de la misericordia* (Barcelona: Planeta, 2015); Juan Carlos Scannone, *El papa del pueblo* (Madrid: PPC, 2017); Massimo Borghesi, *Jorge Mario Bergoglio. Una biografía intelectual.* (Madrid: Encuentro, 2018); Michael Higgins, *The Jesuit Disruptor: A Personal Portrait of Pope Francis* (Toronto: House of Anansi, 2024); Leonardo Boff, *Francis of Assisi, Francis of Rome: A New Springtime for the Church* (Maryknoll, NY: Orbis Books, 2014).

dominates the entire socio-economic system, it ruins society, condemns man, destroys human fraternity, and even, as we see, endangers our common home, our sister and mother earth.[32]

Laudato si' will undoubtedly be the encyclical for which Francis will go down in history; for his commitment to people and to the Earth and for his wise responses to the grave situation both suffer. Francis's ecological perspective is based on a clear religious commitment rather than an ethical one, as he makes clear toward the end:

> The majority of the planet's inhabitants declare themselves to be believers, and this should *encourage religions to enter into a dialogue* with each other *aimed at caring for nature, defending the poor*, and building networks of respect and fraternity. (n. 201)

The "inconvenient" ideas of the environmentalists that made martyrs of some of them, as we have already noted, mark Francis's thinking from the beginning of the encyclical: "Our common home is like a sister. . . . This sister now *cries out to us because of the harm* we have inflicted on her by our irresponsible use and abuse. . . . *We have come to see ourselves as her lords and masters*, entitled to plunder her at will" (n. 1–2). And he repeats in affirmations reiterated until the end of the text: "We may well be leaving to coming generations debris, desolation and filth. The pace of consumption, waste and environmental change has so stretched the planet's capacity." (n. 161). "The *post-industrial period* may well be remembered as one of the *most irresponsible in history*." (n. 165).

---

[32] Available at https://www.vatican.va/content/francesco/es/speeches/2015/july/documents/papa-francesco_20150709_bolivia-movimenti-popolari.html.

These ideas present an inconvenient and difficult challenge to a capitalist-technocratic system predicated on unrestrained consumption, a system only recently responsive to the denunciations environmental activists have been making since the mid-twentieth century. But the most important challenge of Pope Francis, particularly concerning theology and thought, is his new worldview: a *relational* conception of Reality in which everything is connected; a conception that has always been viewed with suspicion in Christian and Western thought as being close to the reviled pantheism.

These ideas of Francis coincide with those expressed several decades earlier by, among others, the German philosopher and Catholic theologian Romano Guardini (1885–1968), the most cited author of the encyclical outside the papal documents:

> Science and technology have brought the energies of both nature and man within our reach in such a way that they can give rise to acute and chronic catastrophes of incalculable dimensions. . . . From now on, human beings will live on the edge of a danger that grows ever greater and affects the whole of their existence. . . . Since Hiroshima, *we know that we live on the brink of disaster* and that we will remain there for as long as history lasts.[33]

Additionally, the writings of Iranian philosopher and essayist Seyyed Hossein Nasr (1933) are pertinent. At the end of the twentieth century, he presciently stated: "The ecological crisis is *of the utmost urgency and gravity*, and those who ignore it *are* simply *self-deceived or dreaming of* nothing."[34] By condemning the environmental assault, Francis aligns himself with a significant portion

---

[33] Romano Guardini, quoted in Jordi Pigem, *Ángeles o robots. La interioridad humana en la sociedad hipertecnológica* (Barcelona: Fragmenta, 2018).

[34] Seyyed Hossein Nasr, quoted by *ibid*. 15.

of present-day humanity, with the most conscious men and women. As far back as the 1990s, a statement from the Union of Concerned Scientists, endorsed by 1700 scientists (many Nobel laureates), cautioned that without significant lifestyle changes, the Earth would soon become "incapable of sustaining life as we know it today."[35] Similarly, Panikkar was convinced that the modern world is at its end. Today we need a profound transformation of consciousness, a *metanoia*: "The world has embarked on a bad road that will lead to a sociopolitical catastrophe if a radical *metanoia* does not take place . . . an anthropological change is necessary, and it is impossible without a spiritual *metanoia*."[36]

Laudato Si': *A Unique Encyclical in the History of the Church's Magisterium*

A decade after its publication (2015), *Laudato si'* remains a groundbreaking encyclical in the history of the Church's Magisterium, a true editorial blockbuster with widespread popularity and unprecedented dissemination in our globalized world.[37] An encyclical that, in the face of so many lies and obfuscation of reality, unequivocally invites us to "look at reality with sincerity" (n. 61); a reality marked by materialism and economism,

---

[35] "World scientists' warning to humanity," quoted by *ibid.* 16.

[36] Panikkar, *La intuición cosmoteándrica. Las tres dimensiones de la realidad*, 28; in English, *The Cosmotheandric Experience: Emerging Religious Consciousness* (Maryknoll, NY: Orbis Books, 1993).

[37] The number of publications on the subject offer ample proof. A few books in Spanish: Enrique Sanz, ed., *Cuidar de la Tierra, cuidar de los pobres. Laudato si' desde la teología y con la ciencia* (Santander: Sal Terræ, 2015); Leonardo Boff, Alex Zanotelli, and Gaël Giraud, *Cuidar la madre tierra. Comentario a la encíclica Laudato si' del papa Francisco* (Madrid: Sanpablo, 2015); in English, Leonardo Boff, Fritjof Capra, and Elizabeth May, *Voices from the Earth Charter Initiative responding to Laudato si'* (Costa Rica: Universidad Técnica Nacional, 2018); Sean McDonagh, *On Care for Our Common Home: Laudato Si'* (Maryknoll, NY: Orbis Books, 2016).

which destroy human beings and the nature in which they live. The world today finds itself in an unsustainable situation; if we are brave enough to be receptive, we will be able to feel "sister earth, along with all the abandoned of our world, [crying] out, pleading that we take another course," because we have never "hurt and mistreated our common home" so much (n. 53). Jordi Pigem pointed this out at the start of one of his illuminating essays, structured around some of the encyclical's texts:

> I found in it an honesty and courage that can be summed up in its invitation to "look at reality with sincerity." If we look at reality with sincerity, we will see that we are in an unusual situation, especially because of what the encyclical identifies as "the main problem," the *technocratic paradigm* that thrives under contemporary capitalism and nihilism.[38]

Francis has given us the first papal encyclical in history on ecology that, in addition to being *environmentalist*, is committed to the ecological conflict. It is a Franciscan encyclical, because the pope very consciously chose the words of the *poverello* of Assisi to give it its name: *Laudato si'*. As we have already seen, this was not the only time that the Church's Magisterium spoke of this topic; but Francis's was not only the first encyclical, but also the first text to directly address a controversial topic in a lucid and courageous manner.

For this reason, after its publication, the encyclical generated both sympathy and hostility, inside and outside the Church. There was support from the media and diverse groups of people worldwide, both scholarly and ordinary, and even from international organizations such as the UN and the United Nations Environment Program (UNEP). The encyclical is *revolutionary* in a literal, albeit peaceful, way: it calls for an *economic, social, and*

---

[38] Pigem, *Ángeles o robots. La interioridad humana en la sociedad hipertecnológica*, 9.

cultural revolution (n.114), and treats the subject in an incisive, courageous, and topical fashion. Unsurprisingly, someone called it "as environmentalist as a Greenpeace boat challenging an oil tanker." Consequently, even left-leaning thinkers such as Michael Löwy ("Considerações sobre o Papa Francisco," online), whose views we read at the start of this chapter, have shown support for the encyclical.

The hostility came, above all, from the conservative sectors of the Catholic Church and other North American Protestant and right-liberal denominations. Some went so far as to accuse the pontiff of being a "heretic" and even a "Marxist pope," as the American Catholic broadcaster Rush Limbaugh called him. The animosity toward the encyclical came especially from the temples of the capitalist market economy, where economic profitability is the most important motto governing society, politics, and life itself. As soon as the encyclical was made public, David Brooks, one of the leaders of US conservatism and a columnist for *The New York Times*, published his critique, speaking of alleged "unscientific claims" and an "exaggerated and reductionist view of reality."[39] The mountains of garbage and the reality of the poor living among them are not seen in the same way from *The New York Times* or from the placid hills of California as from the favelas of Río de Janeiro, the squatter settlements of Quito or the destitute neighborhoods of Bogotá—which I have been able to view—or the slums of Calcutta, Nairobi, etc.

Undoubtedly, 2015 was the year "ecology officially became a Catholic issue," as the Catalan-Spanish collective Cristianisme i Justícia acknowledged.[40] This is reflected in the global resonance

---

[39] *Cf.* David Brooks, "Fracking and the Franciscans," *The New York Times*, June 23 2015, https://www.nytimes.com/2015/06/23/opinion/fracking-and-the-franciscans.html.

[40] Grupo de Sostenibilidad y Ética Cristiana de Cristianismo y Justicia, "El año que la ecología se convirtió (oficialmente) en un asunto católico," 2015, https://blog.cristianismeijusticia.net/2015/01/30/el-ano-que-la-ecologia-se-convirtio-oficialmente-en-un-asunto-catolico.

of *Laudato si'*, as evidenced by media coverage worldwide, from East to West, spanning newspaper editorials, leading scientific and economic journals, Catholic weeklies, and digital platforms.

This encyclical does not aim to present new scientific or economic data; rather, it synthesizes existing data to offer a wise, reflective perspective on these significant challenges. Thus, we find in it:

- Wisdom, not just knowledge. Science and technology offer a good explanation of what is occurring in the atmosphere, oceans, forests, soils, and human societies. But the result of this work has almost always been frustrating. Knowledge demands wisdom, collective reflection, and personal transformation so that it may translate into social change.
- Eco-social involvement. Eco-social challenges are presented in the context of a quest for *integral human development*. The preservation of a healthy environment is a necessary condition for integral human development; hence the insistence on *integral ecology*.
- A special concern for the weakest and most disadvantaged, for those who suffer most from the consequences of environmental degradation: ethnic minorities, Indigenous peoples, migrants, children and the elderly. . . . In short, knowing how to listen *to the cry of the Earth and the cry of the poor*.
- A call to transform ourselves into *custodians* and caregivers of creation, not mere beneficiaries of it.
- A call to *change the conception of our place in the cosmos*. The temptation to dominate creation means an anthropological distortion, a confusion about who we are and our place in the world. We are part of nature and the cosmos, intimately and constitutively linked to them.

The keys to Francis's challenges in *Laudato si'* are twofold.

- A *denunciation of ecological degradation and a call for a* subsequent *ethical response*; the necessary correction of a degradation in which human activity has played a fundamental role.
- A *new worldview*, a *relational* conception of Reality, one close to the complex thought we have discussed. This aspect, which is the most novel and the one that most interests us here, is what has been most ignored, even in congresses about the encyclical.[41] (Is this perhaps because of the danger of a presumed "flirtation" with pantheism entailed in speaking of a Reality in which everything is connected and interrelated?) This aspect is the one that has the most direct relationship with the complexity and relationality of Reality, as we have studied.

Ecological and Social Critiques and Challenges of Laudato Si'

The Fundamental Problem: The "Technocratic Paradigm"

In the first theme of *Laudato si'*, Francis denounces a *system* that seeks to "turn reality into an object simply to be used and controlled" (sec. 11). This critique targets the *technocratic/techno-economic* paradigm dominating thought, science, politics, and economics globally, especially in the West and increasingly the East, which is shaped by market and production focuses—the liberal-capitalist model and market economy. Francis calls it by this name more than any other (sec. 101, 108, 109 . . .), but he also uses the "efficiency-driven paradigm of technology" (sec.

---

[41] *Cf.* congresses such as the International Congress *Laudato si'* of Integral Ecology and Environment of the Catholic University of Murcia (March 2016), available at http://multimedia.ucam.edu/creative-team/laudatosi/Actas_digitales_090317_ LAUDATOSI.pdf.

189), the "undifferentiated and one-dimensional paradigm" (sec. 106) and the "paradigm of consumerism" (sec. 215).

The "one-dimensional paradigm" brings to mind Herbert Marcuse (although Francis obviously does not quote him), a philosopher critical of the *establishment*, one of the fathers of Freudian-Marxism, whose work *One-Dimensional Man*, an essay critical of capitalism, was almost a primer in the 1970s and 1980s for critics of the closed liberal-capitalist system that the US and the West were trying to impose on the whole world. It is the "total fetishism of the commodity."[42] The encyclical explains the *one-dimensional paradigm* as follows: "This paradigm exalts the concept of a subject who, using logical and rational procedures, progressively approaches and gains control over an external object. . . . It is as if the subject were to find itself in the presence of something formless, completely open to manipulation. . . . Human beings and material objects no longer extend a friendly hand to one another; the relationship has become confrontational" (sec. 106).

This dominant technocratic, productive, and economic paradigm is "the heart of the beast that is ravaging the world today," as Pigem excellently puts it,[43] and grows under contemporary materialism and nihilism. A paradigm that the encyclical identifies as "the basic problem" (sec. 106), "omnipresent" (sec. 122), one that destroys "the lives of individuals and the workings of society" (sec. 107). This "way of understanding human life and activity has gone awry, to the serious detriment of the world around us " (sec. 101) and "may overwhelm not only our politics but also freedom and justice" (sec. 53). The entire encyclical is

---

[42] Herbert Marcuse, *El hombre unidimensional. Ensayo sobre la ideología de la sociedad industrial avanzada* (Barcelona: Seix Barral, 1971), 7–9; in English, Herbert Marcuse, *One-Dimensional Man: Studies in the Ideology of Advanced Industrial Society* (Boston: Beacon Press, 1991).

[43] Pigem, *Ángeles o robots. La interioridad humana en la sociedad hipertecnológica*, 87.

a critique of the technocratic paradigm, which has become the true idol that replaces God and religion.

Condemning the Assault on the Environment

In Chapter One, titled "What Is Happening to Our Common Home," Francis provides a synopsis of prevalent environmental concerns regarding ecological damage. We will look at them synthetically, since I believe they are clear and eloquent.

- Pollution, garbage, and the "throwaway culture"

Exposure to atmospheric pollutants produces a broad spectrum of health hazards, especially for the poor, and causes millions of premature deaths. (sec. 20).

These problems are closely linked to a *throwaway culture* which affects the excluded just as it quickly reduces things to rubbish. (sec. 22)

Pollution affects all areas of society: the air we breathe, the things we see (accumulated garbage), and urban acoustics (constant noise). Technology and finance claim to be the only solutions to the problems, but they often cannot see the mystery of the ultimate relationships between things.

- Climate change

Climate change is *a global problem with grave* implications: environmental, social, economic, political and for the distribution of goods. It represents one of the principal challenges facing humanity in our day. (sec. 25)

Climate change is the greatest environmental threat facing humanity. Its consequences might be devastating if we do not drastically reduce our dependence on fossil fuels and greenhouse gas emissions. In this global problem, some (the rich) are more to blame than others (the poor), but the worst impacts fall on the poorest.

- The unfair distribution of water

Access to safe drinkable water is a basic and universal human right, since it is essential to human survival and, as such, is a condition for the exercise of other human rights. (sec. 30)

The issue of access to drinking water as a "basic human right" has been the subject of much controversy, especially among multinational companies aiming to profit from its exploitation and sale. Against the papal insistence on access to drinking water as a universal right, large companies in the sector have said that whoever wants water should pay for it; for this reason, they have harshly criticized Francis's words.

- Pillaging of natural resources and loss of biodiversity

The earth's resources are also being plundered because of short-sighted approaches to the economy, commerce and production. (sec. 32)

For Francis, the loss of biodiversity is not only a practical issue—economic damage and a solution to health problems—but also demands looking "beyond the immediate." On the one hand, biodiversity loss affects human values, "the real value of things, their significance for persons and cultures, or the concerns and needs of the poor" (sec. 190). And, on the other, the value of the species themselves, which have their own rights in this interconnected reality, a right to exist beyond human interests.

- Degradation of the quality of human life and urban social degradation

Nowadays, for example, we are conscious *of the disproportionate and unruly growth of many cities* [especially in the Third World], *which have become unhealthy to live in* (. . .) In some places . . . the *privatization of certain spaces* has restricted people's access to places of particular beauty. (sec. 44–45)

The degradation of individual and social human qualities is denounced in the encyclical, particularly the contribution of growth to the degradation of cities (44), linked to "social exclusion, an inequitable distribution and consumption of energy and other services, social breakdown, increased violence" (46). *Laudato si'* is a plea against urban chaos and the degradation of neighborhoods.[44] The Pope also denounces so-called *gated communities*, which he encountered in Buenos Aires; he alludes to them without naming them, and criticizes this privatization: "'ecological' neighbourhoods have been created which are closed to outsiders in order to ensure an artificial tranquility." (45)

- Unjust distribution of wealth, the North's theft of the South

The rich and the poor have equal dignity. . . . [What does the] commandment "thou shalt not kill" [mean] when "twenty percent of the world's population consumes resources at a rate that robs the poor nations and future generations of what they need to survive." (94–95)

It is well known that today, half of humanity lives below the poverty line. The richest 20 percent of the world's population

---

[44] *Cf.* further analysis in Victorino Pérez Prieto, "Cuidado de la casa común. Una ciudad que cuida de la creación," *Faro*, no. 1 (2017), 30–37.

consumes 85 percent of all the wealth on Earth. This is an unjust reality. The solution to this inequity can only be to "replace . . . greed with generosity . . . an asceticism which 'entails *learning to give*'" (sec. 9). This demands more than politics and economics; it demands a profound conversion, a true *internal revolution* that leads to personal and social commitment.

- The lie of the infinite availability of the planet's resources

[T]he idea of infinite or unlimited growth . . . proves so attractive to economists, financiers and experts in technology. It is based on the lie that there is an infinite supply of the earth's goods. (sec. 106)

The lie of an infinite availability of the Earth's goods leads rich countries to squeeze the planet "dry beyond every limit" (sec. 106). The 2008 witnessed the not only the collapse of the Wall Street bubble, a crisis threatening global economic systems. A week after that fateful September 15 came what was called "Earth Overshoot Day," the *day of surpassing the Earth's natural capacities*. In 2008, humanity consumed 30 percent more than the planet could produce. No comment.

Jordi Pigem calls this a "continuistic mirage": "frivolously letting things continue as they always have." Unlimited economic growth is impossible because the Earth has biophysical and geological limits: "The *ecological footprint* of humanity exceeded the regenerative capacity of the Earth in the nineteen-eighties."[45]

Francis concludes that the response of the world's governments has been ridiculous: "The failure of global summits on the environment make it plain that our politics are subject to technology and finance" (sec. 54). Despite recognizing the positive

---

[45] Pigem, *Ángeles o robots. La interioridad humana en la sociedad hipertecnológica*, 31.

experiences of the Earth Summit (Río de Janeiro, 1992), the Basel Convention (2005), and the UN Conference on Sustainable Development Río+20 (2012), among others, "enforceable international agreements are urgently needed" (sec. 173).

The Earth "is not a commodity" for the indiscriminate exploitation of humans, but "a sacred space with which . . . to interact" (sec. 146), as the *perennial wisdom* of yesterday and today has been saying for centuries.

The New Cosmovision of Laudato Si'

Laudato Si': *An "Integral Ecology," a "Relational" Conception of Reality and a Call to Mystical Communion with All*

Beyond the condemnations and environmentalist proposals, I believe that the greatest contribution of *Laudato si'* is even more innovative and challenging to Christian theology, modern thought, and the world. It is a *new cosmovision,* calling for a truly integral ecology, not only in its social and ethical aspect, a *relational, holistic and non-dualistic* worldview. This was the aspect that most caught my attention in my first reading of the encyclical. It seemed to me to be something particularly novel and revolutionary, given the age-old fear that the Church's ministry and Christian theology have had throughout its history of anything that might sound pantheistic.

This was one of the most important reasons for the Church's fear of the mystics, who, with their vision of Unity in diversity and their tendency to integrate the transcendent God himself into the Whole, denounced that it was forgotten that in Christianity this *transcendent* God is also *immanent*. The institution's fear of mystics—in addition to being a fear of completely free persons, whom they could not fit into their framework—was the fear of radical communion with God, of the process of *divinization* that they sought in mystical union—as if that could "diminish" the divine greatness. But as Panikkar wrote years ago: "*Man is no less man* when he discovers his divine vocation, *nor do the Gods lose their divinity* when they are humanized."[46]

Christian mystics create this mystical union through a path marked, from the time of St. Bonaventure, by *three* classic *ways*:[47] the *purgative, illuminative,* and *unitive* ways. *Purification* disciplines the external human being and leads to internal peace. *Illumination* disciplines rational activity, teaches to know and follow Christ, and to know the Father and oneself. *Consummation* or *union* leads the human being to an awareness of what he is, that his reality is *divine*; it leads him to recognize himself *in* God. St. John of the Cross says: "The soul . . . is so much that it *knows* all these things *to be God in its being* with infinite eminence, that it knows them better in their *being* than in themselves."[48] And Meister Eckhart, taking this union with God to its highest expression, goes so far as to say: "God and I *are one*," and invites us to let God "*be God in you*": "The *depths of God are my depths* and my depths are the depths of God. . . . God asks nothing else of you but . . . that you *let God be God in you*."[49]

The Most Frequently Repeated Declarations in **Laudato Si'**

The *new worldview* that we see in the encyclical, and that we have seen in science, thought, and spiritual experience, is manifested

---

[46] Panikkar, *La nueva inocencia*, 61.

[47] *Cf.* St. Bonaventure, "De triplici via" and "Itinerarium Mentis in Deo," in Bonaventure of Bagnoregio, *Obras Completas* (Madrid: Biblioteca de Autores Cristianos, 1945). *Cf.* a good commentary in Jacques Guy Bourgerol, *Introducción a San Buenaventura* (Madrid: Biblioteca de Autores Cristianos, 1964).

[48] Saint John of the Cross, "Llama de amor viva" [Living Flame of Love], in John of the Cross, *Vida y obras completas*, songs 4, 5.

[49] Meister Eckhart, sermons "Vivir sin porqué" [Living without Why] and "Dios y yo somos uno" [God and I Are One], in Meister Eckhart, *El fruto de la nada* (Madrid: Siruela, 2001), 49 and 53–55.

Green Christian Faith Betrayed ...

here through the declarations repeated over two hundred times in *Laudato si'*. These are the ones most frequently repeated after *ecology* and *environment*:

- Everything is *connected*, everything is *interrelated*, everything is *intertwined*. We are *interpenetrated*.
- All Reality forms a *seamless fabric*.
- We are part of a *universal communion*, with which we are in deep *interdependence*.

Everything Is Connected

The conviction that *everything* in Reality *is connected* is not a casual utterance. Pope Francis himself describes it as one of the "themes which . . . appear as the Encyclical unfolds" (sec. 16) along with others, such as the relationship between the poor and the fragility of the planet, the critique of the forms of power that derive from technology, the real value of each creature, etc. The Pope knows that this interrelational perspective is a "new perspective," a new vision of reality, a new conception: "A *new perspective*, the conviction that *everything* in the world *is connected*" (sec. 16).

This relational perspective of Reality inevitably assumes that "*all* creatures are *connected*, all of us as living creatures are dependent on one another . . . , and everything is interconnected" (sec. 42, 70). This presupposes "sincere love for our fellow human [and non-human] beings and an unwavering commitment" (sec. 91). The logical consequence of the fact that "everything is connected" is that if this connection is lost, the human being crumbles: if "declares independence from reality and behaves with absolute dominion, the very foundations of our life begin to crumble" (sec. 117). This total connection, this interdependence, affects not only human beings, or living beings in general, but all of Reality: "Time and space are not independent of one another, and not even atoms or subatomic particles can be considered in isolation. Just as the different aspects of the planet . . . are interrelated, so too living species are part of a network which we will never fully explore and understand" (sec. 138).

Francis even draws a brilliant theological-spiritual conclusion from this interconnectedness, leading it to the divine Trinity. The Trinity is pure connection, the Trinitarian *perichôresis* of traditional Christian theology, which we have already discussed: "Everything is interconnected, and this invites us to *develop a spirituality* of that global solidarity *which flows from the mystery of the Trinity*" (sec. 240). God is not the *great solitary*, but the *great one in solidarity*, because he is Trinity, the most intimate connection from his essence, and in his action in the world.

Francis traces the relational conception of reality and its consequences back to the biblical narratives themselves, to the Judeo-Christian Bible (sec. 70). This is the spirit of the law of the Sabbath in the book of Leviticus (sec. 71) and the Psalms (sec. 72), as we discussed earlier. But the Pope also draws this relationality from modern science: "In this universe, shaped by *open and intercommunicating systems*, we can discern countless forms of *relationship and participation*" (sec. 79). "[T]he different aspects of the planet—physical, chemical and biological—are interrelated . . . are part of a network " (sec. 138).

"Everything is *intimately related*," he repeats again and again (sec. 137, 142 . . .).

Laudato si' also uses another very eloquent expression: everything is *intertwined/woven together*. "We human beings are united as brothers and sisters on a wonderful pilgrimage, *woven together* by the love God has for each of his creatures and which also unites us in fond affection with brother sun, sister moon, brother river and mother earth" (sec. 92). Because *everything is related, intertwined*, we human beings are intimately united with all of nature and the whole cosmos, and we make *a common journey toward fullness*, as Paul of Tarsus says (Rom 8).

Reality Is a Seamless Fabric

Bruno Latour's felicitous description of reality as a *seamless fabric* (as we saw in Chapter 1) also appears in Francis's encyclical: "The divine and the human meet in the slightest detail in the *seamless garment* of God's creation, in the last speck of dust on our planet" (sec. 9).

In this way, God is present in all Reality, "*intimately* present to each being" (sec. 80). The Spirit of God is in all of Reality, even the most minuscule and intimate. Although there is a "sheer novelty" in the human being, as a "*personal* being within a material universe . . . a particular call to life and to *relationship on the part of a 'Thou' who addresses himself to another 'thou'*" that makes it a subject (sec. 81).

The pope adds something very pertinent, which has been particularly taken up by those who defend the rights of non-human animals: "it would also be mistaken to view other living beings as *mere objects* subjected to arbitrary human domination" (sec. 82). The Spirit is not only in humans, but "in every living creature" (sec. 88). Thus, we can say without shame that dogs have "souls," just as trees and plants have "souls," each in its own way. Certainly, these are souls different from the human soul, but that does not mean that the Spirit of God is only in humans; it is in all living beings, as I have written on more than one occasion.[50] John Paul II himself affirmed this when he said that "animals possess a vital breath received from God"; in the meantime, some media outlets jumped with headlines like: "The Pope opens heaven to animals" (*Corriere della Sera*).

The intimate relationship or *seamless union* of the whole of Reality supposes that human beings walk with the whole of creation toward a common goal, which was already emphasized

---

[50] Victorino Pérez, "Os cans teñen alma?" [Do dogs have souls?], *Luzes*, n. 3 (2014).

in the Letter to the Romans and is taken up by Francis. In consonance with the Pauline message, the Pope went so far as to say on another occasion: "Life after death is not only a gift for believers, but also for animals." "One day we will see our animals again in Christ's eternity" ("Pope Francis and Animals").

We Are Part of a Universal Communion

This is a call to overcome the dualisms that hinder us. For Francis, this *interdependence* of creatures is willed by God (sec. 86). That is why, using another beautiful expression, he says that we form a "universal family" with all that is, a "sublime communion," "we are interpenetrated." "all of us are linked by unseen bonds and together form a kind of *universal family*, a *sublime communion* " (sec. 89). It is not a question of the generosity of human beings; it is a question of *knowledge* and *awareness* of Reality, of what it is and of what we are. For this reason, the encyclical says: "The human person *grows more*, matures more and is sanctified more to the extent that he or she *enters into relationships*, going out from themselves to live in communion with God, with others and with all creatures" (sec. 240).

This call to knowing ourselves to be *interdependent* and *interpenetrated* with everything, to "feel intimately united with all that exists" (sec. 11), is a call—addressed especially to philosophers and theologians—to overcome the dualisms that have colored Western thought and theology for centuries. "Such unhealthy dualisms . . . left a mark on certain Christian thinkers . . . and disfigured the Gospel," says Francis (sec. 98). Moreover, the traditional dualistic and fragmentary perspective of Christian and Western thought has led in general to "loss of appreciation for the whole," and prevents us from finding "adequate ways of solving the more complex problems of today's world" (sec. 110).

Three Final Conclusions

Those of us committed to the holistic paradigm are pleased to see that the encyclical goes beyond a mere denunciation of ecological transgressions, at an ethical and even anthropological level, and speaks of Reality as a *relationship*. For this reason, Raimon Panikkar calls for an *ecosophy*, which goes beyond simple ecology: a "wisdom of the earth" in which science, philosophy, religion, and spirituality interact, to go beyond the anthropocentrism of modern, enlightened and contemporary society, and reach the love that unites the whole of Reality, not just the human one: "The task of the human being is to *cultivate* himself and nature because they cannot be separated."[51] This *wisdom of the earth* must be a global, total wisdom that sees the Earth not as an object but as a *subject*, as a "constitutive dimension of Reality."

For ourselves and our world to have a future, we need a *new way of thinking about the world* and of *thinking of ourselves* in relation to it; a global, *holistic*, relational, interconnected way of thinking, as we have repeated here throughout these pages.

Three conclusions of the encyclical *Laudato si'*:

1. *Laudato si'* is a prophetic denunciation that the destruction of our environment is not inevitable, but a consequence of our sins as predatory human beings. The consequence of the economic interests imposed over the interests of the most vulnerable human beings and Mother Earth herself.
2. This destruction, in which we are all implicated, is the product of a false understanding of the world and our relation with it: The failure to recognize that *we are in relationship*, and that if we break the balance of this relationship, we *are* simply *not*. This must entail "a distinctive way of

---

[51] Panikkar, *Ecosofía. Para una espiritualidad de la tierra*, 119.

looking at things, a way of thinking, policies, an educational programme, *a lifestyle and a spirituality*" (sec. 111).
3. The encyclical is a call to a profound *conversion* (sec. 218), a *metanoia*, a radical change of attitude. A call to live in harmony not only with humans, animals, and plants, but with the entire world, with the whole cosmos, as Teilhard de Chardin called for, and we will see in the last chapter.

The encyclical ends with a call for an *ecological spirituality* (sec. 216). A spirituality that leads to a change of lifestyle that will transform the destructive relationship between human beings and the world of which they are a part, in order to achieve harmony of man-woman, human-nonhuman, matter-spirit. A harmony in which *full attentiveness* at every moment is fundamental: "capable of being fully present," as in a mystical moment (sec. 226). And to know that fullness is in each of these moments: "The universe unfolds in God, who fills it completely. Hence, *there is a mystical meaning to be found in a leaf, in a mountain trail, in a dewdrop*" (sec. 233). *To know oneself in* relationship with others and with Reality, with the awareness that "everything is interconnected, and this invites us to develop a spirituality" (sec. 240).

Two Complementary Texts to the Encyclical: The Post-Synodal Apostolic Exhortation "Dear Amazonia" ("An Ecological Dream") and Pope Francis's Book, A Great Hope: The Stewardship of Creation

Post-Synodal Apostolic Exhortation "Dear Amazonia" ("An Ecological Dream")

The Synod of the Amazon took place in Rome from October 6 to 27, 2019. It brought together three hundred people, including bishops, religious, and lay people, under the theme "Amazonia: New Paths for the Church and for an Integral Ecology," which was also the title of its final document. We hoped that it would be a new Pentecost for the Amazonian Church, the local Churches, and the universal Church. The newness and hope were palpable during the three weeks it lasted, but the reality, in the end, was poorer.

The Pope's post-synodal text *Dear Amazonia*, published the following year (2020), is beautiful. It is full of poetry and commitment, with quotes from Neruda, Galeano, Vinicius de Moraes, Thiago de Lello. . . . "Those poets, contemplatives and prophets, help free us from the technocratic and consumerist paradigm that destroys nature and robs us of a truly dignified existence" (sec. 46). "Only poetry, with its humble voice, will be able to save this world" (Vinicius de Moraes).[52]

It is in line with the ecologistic perspective and commitment of *Laudato si'*; in terms of the cultural, social, political and ecological aspects of this vast area, which is a "multinational and interconnected whole, a great biome shared by nine countries," as Francis points out (sec. 5). But the project was frustrating in some ecclesial aspects because it did not respond to expectations and did not make important decisions that would bring about structural changes in the priestly ministry, with the recognition of married priests and the access of women to the ordained ministry. *Dear Amazonia* is organized in four dreams (sec. 7):

1. A social dream: "An Amazon region that fights for the rights of the poor, the original peoples and the least of our brothers and sisters, where their voices can be heard."

---

[52] *Beloved Amazonia* (Maryknoll, NY: Orbis Books, 2020), includes the text of the Apostolic Exhortation *Querida Amazonia,* the Working Document, and the Final Document of the Synod, "The Amazon: New Paths for the Church and for an Integral Ecology."

2. A cultural dream: "An Amazon region that can preserve its distinctive cultural riches, where the beauty of our humanity shines forth in so many varied ways."
3. An ecological dream: "An Amazon region that can jealously preserve its overwhelming natural beauty and the superabundant life teeming in its rivers and forests."
4. An ecclesial dream: "Christian communities capable of generous commitment, incarnate in the Amazon region, and giving the Church new faces with Amazonian features."

The third chapter is the one that interests us most here, focusing on cultural and ecological issues. In Francis's own words:

1. *The dream made of water.* "In the Amazon region, water is queen; the rivers and streams are like veins, and water determines every form of life" (sec. 43) and "the spinal column that creates harmony and unity" (sec. 45).
2. *The cry of the Amazon.* "[A] painful sensation shared by many of us today . . . the end for so much life, for so much beauty, even though people would like to keep thinking that nothing is happening" (sec. 47). "The cry of the Amazon region reaches everyone because 'the conquest and exploitation of resources . . . has today reached the point of threatening the environment's hospitable aspect: the environment as "resource" risks threatening the environment as "home"'" (sec. 48).
3. *The prophecy of contemplation.* "Frequently we let our consciences be deadened, since 'distractions constantly dull our realization of just how limited and finite our world really is.' . . . This is the way human beings contrive to feed their self-destructive vices" (sec. 53). "From the original peoples, we can learn to *contemplate* the Amazon

region and not simply analyze it, and thus appreciate this precious mystery that transcends us. We can *love it*, not simply use it, with the result that love can awaken a deep and sincere interest. Even more, we can *feel intimately a part of it* and not only defend it" (sec. 55).
4. *Education and ecological habits.* "[A]n integral ecology cannot be content simply with fine-tuning technical questions or political, juridical and social decisions. The best ecology always has an educational dimension that can encourage the development of new habits in individuals and groups . . . encouraged to opt for another style of life, one less greedy and more serene, more respectful and less anxious, more fraternal " (sec. 58).

From the beginning, Francis insists that "everything is connected," specifying now that this "is particularly true of a territory like the Amazon" (sec. 41).

> If the care of people and the care of ecosystems are inseparable, this becomes especially important in places where "the forest is not a resource to be exploited; it is a being, or various beings, with which we have to relate." The wisdom of the original peoples of the Amazon region "inspires care and respect for creation, with a clear consciousness of its limits, and prohibits its abuse. To abuse nature is to abuse our ancestors, our brothers and sisters, creation and the Creator, and to mortgage the future." (sec. 42)
>
> [In the words of the Indigenous people], "we are water, air, earth and life of the environment created by God. For this reason, we demand an end to the mistreatment and destruction of mother Earth. The land has blood, and it is bleeding; the multinationals have cut the veins of our mother Earth" (sec. 42).

In this exhortation, the pope reiterates that the Church must stand by the poor in the face of economic operations that lead to devastation, murder, and corruption, and which deserve the name "injustice and crime" (sec. 9). It is necessary to fight against colonization, the "consumerist vision of human beings" (sec. 33). The ecological dream must unite care for the environment and care for people (sec. 41).

But there is one aspect of this controversial text in which Pope Francis was not bold enough. The Synod Fathers made clear the need to include *ecological sin* among the list of sins. They defined it as "an act of commission or omission against God, against one's neighbor, the community and the environment," which manifests itself in acts and habits of pollution and destruction of the harmony of the environment, as well as in the "transgression of the principles of interdependence and the rupture of the networks of solidarity between creations" and "against justice." Francis himself said shortly afterward about ecological sin: "We must introduce into the *Catechism of the Catholic Church* the sin against ecology, the *ecological sin* against the common home, *ecocide*, because it is a duty."[53] However, although the pope had previously denounced the activities of the capitalist model in very harsh terms and a language of prophetic denunciation of the world economic system, the exhortation says nothing about ecological sin. Admittedly, no pope has ever before gone so far in the categorical nature of his condemnations or in the terms used against the ecocidalists, which make it difficult to look the other way.

A Great Hope: The Stewardship of Creation

This new book by Francis contains the previously unpublished text "A Great Hope" and other texts with the pope's words on

---

[53] XX International Congress of the Criminal Law Association, November 15, 2019.

the stewardship of creation, our common home, from a Christian and ecumenical perspective. The pope sets out his thoughts on the world as God's gift, ecology and environmental protection, the care of creation and the protection of our common home, and integral ecology: "everything is connected."

In addition to the unpublished text, the book also contains texts from *Laudato si'*: sec. 13, 23–26, 32–34, 124 and 209–215. Alongside these texts, the book contains some of Francis's other papal interventions and documents: *Let Us Be Protectors of Creation* (Homily at the beginning of his papacy, March 2013), *Creation Is A Most Beautiful Gift of God* (General Audience, May 2014), *Protecting Human Life, Protecting the Planet* (Address at FAO, November 2014), *Spiritual Foundations for the Care of Creation* (Letter for the Establishment of the World Day of Prayer for the Care of Creation, August 2015) and *The Right to Water* (February 2017).

Francis's new book adds nothing new with respect to the encyclical, but we can highlight a couple of sentences that insist that the ecological crisis is "one of the effects of *a sick perspective* toward ourselves, toward others, toward the world," in which we are "involved in *structures of sin* that provoke evil" and in which the four words that indicate the "path of healing" are: *gift, repentance, offering* and *fraternity.*

> The ecological crisis we are experiencing is one of the effects of *a sick perspective* toward ourselves, toward others, toward the world, toward the time that flows; a sick view that prevents us from perceiving everything as a gift offered (p. 27).

> We are involved in *structures of sin* . . . that provoke evil, pollute the environment, hurt and humiliate the poor, promote *the logic of possessing and power*, exploit natural

resources to excess, force entire peoples to abandon their lands, feed hatred, violence, and war.⁵⁴

We may note his expression "structures of sin" because of its importance concerning the conception of "ecological sin." This terminology is related to a novel view of the new European political theology and, above all, of Latin American liberation theology. Traditional theology insisted that sin was simply something personal, rather than collective, but these theologies say that there is *structural sin* in addition to personal sin. John Paul II referred to the "structures of sin" in some of his encyclicals and addresses⁵⁵ and the *Catechism of the Catholic Church* also speaks of these in one of its sections (sec. 1869). But the pope and the *Catechism* do not use the expression *structural* sin (because of its Marxist resonance⁵⁶) but rather of *structures* that are the fruit of the sins of individuals. On the other hand, the Episcopal Conferences of Medellin and Puebla—imbued with the spirit of liberation theology—clearly use the concept of *structural sin*. The Medellin document (1968) speaks of "sins whose crystallization is evident

---

⁵⁴ Francis, *Una gran esperanza, la custodia de la creación / A great hope, the stewardship of creation* (Vatican City: Libreria Editrice, 2019), 30.

⁵⁵ John Paul II, *Sollicitudo rei socialis*, 36, available at https://www.vatican.va/content/john-paul-ii/es/encyclicals/documents/hf_jp-ii_enc_30121987_sollicitudo-rei-socialis.html. General Audience of August 25, 1999: "*Structures of sin* hinder the development of economically and politically disadvantaged peoples," available at https://www.vatican.va/content/john-paul-ii/es/audiences/1999/documents/hf_jp-ii_aud_25081999.html.

⁵⁶ Karl Marx understood perfectly well the extent to which people immersed in certain socio-economic structures see their possibilities of action curtailed. In the prologue to the first edition of *Das Kapital* wrote: "Here we only refer to *persons* as *personifications of economic categories*, as *representatives of certain interests and class relations*. Whoever, like me, conceives the *development of the economic formation of society* as a *natural-historical process*, cannot hold the individual responsible for the existence of *relations in which he is socially a creature*, even if subjectively he considers himself far above them."

in *unjust structures.*" And the Puebla document (1979) says: "There are many causes of this unjust situation, but at the root of them all is sin, both in its *personal* aspect and in the *structures themselves*" (sec. 1258).

Following the encyclical *Laudato si'*, Pope Francis published an apostolic exhortation, *Laudate Deum*. This new text, published in 2023, complements the vision on the care of the common home presented in *Laudato si'*, specifically addressing the climate crisis and the lack of sufficient responses to it.

5

Toward an Ecotheology and an Ecospirituality[1]

*In the beginning—before spacetime—was the
   Word . . . (Amorous word). . . .
All things love, and He is the love with which
   they love. . . .
They are the two choruses which take turns to
   sing . . .
Creation is a poem . . .
Things, not created by calculus
but by poetry.
By the Poet ("Creator"=poiētés). . . .
The cosmos knows itself through us . . .
Our own consciousness, also the consciousness of
   it all.*

ERNESTO CARDENAL, Cosmic Canticle

---

[1] This chapter is partly indebted to other works that I have published previously, some of them referred to in the bibliography.

> *Today, however, this holistic vision seems to be the undimmed hope of an ever-growing number of people and the explicit goal of human consciousness. Man . . . has never sought partial truths. . . .*
>
> *The entire reality counts, matter as much as spirit . . . science as much as mysticism, the soul as much as the body.*
> *. . .*
>
> RAIMON PANIKKAR,
The Cosmotheandric Experience

> *For the Christian, the true "Theory of Everything" is Trinitarian theology.*
> JOHN POLKINGHORNE, The Trinity and an
Entangled World: Relationality in Physical Science and Theology

TOWARD AN ECOTHEOLOGY FROM A RELATIONAL CONCEPTION OF REALITY

Ecotheology and Complexity

I have been thinking and saying for years that Christians in the twenty-first century must either be *ecologists* and *ecopacifists* or seek an *ecotheology* and an *ecospirituality*; otherwise, they will not be good Christians, disciples of Jesus of Nazareth. They must seek *justice, peace, and communion with all of creation*, establishing just relationships with their brothers and sisters, with the Earth and with the cosmos, feeling deeply that "*we are part* of the Earth and it *is part of us*," as Chief Seattle said. Furthermore, they will either seek the wisdom-spirituality of the Earth (*ecosophy*) with holistic sensibility, recognizing the *interdependence of all with all* knowing that "the entire reality counts, matter as much as spirit," as Raimon Panikkar says, or they will have no future. Because life and the cosmos live and die with us: we are the consciousness of the universe, but without it, we are not.

That is why I think and believe that in the theological task of the twenty-first century, *ecotheology* should occupy a dominant place in theology and thought. Moreover, ecology cannot be simply one *more* element of this theology, but a *backbone* of it all, as a constitutive dimension of faith and life. It must be a perspective that puts an end to centuries of anthropocentric and Eurocentric vision, so contemptuous of "the other" and of non-human life, in order to illuminate a new image of God and Reality. An image of the Divinity marked by the radical relationality of all that *is*.

And this ecotheology must take into account what science and complex thought have taught us, as we saw in an earlier chapter. Theological reflections based on complexity have already been developed. In 1993, the Vatican Observatory co-sponsored a groundbreaking conference on this, which was subsequently published.[2] The well-known English physicist and theologian John Polkinghorne, whose way of relating complexity and Trinity will be discussed below, published *Quantum Physics and Theology: An Unexpected Kinship* (London, 2007). The Australian scholar and bishop Stephen Pickard also developed a Trinitarian theology based on complexity in *Seeking the Church: An Introduction to Ecclesiology* (London, 2012). In the same vein, Professor Kester Brewin elaborated a Christology in *The Complex Christ: Signs of Emergency in the Urban Church* (London, 2004). And there are more. A key figure in theological reflections from the perspective of complexity is the American biologist and theologian Stuart Kauffman, one of the most relevant in the field

---

[2] Robert Russell, Arthur Peacocke, and Nancey Murphy, eds., *Chaos and Complexity: Scientific Perspectives on Divine Action* (Vatican City: Vatican Observatory Publications, 1997).

of biological complexity, with his work *Reinventing the Sacred: A New View of Science, Reason, and Religion* (New York, 2008).[3] Other relevant works, not included in the article from which we have taken the above data, are those of the American Catholic theologian John Haught: "Chaos, Complexity and Theology" (American Theological Association, 1994) and *Christianity and Science: Toward a Theology of Nature* (2007), in which he collects his reflections on the subject, as does the Lutheran theologian Paul Hinlicky in *Divine Complexity: The Rise of Creedal Christianity* (Fortress Press, 2010).

Approaching this ecological and complex perspective presupposes for Christian faith and reflection a process similar to that which the Sacrament of Reconciliation proposes to Catholics. First of all, a *deconstructive work* ("examination of conscience"): discovering the conflicts with science and the ecological crisis, in which both Christians and non-Christians are to blame; and erasing the dualistic, anthropological and theologically anthropocentric, domineering and predatory conception of nature that has done so much damage to nature and ourselves. And together with this, correcting the ignorance surrounding what Reality *is*, according to what the new physics and new biology can teach us. For this, an intercultural and multidisciplinary dialogue is essential, as well as an interreligious one that would consider what current science, anthropology, and the phenomenology of religion tell us.

Second, a *labor of reconciliation* with nature and the cosmos ("sorrow for sins and purpose of amendment"): placing ourselves

---

[3] *Cf.* with numerous bibliography in Tim Harle, "Complexity and Theology Readings," Susanna Wesley Foundation, 2017, https://susannawesleyfoundation.org/wp-content/uploads/2017/02/Complexity-and-Theology-for-Keith-Elford-SWF-latest.pdf. At the beginning of this paper we are told that the origin of this reading list "is the result of a long conversation with Keith Elford and Sue Miller of the Susanna Wesley Foundation in November 2016." Regarding Stuart Kauffman, there is a doctoral thesis in Spanish: Alfredo Pérez Martínez, "La obra de Stuart Kauffman. Aportaciones a la biología del siglo XXI e implicaciones filosóficas" (Universidad Complutense de Madrid, 2005).

before the God of forgiveness who always patiently awaits the *return home* (*oikos*) of his lost sons and daughters, the return to total equilibrium in love.

Last, a *constructive task* ("purpose of amendment, to confess one's sins, receive absolution and do penance"): to fulfill what has been discovered, to remake our life, to rebuild the broken harmony; to elaborate a new theology, an *ecotheology* and a *complex theology* that discovers and manifests a God in intimate connection with human beings—men and women—with the cosmos and with all that *is*. A non-dual connection that does not fall into either a destructive dualism or a monism that denies Reality as it is: identity and diversity coexist and both are real; the search for a harmonious synthesis. A connection that helps us to be one, unified, and walk the paths that start from a non-dual heart that allows us to *be all in all*.

Finally, it is a matter of developing a *complex ecotheology* that knows that to say "God is *love*"—as Jesus of Nazareth, the Christ, the definitive Word of the Father, pointed out—is to manifest that God is *communion*, an intimate Trinitarian relationship *ad intra* (Father/Mother-Son-Spirit) and *ad extra* (God-Human Being-Cosmos). An *ecotheology that is ecotheological* and *complex*, that knows how to manifest that the human being and all creation are called to *christification*, to the fullness of life in Love; indissolubly united in the way of Love.[4]

This is what I believe a true *complex ecotheology* should entail: developing a new and timely theological conception on the level of today's world and of the evolution of contemporary thought and science. A theology in keeping with the aspects of the new science and philosophy reviewed here, one which can in turn learn

---

[4] *Cf.* Victorino Pérez Prieto, "La ecoteología en el quehacer teológico del siglo XXI," En el décimo aniversario del Equipo de Investigación Ecoteología, de la Facultad de Teología Pontificia Universidad Javeriana de Bogotá, 2012, http://www.ecoteologiapuj.blogspot.com/2012/10/mensaje-de-victorino-perez-prieto.html.

from the wisdom of different cultures and religions. As has been attempted in the past, we must develop a new way of conceiving God/Divinity and our relationship with Him. It is a matter of having the courage to think imaginatively in order to produce images/metaphors of God—the unknowable Mystery, personal and impersonal at the same time—that are meaningful to us here and now, as others were in the past, and to find the most appropriate ones while indicting the old ones, which have become obsolete.

This new conception will require a transition from a *dominating God separated from the world,* who rules from on high like an absolute monarch, to a *God who embodies a Trinitarian Relationship / Communion in Solidarity,* who is *Companion, Father-Mother, Lover, and Friend.* But also a shift toward a God whose *Sacrament* is the world: the *World* as the *Body of God* and God as the *Spirit of the World.* A God indissolubly linked to his creation, which is not something foreign to him, but an expression of his Being. All this to see the *seamless fabric* that forms the whole of Reality.[5]

A New Way of Conceiving God and Our Relationship with Him

First. *From 'Dominion of the Lord' to 'Gardener's Care': We Are 'Part' of Nature and the Cosmos, Not 'Above' It.*

The traditional image of God as absolute *Lord Almighty, dominator* of heaven and earth from up high, *distant and transcendent,*

---

[5] For this new way of conceiving God that I have developed in recent years, I was initially inspired by the second part of the work of a great American feminist theologian, the recently deceased Sallie McFague (1933–2019), who speaks of God as *mother,* as *lover* and as *friend*: *Modelos de Dios. Teología para una era ecológica y nuclear* (Santander: Sal Terræ, 1987); in English, *Models of God: Theology for an Ecological, Nuclear Age* (Minneapolis: Fortress Press, 1987). I have worked on this idea in my previous books *Do teu verdor cinguido. Ecoloxismo e cristianismo* (La Coruña: Espiral Maior, 1997) and *Ecologismo y cristianismo* (Santander: Sal Terræ, 1999).

untouchable, and the world as *his property* with which he can do whatever he wants, is one of the most deep-seated reasons for the despotic spirit of humans on Earth.

> The idea of God as "the Almighty" took hold in Western Europe.... Divine *omnipotence* was seen as the preponderant quality of his divinity: God is the Lord and can do with the world as he wills. He is *the absolute subject*, and the world the passive object of his lordship.[6]

Moltmann's words describe a conception of God that—especially in the West—relates to the world *from outside*. Just like the monarchs of old, ruling from their inaccessible palaces, he encompasses the world with his absolute power, his *benevolent* dominion, as do all lords who place themselves above their subjects. In this image, as Sallie McFague says, "God *has no world* and the *world has no God*. The world is *empty* of God's presence for it is too humble to be a *real residence*. Time and space are not filled with God."[7] To twist the well-known words of Jesus of Nazareth, his kingdom "is not of this world," but of another. Therefore, he acts *on* the world, not *in* the world or *from* the world. A dualistic hierarchical perspective that has nourished numerous forms of oppression.

With the withdrawal of this "Almighty God" from the world, following a secularization of the West that has expelled God from its daily activities, man prevailed—an inadequate, warped "image" of Him. This is the *all-powerful human*; one who, through dominion over the earth, pretends to more closely resemble the old image of God. "As the *image of God on earth*, man had to understand himself as sovereign, to place himself before the

---

[6] Moltmann, *La justicia crea futuro. Política de la paz y ética de la creación en un mundo amenazado*, 81.

[7] McFague, *Modelos de Dios. Teología para una era ecológica y nuclear*, 119.

world and subdue it, . . . to be lord and master of the earth."[8] In this manner, we would wish to become like God not for his goodness, but because of our *power as a capacity for* unlimited *dominion* over the world.

As long as our relationship with nature is governed by the conviction that nature is fully submissive to humans—as Descartes and Bacon wanted—there is no hope for either nature or for human beings themselves. We are not only experiencing an ecological crisis, but a crisis regarding the very idea of the world. We need a new worldview, a change in values and beliefs that will suppress our unending drive to dominate nature. For we are part of nature, and a conviction in the interconnection between natural and spiritual processes must gradually prevail. We need a *new ecological consciousness*, a true *paradigm shift*, a *new way of thinking about the world*, seeing reality in a complex, global, holistic way. And, consequently, we need a new theology.

An ecological, evolutionary and complex perspective has shown us that what characterizes Reality are structures of relation and relativity, processes of transformation and open changes. In this new organic or mutualistic model, a being does not *enter into relation with* another, but *is* itself *in relation*. We must learn to increasingly think of ourselves as gardeners, guardians and lovers, co-creators and friends of a world that gives us life and *is* our life.

This new ecological consciousness must include an evolutionary framework and the human responsibility it entails. It must also include a serious, realistic conviction that the Spirit also permeates nature and the cosmos; not in the sense of returning to the old sacralization of nature, but of learning what history, science, and spirituality have taught us. From Teilhard de Chardin and modern physics, we can better understand the mystics, who, centuries ago, already spoke of a spiritual and mystical

---

[8] Moltmann, *La justicia crea futuro. Política de la paz y ética de la creación en un mundo amenazado*, 82.

understanding of the nature we are in relationship with. We are flesh that has emerged from the earth and has been spiritualized: clay and stardust, not disembodied spirits.

Second. *God as Father-Mother, Companion, Lover, and Friend*

In contrast to the vision of a static, *all-powerful* God, the emphasis is on dynamic action. This idea of God is at the core of all liberation theologies, as well as modern process theology and feminist theology. In contrast to seeing God as lord, king, and patriarch, which Rosemary Radford Ruether aptly called "the tyranny of the absolutizing imagination," models of God as *Father-Mother, Companion, Lover, Friend* emerge that manifest love and interdependence in the face of power as dominion. A God who manifests Himself as a *Thou* in an intrinsically loving relationship with all that exists, particularly with humans, who represent the maximum relationship of otherness with Him. But we must also bear in mind that many personalist images of God maintain imperialist ideas (king, sovereign, owner, omnipotent . . .), which, moreover, lead to real dead ends: "How is it that God, being a kind father, allows innocent children to die of hunger, if he is also omnipotent and all-powerful?"

God the Father-Mother. The image of God as *Father* is the preferred expression of Jesus of Nazareth in speaking of God, and the summit of the revelation of God made by biblical history. The God of Jesus wants to be a real Father-Mother, "not in a super-protective way that avoids difficulties, keeping us in dependence." But if Christianity has never denied the paternity of God, the reality is that, as Torres Queiruga—a theologian who frequently resorts to the idea of God as Father—confesses,

> We are not capable of believing in God's love: from God who is father-mother without limits of selfishness, without restriction of trauma or our own need. . . . We need a long

time to reach a minimal conviction that, if God is love, this means that his whole being consists of loving us; that he neither knows nor wants, nor can do anything else. We were not created to give glory to God, but we ourselves are his glory.[9]

But God the Father is also *Mother*. The prophet Hosea beautifully describes God's maternal traits: "I taught Ephraim to walk, and I raised him in my arms.... With cords of tenderness, with bands of love I lifted him; I was to them as one who lifts up a child to his cheeks and bends down to him" (Hos 11:1–4). Paul Tillich even prefers the image of God as *Mother* to that of God as *Father*, since the image of God as Mother better illustrates the gift of life, in keeping with the maternal quality of giving life and embracing it. God the Mother is the manifestation of unconditional love (*agape*), which is given without expecting anything in return: the mother loves her children regardless of whether they are "good" or "bad," although she is not indifferent to their goodness or badness. Creation is the *maternal activity* of God the Mother, and justice is her *maternal ethics*.

God as Companion. Curiously, it was not a professional theologian, but a mathematician who became a philosopher, A. N. Whitehead, whom we discussed earlier, who offered one of the most beautiful images of God: the "great companion" who walks with us as a "fellow-sufferer" who truly "understands" us: "God is the great companion, the fellow-sufferer who understands."[10] God is not something static and outside of Reality, but deeply "immanent" in the world and committed to the march of history, in a personal relationship and with a commitment to love. The importance of this expression lies precisely in the fact

---

[9] Andrés Torres Queiruga, *El Dios de Jesús. Aproximación en cuatro metáforas* (Santander: Sal Terræ, 1991), 34. *Cf.* by the same author *Creo en Dios Padre. El Dios de Jesús como afirmación plena del hombre* (Santander: Sal Terræ, 2001).

[10] Whitehead, *Proceso y realidad*, 471.

that—as Torres Queiruga, a great admirer of Whitehead says—it "breaks the normal scheme: that of God above us, commanding, demanding and judging, not as a companion and even an accomplice, but as our rival and our master."[11]

A loving God. God is also *Lover* (*eros*), in a daring metaphor with which Sallie McFague also speaks of the God of love. A daring metaphor that may seem revolutionary, which brings God's love closer to the dimension of eroticism: a loving passion that seems to "soil" the unconditional nature of God's love. And yet . . . how much passion has not been attributed to God when speaking of the "divine wrath"! Moreover, despite the novelty of this approach, it is not groundbreaking, for the *loving* God is present in the Bible in the Song of Songs, a book that the mystics did not hesitate to embrace in all its erotic weight. Bernard of Clairvaux takes the words "May he kiss me with a kiss from his mouth" (Song 1:2) as an analogy of the mystical incarnation and union.[12] And the erotic dimension of the writings of Teresa of Ávila or John of the Cross is also well known. The amatory image firmly illustrates God's passion for his world and his extraordinary intimacy with it. Moreover, this image expresses like no other the reality of reciprocal love, of loving and being loved. Salvation is the *loving activity* of this loving God.

> God as lover is only one who loves the world not with the fingertips but totally and passionately, taking pleasure in its variety and richness . . . delighting in its fulfillment. God as lover is the moving power of love in the universe, the desire for unity with all the beloved, the passionate embrace.[13]

---

[11] Torres Queiruga, *El Dios de Jesús. Aproximación en cuatro metáforas*, 17.

[12] "Let the mouth that gives the kiss be the Word becoming Flesh. Let the Flesh [Human Nature] which is assumed be the mouth that receives the kiss. . . . Happy kiss! . . . in which God is united to Man!" Quote taken from McFague, *Modelos de Dios. Teología para una era ecológica y nuclear*, 212.

[13] *Ibid.* 217.

God as Friend. Finally, we can speak of God as *Friend* (*philia*); an encounter in which we reach a reciprocal and free relationship, in which we let the friend be himself or herself. Attraction, joy, freedom, trust. Friendship has a certain similarity to the erotic encounter, but without the passionate-sexual component. Therefore, it is also a common experience for the mystics, whose religious experience of closeness to the divine, to the mystery, is manifested in the love of mixed *philia* and *eros*. *Divine Providence*, the sustenance in the solicitous care of the world, is the *friendly activity* of this God Friend, and companionship its *ethics of friendship*.

The Galician-Spanish theologian Xosé Antón Miguélez, in his beautiful "Letter of God," uses these images profusely, and does not hesitate to apply them with passion and intimacy, although some may think that he reaches an excessive anthropomorphism and "familiarity" with God. But this is the freedom of the poet and the mystic.

> I urgently need friends, children, lovers who will always trust in my total and unreserved love for them and for everyone. . . . I need your faith and trust, my friend. I need people who have faith in life . . . faith in people, . . . faith in themselves. . . . People's loves are the best school for knowing my love for you and for everyone. Whoever loves knows me. The more you love, the more you will know me.[14]

Third. *From a* Monarchical *Conception to God as a* Trinitarian Relationship *and Communion in Solidarity*

The Christian challenge today is to go beyond the image of God as an Almighty *Lord*, *monarch* and *absolute Lord* of all, who

---

[14] Xosé Antón Miguélez, *Tenemos carta de Dios* (Barcelona: Centre de Pastoral Litúrgica, 1996).

is in his kingdom, outside this world, separated by an inaccessible transcendence. Instead, we must recover the wisdom of the best of Christian religious tradition and rediscover what was destroyed in the Modern Age by this absolute image of God and the concept of individuality. To rediscover God as *relationship*, as otherness, as *communion in solidarity* with everyone and everything from his very essence. In the face of the absolute and despotic monotheism of God as essence and individual, the Christian faith proclaims its faith in the Trinity as communion and relationship. Says Moltmann, "The only thing we need is to return to the original wisdom of our own tradition. . . . It is a matter of rediscovering the *one and triune God*."[15]

It is a matter of rediscovering that God is not a *solitary* Being, but rather a *solidary/communitarian* Being, rich in relationships *ad intra* and *ad extra*; moreover, God is *pure relationship*. The world is the expression of this love. If we want to aspire to be truly *the image of God*, humans have to resemble God not in the *power* of the Lord *over* nature and matter, but in *communion with* it and in life-giving reciprocity. The Spirit of God is present in all that exists, and every living thing lives from this source. From both an environmentalist and feminist perspective, Sallie McFague writes:

> I have come to see patriarchal as well as imperialistic, triumphalist metaphors for God in an increasingly grim light: this language is not only idolatrous and irrelevant . . . but it may also work against the continuation of life on our planet . . . we must ask whether the . . . imagery for the relationship between God and the world is helpful or harmful.[16]

---

[15] Moltmann, *La justicia crea futuro. Política de la paz y ética de la creación en un mundo amenazado*, 83.

[16] McFague, *Modelos de Dios. Teología para una era ecológica y nuclear*, 9–10.

Therefore, the premises that a theology for today should take into account are: *the relational conception of Reality*, which implies a greater appreciation of the world and a moderate admiration for technology; the *importance of language in the challenges that other religious* interpretations pose to the Judeo-Christian tradition; the *displacement of the masculine-white-Western and the relevance of the dispossessed*, of the poor; an *apocalyptic sensibility*; growing appreciation of the radical and total *interdependence of all forms of life*. This core problem is also related to other problems of domination: rich over poor, white over Black, man over woman. The alternative to this type of power cannot be other than the power of love, otherness, and radical relationality.

For this reason, many of us believe that the new image of God implies a return to the Trinitarian God of the early days of Christian thought. The divine Trinity, far from being a theme of the past—"something from medieval theology that was imposed on us during catechism," as I have sometimes heard it described when discussing it—is a current theme, which is returning with force to Christian theology and religious experience, and which even seeks a point of confluence with the empirical sciences and contemporary human sciences. *God is relationship* and—as we have seen here from the beginning—*the world* that the latest physics has been showing us, both the macrocosm and the microcosm, is *pure relationship*; the human being is also relationship and "the Trinity is the best community," as Leonardo Boff titled one of his books.[17] The Trinity, in short, is perfect *unity in diversity*.

---

[17] Leonardo Boff, *La Santísima Trinidad es la mejor comunidad* (Madrid: Paulinas, 1990), and especially his previous book, *La Trinidad, la sociedad y la liberación* (Madrid: Paulinas, 1987); in English, *Holy Trinity, Perfect Community* (Maryknoll, NY: Orbis Books, 2000) and *Trinity and Society* (Maryknoll, NY: Orbis Books, 1996). I myself confirmed the interest in a Trinitarian God through the positive reception to a book I published years ago, a dense volume of theology of over 500 pages: *Dios, Hombre, Mundo: La trinidad en Raimon Panikkar* (Barcelona: Herder, 2008).

This is a true "revival and renewal of Trinitarian theology," as John Polkinghorne—scientist and theologian, professor emeritus of mathematical physics at Cambridge University, president and founder of the International Society for Science and Religion—acknowledges in the interdisciplinary collection *The Trinity and an Entangled World*.[18] Here, Polkinghorne oversees a series of complex pieces by physicists, philosophers, and theologians on the theme of the Trinity in the theology of yesterday and today, in relational ontology and the relationality of modern physics. Relational ontology and quantum physics invite us to rethink the Christian faith from its Trinitarian roots, from a time when the Trinity had not yet become an idle and useless dogma, with little relation to Christian life. They help us rediscover that, as Rahner wrote, "the *economic* Trinity—the *Deus ad extra* or the *Deus pro nobis* present in salvation history—is the *immanent* Trinity, the *Deus ad intra*." Polkinghorne introduces the book with these eloquent words, which many of us share wholeheartedly:

> Science has increasingly found that concepts of atomism and mechanism . . . are unable to fully express the character of physical reality. . . . The history of twentieth-century physics can be read as the story of the discovery of many *levels of intrinsic relationality present in the structure of the universe*.

To conclude his introduction, he states:

---

[18] John Polkinghorne, *La Trinidad y un mundo entrelazado. Relacionalidad en las ciencias físicas y la teología* (Estella: Verbo Divino, 2013); in English, *The Trinity and an Entangled World: Relationality in Physical Science and Theology* (Grand Rapids: William B. Eerdmans Pub. Co., 2010). *Cf.* a critique of this book in Victorino Pérez Prieto, "Reseña: "La Trinidad y un mundo entrelazado. Relacionalidad en las ciencias físicas y la teología"," *Análisis* 47, no. 87 (2016).

Just as physicists in their own domain have found relationality to be more extensive and more surprising in its character than prior expectation would have led them to anticipate, so philosophers and theologians should be open to the possibility of unexpected discovery and counterintuitive insight.[19]

This is "holistic connectivity in the physical world" and the relationality of the Trinitarian God in theology. In his paper "The Demise of Democritus," included in the book, Polkinghorne speaks of the "intrinsic relationality" of all Reality ("nature is intrinsically relational"), from the most elementary (particles and fields) and the biological to humans "in an ever-increasing" relationality and to God himself, Father-Son-Spirit. Thus, he boldly concludes that "for the Christian, the true 'Theory of Everything' is Trinitarian theology."[20] The book's most innovative perspective comes from the Orthodox theologian and bishop John Zizioulas in his critique of atomistic individualism and defense of a *Trinitarian relational ontology* based on communion; through his work, he has created a magnificent interaction between modern science and theology. His thesis is the precedence of *relationship* over *being* in God—as opposed to that of *being* over *relationship*, which was the dominant framework starting with Aristotle—as it would exist in the Church Fathers Basil of Caesarea, Gregory of Nazianzus and Gregory of Nyssa. Together with Zizioulas—although the Church Fathers are not mentioned in his work—we should mention the Trinitarian theology of Jürgen Moltmann,[21] of Gisbert

---

[19] Polkinghorne, *La Trinidad y un mundo entrelazado. Relacionalidad en las ciencias físicas y la teología*, 11 and 15.

[20] Ibid. 30.

[21] Jürgen Moltmann, *The Trinity and the Kingdom* (Minneapolis: Fortress Press, 1993).

Greshake[22] and of the *theanthropocosmic* perspective of *radical relativity* of Raimon Panikkar[23] (God "is not and has no *substance*" because "he is *pure relationship*"), which is accompanied by the notion of *radical relativity* or *total reciprocity*. We should also consider Leonardo Boff and other contemporary theologians.

To speak, then, of God as Trinity is to speak of God as *pure relationship*, of the essential relationality of the triune God, of which the Greek and Latin Church Fathers[24]—among whom the three Cappadocian Fathers and the theologians of the Middle Ages, especially Richard of St. Victor, Bonaventure, and Thomas Aquinas, are the most important—had already spoken. For Richard of St. Victor—writing a century before Bonaventure and Aquinas (1110–1173)—the Christian God is essentially a *mystery of love*, an *interpersonal encounter* of love and a mystery of *Trinitarian communion*, in which persons emerge from one another. Richard of St. Victor *deduces* the three divine persons, Father-Son-Holy Spirit, from the demands of divine love, happiness, and glory: if

---

[22] Gisbert Greshake, *El Dios Uno y Trino. Una teología de la Trinidad* (Barcelona: Herder, 2002).

[23] Raimon Panikkar, *The Trinity and the Religious Experience of Man; Icon-Person-Mystery* (Maryknoll, NY: Orbis Books, 2009).

[24] The Holy Fathers are the creators of two brilliant complex expressions that have been revived in contemporary theology: *perichôrêsis* (from the Greek Fathers) and *circumincessio* (from the Latin Fathers). These expressions seek to think about *unity in the Trinity* and the *Trinity in unity* simultaneously; God *as relationship* rather than God *as substance*. These assertions state that the divine reality is *relationship, communion, interaction, constitutive interpenetration*. In contemporary theology, Walter Kasper uses these expressions as "communal unity open to the integration of the world and history in the divine fullness" (Walter Kasper, *The God of Jesus Christ* (Chestnut Ridge, NY: Crossroad Publishing, 1986)). See also Jürgen Moltmann and Leonardo Boff, in the works cited in the previous notes. For Raimon Panikkar, *perichôrêsis* is the *radical* divine *relationality*: "Without patristic *perichôrêsis* or *advaita* thought, the Trinity is pure contradiction, gibberish, one in three, three in one" (Panikkar, *La Trinidad. Una experiencia humana primordial*, 68).

there were no *otherness*, one could not speak of *love*; the person is not to be defined within the horizon of generic *substantial being*, but from the fact of being a specific *relational subject*. For this reason, the divine person is essentially formed by *relationality*. The divine person is *communion* as a manifestation of the fact that *God is love, and love cannot exist without relationship*.[25]

Bonaventure (1217–1274) has been referred to as having a "Trinitarian obsession": "Eternal life consists only in this," he says, "that the rational spirit, which flows from the Holy Trinity and is the image of the Trinity, as if making a mental circle, returns, through memory, intelligence and will, to the Most Holy Trinity." Finally, to Thomas Aquinas (1224–1274) belongs the well-known statement *Deus est relatio*: God is *relation without substance* or accidents.[26] After a decline with the coming of Modernity (17th century), Trinitarian theology experienced a strong resurgence in the theology of the second half of the twentieth century, curiously hand in hand with science—with which it had clashed most fiercely during the eighteenth and nineteenth centuries—and specifically the new science of complexity and relationality.

Fourth. *The World as the Body of God:* Panentheism *and* Cosmotheandric *Reality*

Another possible metaphor for God, which seems very appropriate for the new relational and ecologistic mentality, is to speak of the *world as God's body*, as a material expression of God, as God's sacrament—not something foreign to Him, but an expression of Himself. Using a maternal image, Sallie McFague is not afraid to say that "the universe is bodied forth from God. . . . It is not

---

[25] Richard of St. Victor, *De Trinitate iv*, 17–18, p. 22.

[26] *Cf.* Bonaventure, *De Myst. Trin.*; Thomas Aquinas, *Sum. contra Gentiles*, 1,14; *Sum. The.* 1, q. 28. 1–4.

something alien to or other than God but is from the *womb*, formed through *gestation*."[27] How would believing-religious people feel and act if they really perceived the world as *God's body*? In all probability, they would feel and act differently.

In the monarchical-imperial model of understanding God, as we have seen, the predominant image was dangerous, for it situated him as a lord and ourselves as his servants, and this sustained an authoritarian type of religion. In this image, God controls the world with dominion and benevolence, inhibiting human responsibility. This image of sovereignty encourages actions of control and use of the non-human world at the discretion of human beings.

In the conception of the world as *God's body*, the terms change in a fundamental way, since God himself enters into the weakness of matter. God's action in the world now proceeds from within, overcoming dualisms that are no longer sustainable. In addition, overcoming the authoritarianism of the old model, this metaphor makes God more "vulnerable," which helps us to better understand the "crucified" and "powerless" God of the cross. This model also even suggests that *God loves bodies*, which is a strong challenge to the dualistic Christian tradition that opposes the bodily/sexual, the material, and sees the spiritual as superior. The other perspective assumes that matter is good and that bodies are worthy of love; it assumes God's love for all creatures. In this conception, divine reality appears as *relational*, the quality that characterizes Reality: everything is related. God himself is part of this relationship; he has always existed with himself as relationship. God himself is relational in himself and is in relationship with all of Reality.

Even so, we should remember that we are also presenting a *metaphor* about God, not a *description* of the Divine. Therefore, the expression *cannot* lead either to the old *sacralization* of nature,

---

[27] McFague, *Modelos de Dios. Teología para una era ecológica y nuclear*, 187.

or to a simple descent into *pantheism*; God is not reduced to the world, and neither one is identified. As Panikkar indicates, pantheism is "an error by *defect* and not by excess," and it is that the Divinity is *more* than the *panta* of pantheism. "God *is in* everything, but God *is not exhausted in* that everything."

> *All is God,* says pantheism, and it is true, but God *cannot be reduced to any all.* Pantheism *limits God*, it does not have the audacity to affirm that in such a way everything is God, that God is not even this everything, because everything is never totalized. . . . Pantheism lacks the *experience of nothingness*, non-experience.[28]

Teilhard de Chardin expressed pantheistic sympathies, trying to situate pantheism in a Christian context: "What I am proposing to do is narrow the gap between pantheism and Christianity by bringing out what one might call the *Christian soul of pantheism* or the *pantheist aspect of Christianity*."[29] For him, the identification of pantheism with Spinozism, theosophy, monism, etc., is "false, unjustified and dangerous." On the contrary, this "is only the *defective form* in which is expressed a well-justified (and moreover, ineradicable) tendency in the human soul, a tendency which can be fully satisfied only in Christianity . . . to recognize the *importance, in one's religious calculations, of the* Whole."[30] Alone in the equilibrium between God and the cosmos, forming part of the Whole, "peace can be established in our faith," affirms Teilhard.

---

[28] Raimon Panikkar, *La experiencia de Dios* (Madrid: PPC, 1994), 52.

[29] Pierre Teilhard de Chardin, "Panteismo y Cristianismo" in *Como yo creo*, 65–84; in English, the essay is found in the collection *Christianity and Evolution* (London: Harcourt, 1969).

[30] *Ibid.* 66. And further on: "Fundamentally, we have but one passion: to become one with the world which envelops us without our ever being able to distinguish either its face or its heart," p. 67. "The Whole cannot reveal itself to us without our recognizing in it God," p. 69.

Then, using an expression dear to him, he says that the "Christian transposition of the pantheist tendency" must come through the encounter with the *cosmic Christ*. In him is "Christianized" the concern for the Whole, "the religion of the Whole." He is "the principle of universal consistence," the "Center of the World."[31]

To overcome the contradictions of pantheism, a new concept emerged more than a hundred years ago, which was lost in the philosophy of the nineteenth and early twentieth centuries and which has made its way back at the end of the twentieth and beginning of the twenty-first: *panentheism*. God *in everything* and *everything in God*. "*All-in-God*"; God intimately immersed in the process of cosmogenesis, but not lost in it. The concept has very Pauline theological roots: "In him we live and move and exist" (Acts of the Apostles 17:28), Paul said in his speech at the Athenian Areopagus. But the concept did not grow philosophically until the nineteenth century, with the German Karl Christian F. Krause.[32] Fascinated by the divine brilliance of the universe, Krausist panentheism seeks an organic vision of Reality, linking unity and diversity, going from God to the human being and nature. Krause believes that modern science—which must have religious intentionality—must be able to unite analysis and synthesis, original and absolute consciousness of the Divinity, and derived and particular consciousness of its manifestations. It is God who unifies the diverse aspects of Reality.[33]

Pantheism affirms that *everything is God* and *God is nothing more than this material everything*; there is an identification between

---

[31] *Cf. Ibid*. 75 and ff.

[32] Karl Christian Friedrich Krause (1781–1832), epigone of the great philosophies of Fichte and Schelling, of whom he was a student at the University of Jena, expresses this concept above all in his work *The Ideal of Humanity and Universal Federation* (South Yarra, Australia: Leopold Classic Library, 2016). *Cf.* the works of Rosemary Radford Ruether in *Concilium*, n. 287 (2000) and n. 256 (1994).

[33] *Cf.* "Krause," *Encyclopædia Universalis*, Paris, 1990.

God and the world, with no difference between the two: *Deus sive natura*, in Spinoza's famous utterance. On the other hand, *panentheism* affirms that, although God *is in everything*, God *is more than* this material whole; God is not completely identified with the world and is not reduced to material reality, for God is more than the world; he surpasses it, but both are open, one before the other in an intimate relationship. God is immersed in all material reality. In the best biblical wisdom, everything exists *"from* God," *"through* God" and *"in* God" (*cf.* Proverbs 8, Wisdom 11); everything lives from that "source of life" which is the divine Spirit.

Leonardo Boff embraced this concept, which for him demonstrates the important category of *transparency*, as an expression of the "presence of transcendence within immanence"[34]. Divine transcendence becomes transparent in worldly immanence; the world is no longer opaque, but transparent, charged with meaning and purpose. Precisely the opposite of the famous expression of the French biologist and Nobel laureate Jacques Monod: "Man is alone in a world that is blind and deaf to his groans." Teilhard de Chardin saw this spiritual transparency like no one else: "The great mystery of Christianity is not exactly the appearance, but *the transparency of God in the Universe.*"[35] God becomes transparent in the cosmos in a thousand ways, in every expression of life and love; but he became exceptionally transparent in Jesus Christ, the incarnate Word.

On the other hand, the concept of *panentheism*—which we find very valuable—seems insufficient to Raimon Panikkar: "I like the concept of *panentheism* only in part; what I don't like is that we put the Divinity in *a separate circle.*" For Panikkar, it is necessary to arrive at a new conception, which he draws from

---

[34] Boff, *Ecología. Grito de la tierra, grito de los pobres*, 193.

[35] Pierre Teilhard de Chardin, *El medio divino* (Madrid: Taurus, 1967), 141; in English, see *The Divine Milieu Explained: A Spirituality for the 21st Century* (Mahwah, NJ: Paulist Press, 2007).

the Hindu wisdom of *advaita* ("non-duality"); which allows us to say without condescension "that *matter is divine*, or that God *is* in matter, or that he is *human*."[36] It does so through a concept and a formulation that we have already seen and which, without undervaluing the rich contribution of panentheism, seems to me the most valuable elaboration of the relationship between God/Divinity and the World in years: the *cosmotheandric/theanthropocosmic* vision of Reality, in which God-Human Being-Cosmos appear wholly related and involved:

> What counts is the whole reality, matter as much as spirit, good as much as evil, science as much as mysticism, soul as much as body.... It is not a question of regaining the innocence we had to lose to become what we are, but of conquering a new one.
>
> Without denying differences, and even recognizing a hierarchical order within the three dimensions, the cosmotheandric principle stresses the *intrinsic relationship* among them.[37]

God is in intimate relation with the human being and the cosmos. He is the abyssal dimension, at once transcendent and immanent, here and beyond the world and human beings, the constitutive principle of all beings. The *theandric* perspective already had a long tradition in Western Christian thought of expressing the harmonious union without confusion between the divine and the human. With the addition of the third term (*cosmos*), a vision that assumes the whole and eternal Reality, matter and spirit, science and mysticism appears. Although the experience of totality is properly mystical, more ineffable than

---

[36] Victorino Pérez Prieto, "El pensamiento cristiano es trinitario, simbólico y relacional. Encuentros con Raimon Panikkar," *Iglesia viva*, no. 223 (2005), 77.

[37] Panikkar, *La nueva inocencia*, 53–54.

analytical ("physicists now speak like mystics," as we read in Ernesto Cardenal). God is not only the God of humanity, but also of the world, and the human being exists "with the firmament above, the earth below and the companions around.... To isolate man from God and the world is to strangle him."[38] Panikkar goes quite far in this interconnection between God, the world, and the cosmos, to end up "apologizing" for his audacity by saying, "Man is no less man when he discovers his divine vocation, nor do the Gods lose their divinity when they are humanized."[39]

James Lovelock—the father of the "Gaia hypothesis"—himself said something similar many years ago in his well-known book, where he conceived of the Earth as a single organism called Gaia, without falling into the error of divinizing Gaia ("In no way do I see Gaia as an alternative God"). He knew that the battle was between a flat reductionism and a self-organized vision of the universe: "I tried to show that God and Gaia, theology and science, . . . are not separate, but form a single line of thought."[40]

TOWARD A NON-DUAL ECOSOPHICAL ECOSPIRITUALITY

We Need to Open "The Third Eye" for a Total Non-dual Vision of Reality

Theology and spirituality/mysticism are—or should be—closely linked, but they are not the same thing, above all because of their methodology. There is a well-known phrase attributed to Karl Rahner—one of the most important theologians of the twentieth century—but which was actually first uttered by my great

---

[38] *Ibid.* 57.
[39] *Ibid.* 61.
[40] James Lovelock, *Gaia. Una nueva visión de la vida en la Tierra* (Barcelona: Orbis, 1982), 228 and 233, and ch. 9 ("Dios y Gaia"); in English, *Gaia: A New Look at Life on Earth*.

teacher Raimon Panikkar: "The Christian of the twenty-first century must be a *mystic* or [he or she] will not be a Christian." The phrase seems to me magnificent and one that should be repeated over and over: philosophical-theological reflections, laws, norms, rites, and even social praxis itself do not liberate, even if they can be of help on our life's journey. What liberates us is the Spirit, life lived intentionally, the *full experience of life* in communion with our brothers and sisters, with the world and with God, as the great master Jesus of Nazareth, the Liberating Christ, said and did.

As I have said before, to this statement I like to add that Christians of the twenty-first century must also be *ecopacifists* and seek *ecospirituality*, or they will not be good Christians, disciples of Jesus of Nazareth. They must seek a peaceful balance with their fellow brothers and sisters, but also harmony with nature and the cosmos of which they are a part; with brother wolf, sister ostrich, hummingbird and lark, with tree and stone, with water and wind, with the whole cosmos. They should seek *justice, peace, and integrity with all creation*, creating for themselves just relationships with the Earth and the cosmos. They must seek the wisdom and spirituality of the Earth, with holistic sensitivity, recognizing *the interdependence of all with all*. Otherwise, they will not *be*, they will have no future, because life and the cosmos live and die with us: we are the *consciousness* of the universe.[41]

Vandana Shiva—the Indian ecofeminist quoted earlier—says that there is an intimate relationship between ecologism, ecofeminism, and spirituality: the *interconnectedness of all things*, which was already known to our ancestors, the recognition of the interconnection. For her, spirituality is the knowledge that everything is interconnected in matter and spirit. "Relationships cannot be

---

[41] *Cf.* Pérez Prieto, "La ecoteología en el quehacer teológico del siglo XXI". Also "Nel cuore di un cristianesimo ecologista: l'intima connessione tra materia, coscienza e infinito," *Adista*, no. 5 (2013).

measured in inches and feet," she says, but "must be lived." There is a holistic, multidimensional interconnectivity in spirituality. Wholeness and spirituality are not distinct, and recognizing the wholeness of each person and each species is itself spirituality.[42]

This spirituality/mysticism is the return to oneself, to one's own unified center, to one's own *consciousness*, which is part of the Consciousness of all Reality. Faced with the constant departure from oneself, the estrangement and alienation from the center, it is a matter of seeking union. It is a non-narcissistic self-absorption, which is the opposite of egocentrism. It is about *entering into Silence*:[43] external and internal, contemplative, mystical silence. Mysticism, present throughout the history of humanity from East to West, seeks an integral experience of Reality, a life in plenitude: the consciousness of *profound communion with all of Reality*. Raimon Panikkar defines it as a "full experience of life," to which every human being is called: "integral experience of life" or of Reality, rather than ecstatic experiences or conceptual lucubrations.[44]

To live fully is to live consciously, with full attention; to open our eyes to Reality beyond all mediation; to dare to see it beyond our ideas and beliefs, fears and desires, beyond reason. For the realm of the real overflows the intelligible, since reason is limited. It is not a matter of renouncing reason but of relativizing it in order to reach the transrational as well. For this reason, the mystics have been called "those inveterate seekers of the Real." They have been

---

[42] *Cf.* Shiva, "Ecofeminismo, derechos de la naturaleza, suma kawsay. Diálogo con mujeres ecuatorianas y conferencia".

[43] There is an extensive bibliography in Spanish on the concept of silence: the successful book by Pablo D'Ors, *Biografía del silencio* (Madrid: Siruela, 2012); Teresa Guardans, *La verdad del silencio* (Barcelona: Herder, 2009); Sara Maitland, *Viaje al silencio* (Barcelona: Alba, 2010); Marià Corbí, *El conocimiento silencioso. Las raíces de la cualidad humana* (Barcelona: Fragmenta, 2017), and others.

[44] Panikkar, *De la mística. Experiencia plena de la vida*, 20–23. *Cf.* also my work "La interioridad en las tradiciones religiosas no cristianas," in *Hacia una teología de la interioridad*, ed. Elena Andrés and Carlos Esteban Garcés (Madrid: PPC, 2019), 95–140.

men and women who have known how to reach the "hidden depths that lie in the heart of people and things; a depth and a spaciousness that, from time to time, are illuminated."[45] The mystics have known how to reach the depths of Reality. The mystical experience requires having *all three eyes* wide open—the sensitive/empirical, the rational/philosophical, and the spiritual/contemplative—in order to fully enjoy all that *is*. We will see this later.

Teilhard de Chardin, scientist and theologian, but also a great contemporary mystic that we have quoted several times here ("my poor trifling existence was one with the immensity of all that is"), beautifully captured the challenge of the mystical union/communion between God and creation, the union with All, which is at the basis of an eco-spirituality:

> Poets, philosophers, and mystics—the long procession of those who have been initiated into the vision and *cult of the Whole*—have left behind them a central wake which we can follow unmistakably from our own days right back to the most distant horizons of history . . . the essentially modern work of philosophic criticism and scientific research which has been carried out for the last two or three centuries in every field of terrestrial knowledge, is all leading in the same direction . . . to a magnification and solidification of *the universe as one bloc.*
>
> . . . the vital question for Christianity today is to decide what attitude believers will adopt towards this *recognition of the value of the Whole*, this "preoccupation with the Whole." Will they open their hearts to it, or will they reject it as an evil spirit? [46]

---

[45] Javier Melloni, *Voces de la mística*, vol. I, II (Barcelona: Herder, 2009, 2012), 11.

[46] Teilhard de Chardin, "Panteismo y cristianismo," 69–70 and 73 (in *Como yo creo*); in English, the essay "Pantheism and Christianity" is in the collection *Christianity and Evolution*.

"Physicists now speak like mystics," sang Ernesto Cardenal. And David Bohm—one of the best quantum physicists of all time—says about the mystical dimension: "We could imagine the mystic as someone who is in contact with the frightening depths of matter or of the subtle mind, no matter what name we give it."[47] This unfathomable experience, present in all the great religions, is based on the conviction and the assumption that "there is an infinite Reality yet to be unveiled—as Javier Melloni states—and that the human being is only at the start of his potential."[48] The core of religious traditions is deeply mystical; their sacredness surpasses the reality that is seen with the eyes; the *excess* of this perspective is the true sign of sacredness, and "the grasping of these roots can only be done with the cleansing of the heart," as Melloni immediately adds alongside other masters.

Centuries ago, the great Spanish mystic John of the Cross used the image of a mountain and several verses to sketch out his vision of the mystical union of the human being with God in one of his most sublime works: *Ascent of Mount Carmel*. The last verses of this text also fascinated Edgard Morin. They seemed to him an expression of complex thought, as we have seen above. They express a constant path, always open to what is greater than our reason and our knowledge.

> To reach satisfaction in all
> desire its possession in nothing.
> To come to possession in all
> desire the possession of nothing.
> To arrive at being all
> desire to be nothing.

---

[47] In an interview in Renée Weber, *Diálogos con científicos y sabios. La búsqueda de la unidad* (Barcelona: La Liebre de Marzo, 1990). Also in a magnificent book cited earlier: Wilber, *Quantum Questions: Mystical Writings of the World's Great Physicists*.

[48] Javier Melloni, *Vislumbres de lo Real* (Barcelona: Herder, 2007), 12.

> *To come to the knowledge of all*
> *desire the knowledge of nothing.*
> *To come to the pleasure you have not*
> *you must go by the way in which you enjoy*
> *not.*
> *To come to the knowledge you have not*
> *you must go by the way in which you know not.*[49]

The experience of encountering the deepest Mystery of Reality cannot be expressed except in the words "I know not what, of which they are darkly speaking," as John of the Cross himself said brilliantly in his *Spiritual Canticle*. We will return later to this mystic of the Spanish Golden Age.

I said earlier that ecologism is a *new humanism*. This humanism calls for a *new*, ecological *spirituality* as a response to a current ecological crisis caused by predatory human activity. For this spirituality we need even more a *totalizing vision of Reality* that goes beyond the moral-ethical demands of the ecological crisis discovered by ecologism to a *total empathic connection with a Reality* in which we feel truly immersed. A spirituality that, in the words of Leonardo Boff, "allows for *a unique* and surprisingly new *religation of all our dimensions* with the most diverse instances of planetary, cosmic, historical, psychic and transcendental reality."[50] We need to open ourselves up to a radical ecological spirituality.

This *ecosophical spirituality* demands a connection with Reality in order to reach a *communion* with Everything, with the cosmos—not only "living" nature, but the whole reality of matter—and with the Spirit, with God. Being part of the cosmos, it is essential for us to live in harmony with it in order to be at

---

[49] St. John of the Cross, "El monte de perfección," in John of the Cross, *Vida y obras completas*, 435.

[50] Boff, *Ecología. Grito de la tierra, grito de los pobres*, 99.

peace with ourselves. As Raimon Panikkar says, "man, on the one hand, is *part of the universe* and, on the other hand, is *the crossroads of the entire cosmos.*" Moreover, "he becomes all the more human the more the destiny of the universe comes to be realized in him"[51] "When one has experienced that *God is in everything*, that *everything is in God* and that nevertheless *God is* nothing of that which *is*, then one is close to *realization.*"[52]

An ecosophical spirituality implies going beyond the *materiality of matter*. It implies going beyond the purely empirical perspective of material reality that places us before it as something neutral, alien to the spirit, to finally open ourselves to its *spiritual* dimension: matter, even inert matter, is inhabited by the Spirit!

In other words (ones rarely used these days), we need to open the third eye to achieve a radical ecosophical spirituality. It is necessary to go beyond the vision provided by the *first eye* (the corporeal-empirical, the sensitive) and the *second eye* (the rational, which allows us to analyze and understand Reality) to activate the vision of the *third eye* (the spiritual-contemplative-mystical eye, the eye of faith, which allows us to enter the depths of Reality). The *third eye* is the inner eye, the eye of the mind, the eye of the heart, the eye of faith/contemplation, the eye of the spirit and the spiritual, the *organ* of the soul. It is the entrance to the inner realm and the depth of the Self, a state of higher consciousness associated with mystical and spiritual experiences, to the encounter with the Mystery and with what *we are*, to the clairvoyance of vision. Although many associate it only with Hinduism and Buddhism, the *third eye* is present in many cultures, from Egypt to India, passing through pre-Columbian American cultures and the Christian West.

In Christianity, from the *non-dualistic* mystical thought, the concept of the *third eye* represents how the mystics *see*. It appears

---

[51] Panikkar, *La nueva inocencia*, 121.
[52] Panikkar, *La Trinidad. Una experiencia humana primordial*, 60.

clearly from the beginnings of Christian spirituality, with Dionysius the Areopagite, to John of the Cross and contemporary mystics. The *first eye* is used for sensory information, the *second eye* for reflection as the eye of reason and the *third eye* to go beyond, to achieve a higher level of vision and consciousness: "to have the mind of Christ." The Gnostics already saw a symbolic reference to the third eye in a well-known text of the Apocalypse, in the message of the angel to the sixth of the seven churches of Asia (Philadelphia): "Behold, I have left before you an open door which no one can shut" (Revelation 3:8).[53]

The theologian Hugo of St. Victor (1096–1141), a predecessor to the Scholastic greats Bonaventure and Thomas Aquinas, offered—in twelfth-century Paris—the first Christian reflection on the three eyes of knowledge, which would later be taken up by St. Bonaventure.[54] His thought draws from Plato and Plotinus, Augustine of Hippo and Dionysius the Areopagite. The Greek tradition speaks of three realities in knowledge: *ta aisthêta* (the sensible), *ta noêta* (the mental) and *ta mystika* (the mystical). Hugo of St. Victor affirms that God placed the human being in paradise with three eyes: one *corporeal* (*oculus carnis*, sensitive eye), another *rational* (*oculus rationis*, eye of reason) and a third, the eye of *contemplation* (*oculus fidei*, eye of the spirit). In the utopian vision of a beginning in Edenic innocence, which in reality is the fullness of a future end, Adam and Eve had all three eyes open, but as a result of sin they had to leave paradise; as a result the first eye was weakened, the second confused, and the third blinded. It was the task of all human history to improve the vision of the first eye and to recover the vision of the second and third. To be "out of paradise" is to no longer perceive the Presence or "see"

---

[53] *Cf.* Victorino Pérez Prieto, "Los tres ojos del conocimiento: Ciencia, Filosofía y Teología," *Complessità* XIII, no. 1–2 (2018), 46–72.

[54] *Cf.* Pérez Prieto, "Los tres ojos del conocimiento en San Buenaventura. De la reductio Bonaventuriana al pensamiento complejo de Edgar Morin y la perspectiva cosmoteándrica de Raimon Panikkar."

God. Jesus of Nazareth and the Gospels proclaim this biblical wisdom: "Blessed are the pure *in* heart, for they *shall see* God" (Mt 5:8). "The eye is the lamp of the body. If your eye is healthy, your whole body is enlightened; but if your eye is diseased, all will be in darkness. And if the light that is in you is darkness, how great will be the darkness" (Mt 6:22–23). Augustine of Hippo said that our only task in this life is to "cure the eye of the heart," which allows us to *see* God.

Knowledge is not only tied to empirical science and rational reflection (philosophy), however important they may be; a contemplative perspective (theology and spirituality) is also necessary, since Reality is much larger than what is uncovered by empirical and rational knowledge. A well-known text by Carl Jung says: "Your vision will become clear only when you can look into your own heart. Who looks *outside*, dreams; who looks *inside*, awakes." While the eyes on our face look outward and see only the material world, there is an inner eye, the spiritual perception, which looks inward and sees Reality in depth: the *third eye*. The secret lies in balancing the *duality* and *unity* of our being in order to awaken the third eye, and thus to achieve a complete vision. The mystical experience that opens the *third eye* is the fullness of living, of authentic living. For this reason, Raimon Panikkar defines mysticism as "the fullness of life."

This is the path of mystical vision, a path to which every human being is called, not just exceptional beings—although there are different levels. It is a path related to what John of the Cross said: "To come to the *knowledge you have not,* you must go by the way *in which you know not*." It is a path open to the Spirit which blows where, when, and how it wills, as the Gospel affirms (*cf.* Jn 3:8).

We will examine three texts from three important Christian mystics who are distant from each other in time (between the twelfth and twentieth centuries), but very similar all the same.

Learning from Three Great Ecological Mystics: Francis of Assisi, John of the Cross, and Pierre Teilhard de Chardin[55]

> *If the world is already so beautiful when we behold it,*
> *Lord, with your peace in our eyes,*
> *what more could you give us in another life?*
> *And so I am heedful of the eyes and the face*
> *and the body you have given me, Lord, and this heart*
> *which has never yet halted, and I greatly fear to die.*
> ....
> *This world, be it as it may,*
> *so varied, so vast, so much of time,*
> *this earth, with all that grows in it,*
> *is my homeland, Lord, and could it also*
> *not be a heavenly home?*
> *I am a man, and my measure is human*
> *for all I can believe and hope:*
> *If my faith and hope remain here,*
> *will you blame me for it in the afterlife?*
> *Beyond me I see the sky and the stars,*
> *and there I should still want to be a man:*
> *If you have made things so beautiful to my eyes,*
> *if you made my eyes and senses*
> *for them, why close them seeking another world*
> *if for me there will be no other like this!*[56]

---

[55] *Cf.* For references and an extensive bibliography on the ecologist perspective of St. John of the Cross, St. Francis and Teilhard, see the chapter "Tres místicos cristiáns ecoloxistas" in Pérez Prieto, *Do teu verdor cinguido. Ecoloxismo e cristianismo*, 37–50.

[56] Joan Maragall, *Canto espiritual*, taken from Josep Maria Castellet/Joaquim Molas, *Ocho siglos de poesía catalana* (Madrid: Alianza, 1976), 23.

These verses by the Catalan poet Joan Maragall (1860–1911), a poet who was religious and at the same time intensely vitalist, express a passion for all Reality, and are a wonderful introduction to three exceptional Christians. Despite being separated by several centuries and very different realities and styles, these mystics and poets share a common love for God and all Reality—for all that exists, not only human reality. For the *poverello* of Assisi, the poet-mystic of Ávila and the French scientist-theologian-mystic Teilhard de Chardin, there is a passion for a whole material reality that manifests the presence of God without conflicting with their faith, their spirituality, or their scientific honesty. The mystical experience is at the base of this passion. These mystics are accustomed to experiencing God in an all-encompassing way. For this reason, they have no difficulty *feeling themselves in the world* and, simultaneously, in *feeling themselves in God*, harmoniously, without fissures, in a deep, true and radically holistic experience. From this authentic *religation* with the Divinity, which they experience while remaining very close to the earth, being deeply immersed *in it* rather than *on it*, a true non-dual *eco-spirituality* is born.

Francis of Assisi (1181–1226):
The Mystic of Cosmic Brotherhood-Sisterhood

The Canticle of the Creatures
or Laudes creaturarum

Praised be you, my Lord
with all your creatures,
especially Brother Sun,
who is the day through whom
you bring us light.
And he is lovely, shining

> with great splendor,
> for he heralds you, Most High.
> Praised be you, my Lord,
> through Sister Moon and Stars.
> In heaven you have formed them,
> lightsome and precious and fair.
> And praised be you, my Lord,
> through Brother Wind, through
> air and cloud, through calm
> and every weather by which
> you sustain your creatures.
> Praised be you, my Lord,
> through Sister Water,
> so very useful and humble,
> precious and chaste.
> Praised be you, my Lord
> through Brother Fire,
> by whom you light up
> the night, and he is
> handsome and merry,
> robust and strong.
> Praised be you, my Lord,
> through our Sister, Mother Earth,
> who sustains us and directs us
> bringing forth all kinds of fruits
> and colored flowers and herbs. . . .
> O praise and bless my Lord,
> thank him and serve him
> humbly but grandly![57]

Lynn White, the first to accuse Christianity of being at the root of the evils denounced by ecology, suggested in 1967 that

---

[57] Posted at www.stanthony.org.

St. Francis be proclaimed "the patron saint of ecologists" because he wanted to overthrow the absolute monarchy of man over nature in order "to establish a *democracy of all* God's *creatures*." Ten years later, in November 1979, John Paul II declared St. Francis patron. Max Scheler went so far as to say of Francis that he was "the most sublime example of the *spiritualization of matter* and, at the same time, of the *materialization of the spirit* that was ever made known to me." Hermann Hesse wrote: "Francis united heaven and earth in his heart and lit the earthly and mortal world with the flame of eternal life."[58] Finally, Ian Bradley also states that Francis of Assisi is "the most outstanding example of a Christian saint, committed to his faith and life, in loving communion with the natural world."[59] Indeed, rarely would there be so much consensus around a person who, as his first biographer, Thomas of Celano, had already written, "embraced all the beings of creation with a love and devotion never seen before. Francis showed such fervor and veneration for nature that he established an eternal peace with the Earth, loved as Mother and sister, and with all creatures." Thomas of Celano also beautifully summarizes the ecological attitude of St. Francis:

> He was filled with ineffable joy every time he looked at the sun, contemplated the moon and directed his gaze towards the stars and the firmament . . . when he met the flowers, he preached to them as if they were endowed with intelligence, and invited them to praise the Lord. He did so with the most tender and touching candor,

---

[58] *Cf.* the quotes in Leonardo Boff, *Francisco de Asís. Ternura y vigor* (Santander: Sal Terræ, 1990), 36–37; in English, *Francis of Assisi: A Model for Human Liberation* (Maryknoll, NY: Orbis Books, 1996). A good commentary can be found in Éloi Leclerc, *El cántico de las criaturas* (Oñate: Editorial Franciscana Arantzazu, 1977). *Cf.* Carlos Díaz, *Ecología y pobreza en Francisco de Asís* (Oñate: Editorial Franciscana Arantzazu, 1986).

[59] Bradley, *Dios es verde. Cristianismo y medio ambiente*, 139.

exhorting to gratitude the wheat fields and the vineyards, the stones and the forests, the flatness of the fields and the currents of the rivers, the beauty of the orchards, the earth, the fire, the air and the wind. Finally, he gave the sweet name of sisters to all creatures, whose secrets, in a marvelous way and unknown to all, he divined as one who already enjoys the freedom and glory of the children of God.[60]

Only those who have listened to their symbolic resonance within the soul can live in such intimacy with all beings, thus uniting environmental ecology with a mental and deep ecology, knowing themselves to be part of the *seamless fabric* of reality. Francis never placed himself above things but at their feet, truly as a brother and sister, and discovered the bonds of consanguinity that unite us all, feeling himself intimately linked to the *maternal Father*, creator and universal provider. Francis's passion for a *mystical union with the whole cosmos* is linked only to his desire for union with Christ the Lord, the manifestation of God as Love: "He looked everywhere and followed the Beloved via the traces imprinted on his creatures," writes St. Bonaventure.[61] Francis sings to the Creator, who loves him *with and in all creatures*, for all are his *sisters*: creatures and humans have arisen equally from the maternal love of God. For this reason, Leonardo Boff rightly writes that Francis "lived the new *paradigm of fraternity*, of benevolence, of coexistence with nature, intimately linked to everything." If from 1500 until today, Christians have lived as disciples of Pietro Bernardone—Francis's father, a man of the bourgeoisie and merchant power—"now we should all become disciples of

---

[60] See "Vida de San Francisco de Asís. Vida primera," in Thomas of Celano, *Escritos y biografías* (Madrid: Biblioteca de Autores Cristianos, 1971); in English, *The Life of St. Francis and the Treatise of Miracles* (Phoenix: Tau Publishing, 2017).

[61] Bonaventure of Bagnoregio, *The Life of St. Francis of Assisi* (Charlotte, NC: TAN Books, 2010), Chapter viii.

St. Francis if we want to rescue the sacredness of the earth in a new paradigm.[62]

The *Canticle of the Creatures* or *Laudes creaturarum* is Francis's masterpiece of cosmic fraternity; a true mystical hymn, but also an "ecological manifesto" *avant la lettre*. This beautiful poem-prayer expresses the profound union of God with the whole cosmos. In it, Francis sings of the love of God, who wants the world to be interwoven and in harmony. The song becomes a magnificent example of *ecological mystical poetry*, and reveals the exceptional religious experience of the saint of Assisi, the *unity* and coherence he had in himself and *with all of Reality*, thus overcoming the old dualisms. This jewel of mystical poetry and literature is the hymn of an ontological poet and mystic who "attained the transfiguration of the universe and the discovery of *pan-relationality* with all creatures."[63]

Francis has a *cosmic experience of the sacred*, a communion with God in the depths of Reality. This is what the religious experience of the *Canticle* expresses. In Francis, the cosmic dimension is inseparable from his spiritual-mystical life. Union with God is found by way of Christ, by way of the incarnation. In this way, as the Franciscan Éloi Leclerc states:

> All the originality of Francis's religious experience derives from the synthesis he was able to achieve between these two dimensions: that of the most intimate and personal *evangelical mysticism* and that of the most enthusiastic *cosmic mysticism*. Francis magnificently incorporates into his life of union with the person of Christ the great cosmic religious

---

[62] Leonardo Boff, "Teologia della liberazione ed ecologia: Una lotta comune per la sinfonía del creato," *Adista*, no. 44 (June 1996). *Cf.* also in *Francisco de Asís. Ternura y vigor*, and the chapter "All the Ecological Cardinal Virtues: St. Francis of Assisi," in *Ecología. Grito de la tierra, grito de los pobres*, 253–272.

[63] Boff, *Ecología. Grito de la tierra, grito de los pobres*, 264.

emotion of the pantheist religions. He unites the Sun and the Cross.[64]

The *Canticle* is filled with the experience of the *interrelatedness of everything*; that is, the union with the whole, which forms the basis of environmentalism and complexity. At the same time, a *transformative utopia* emerges from the *Canticle*, which is committed to the fact that beyond this broken world, the *harmony of all* in justice and peace is possible. The *Canticle* expresses the mystique of *cosmic fraternity*, based on *respect for what is different* and, above all, on *love that renounces possession and dominion*. This universal fraternity is a consequence of St. Francis's way of *being poor*—his marriage to "Lady Poverty"—because poverty is humility (to know oneself to be earth = *humus*, to be attached to the earth), as well as of his ecological asceticism, a magnificent reading of the three R's of ecology. Poverty leads him to a new yet ancient way of being in the world: no longer *over* things, but *at the foot of* them and even *within* them, to establish a true *cosmic democracy*. His song is a profound affirmation that everything is interrelated. The relationship of creatures with the cosmos, the communion of everything, is a total brotherhood-sisterhood, a relationship that has its roots in knowing how to understand what truly is.

Finally, the motto of Francis of Assisi, *Deus meus et omnia* is a cosmic slogan that manifests a non-dual vision of Reality. It is a call to the men and women of today, who need, as never before, to recover the broken harmony with God and with the whole reality of threatened nature. It is a call to an ecosophical commitment that knows how to unite an *external ecology* (harmony with nature and with the whole cosmos), a *social ecology* (a commitment to the beings of Nature, especially the poorest, the greatest victims of an unjust social structure that murders human

---

[64] Leclerc, *El cántico de las criaturas*, 17.

beings) and an *eco-spirituality*, an inner, spiritual, mystical ecology; a union with the Source—God, the Mystery, Meaning—that leads to peace with oneself and with All.

John of the Cross (1542–1591): An Ecologist Mystic

Spiritual Canticle

Where have You hidden Yourself
And abandoned me in my groaning, O my Beloved?
You have fled like the hart,
Having wounded me.
I ran after You, crying; but You were gone . . .
In search of my Love
I will go over mountains and strands;
I will gather no flowers,
I will fear no wild beasts;
And pass by the mighty and the frontiers. . . .
A thousand graces diffusing
He passed through the groves in haste,
And merely regarding them
As He passed
Clothed them with His Beauty. . . .
My Beloved is the mountains,
The solitary wooded valleys,
The strange islands,
The roaring torrents,
The whisper of the amorous gales;
The tranquil night
At the approaches of the dawn,
The silent music,
The murmuring solitude,
The supper which revives, and enkindles love. . . .

St. John of the Cross's vision is not always as clearly ecologic as that of St. Francis, but the Spanish saint, who shines with his own light from the summit of mysticism and poetry,[65] far from being lost in the heights, also shows himself to be a lover of sensitive reality, to which he feels intimately linked. Thus he becomes another radical ecologist *avant la lettre*: "The soul is much moved to the Love of its Beloved God, by the consideration of creations, seeing that they are things that by his own hand were made, and therefore his 'trace' remained in them," writes the holy mystic in his commentaries on the *Spiritual Canticle*. In fact, for the mystic, in the end, "I no longer have any other occupation, for loving alone is my exercise," as he confesses in the *Spiritual Canticle* (definitive text 28).

John of the Cross was a man in love with nature, and through it, he reached God, his Beloved: one can and should ascend toward God via sentient things, through nature. This is how he taught his novices, as many witnesses testify. Jerónimo de la Cruz tells us: "He used to pray looking at the rivers, the fountains, the sky, the grass, and he said he saw in them *something* of God." Juan de Santa Ana speaks of his love for the cosmic night: "He went out into the fields singing psalms, especially at night . . . he spoke of the beauty of the sky and the light of the stars . . . and other things of the harmony of the heavens."[66]

The Castilian and universal mystic presents himself as a symbol for *knowing how to read* nature as a creation of God, rescued and redeemed by Christ and left to our care; a gift from God,

---

[65] Words of praise for the stature of St. John of the Cross abound, not only among Catholics, but also among Protestants and other religions. Paul VI called him "a heavenly and divine man" and the Evangelical Church pastor Ernst Schering said: "Teresa of Jesus and John of the Cross are, without doubt, the two most prestigious mystics who have ever lived." Quotes taken from the "Prologue" to John of the Cross, *Vida y obras completas*, xxviii–xxxi. He was declared patron saint of poets in 1952.

[66] Quotes taken from José Vicente Rodríguez, "San Juan de la Cruz y la ecología," *Revista de Espiritualidad*, no. 182 (1987), 123–126.

a great space for human beings to meet with Him, a workshop for a *cosmic-divine poetry*, perfectly integrated into prayer. And as an expression of communion with All: the *Deus meus et omnia* of Francis of Assisi, one of the few authors he quotes in the commentaries of his *Spiritual Canticle*, clearly manifests this communion. In explaining stanzas 13–14 of the *Canticle*, the mystic says:

> For in the ecstatic communications of God the soul feels and understands the truth of the saying of St. Francis: "God is mine and all things are mine." And because God is all, and the soul, and the good of all, the communication in this ecstasy is explained by the consideration that the goodness of the creatures referred to in these stanzas. . . . Inasmuch as the soul is one with God, it feels all things to be God according to the words of St. John: "What was made, in Him was life." (Jn 1:4).
>
> *Commentary on Canticle 14–15.5*

In the *Spiritual Canticle*, John of the Cross constantly refers us to nature and to God. St. John's vision of creation is the gaze of the sensitive and contemplative human being, but at the same time of the religious believer and the theologian, who discovers God's imprint in the universe, in a cosmos of which he is an indissoluble part. The created things have been "planted by the hand of the Creator"; on them the Creator "poured a thousand graces," and by that means left them "clothed in their beauty." (*Commentary on Canticle* 5): "clothed with admirable beauty and supernatural virtue derived from the infinite supernatural beauty of the face of God, whose beholding of them clothed the heavens and the earth with beauty and joy," says the poet in his commentary on the *Canticle*. The human being cannot but deeply respect the beauty of nature and the reality of things in their element, not needlessly mistreating, not even to create a bouquet of flowers: "I will not pick the flowers."

The verses of Stanza 4 of the *Canticle* show the sacred dialogue between the human being and the cosmos: "Oh groves and thickets/Planted by the hand of the Beloved. . . . Tell me, has he passed by you?" The questioned creatures respond in chorus in stanza 5: "A thousand graces diffusing/ He passed through the groves in haste. . . . Clothed them with His beauty."

The poet himself comments on his verses[67] expressing his harmonious relationship with nature and the cosmos, in the search for the Beloved, the God who dignifies all creation:

> The soul, then, in this stanza addresses itself to creatures inquiring after the Beloved. And we observe, as St. Augustine says, that the inquiry made of creatures is a meditation on the Creator, for which they furnish the matter.
> *Commentary on Canticle 4, 1.2*

From the perspective of John of the Cross, all of nature is bathed in God's love; the whole universe is bathed in his love, for as the mystic himself says in his commentary on the Canticle: "To *look upon* God is to *love* and to do mercy" (*Commentary on Canticle* 19.6). The mystic expresses his experience of God and his experience of the world. The rivers and the mountains sound like a "quiet music" that manifests the divine presence, and the valleys the "murmuring solitude" of nature that expresses the music of the Creator:

---

[67] The commentary that John of the Cross provided for the *Spiritual Canticle* has a long title by the same author: "Declaration of the Songs that Deal with the Exercise of Love between the Soul and the Bridegroom Christ, in which They Touch on and Declare Some Points and Effects of Prayer, at the Request of Mother Ana de Jesús. Year 1584." John of the Cross, *Vida y obras completas*, 703–808.

[*In the silent music*], the soul discerns a marvelous arrangement and disposition of God's wisdom in the diversities of His creatures and operations. All these, and each one of them, have a certain correspondence with God, whereby each, by a voice peculiar to itself, proclaims what there is in itself of God . . .

. . . This is the *silent music*, because it is knowledge tranquil and calm, without audible voice; and thus the sweetness of music and the repose of silence are enjoyed in it. The soul says that the Beloved is silent music, because this harmony of spiritual music is in Him understood and felt . . .

[*The murmuring solitude*] . . . is almost the same as the silent music. For though the music is inaudible to the senses and the natural powers, it is a solitude most full of sound to the spiritual powers. These powers being in solitude, emptied of all forms . . . may well receive in spirit, like a resounding voice, the spiritual impression of the majesty of God in Himself and in His creatures. . . . and thus all these voices together unite in one strain in praise of God's greatness, wisdom, and marvelous knowledge.

Commentary on Canticle, 14–15, 25, 26, 27

This is what it means for the mystic to live in harmony with all of creation, listening to the cosmic echo, the marvelous symphony of creation.

Pierre Teilhard de Chardin (1881–1955): The Mystic of Matter

Hymn to Matter

Blessed be you, harsh matter, barren soil, stubborn rock. . . .

Blessed be you, mighty matter, irresistible march of evolution, reality ever newborn; you who, by constantly shattering our mental categories, force us to go ever further and further in our pursuit of the truth.

Blessed be you, universal matter, immeasurable time, boundless ether, triple abyss of stars and atoms and generations: you who by overflowing and dissolving our narrow standards or measurement reveal to us the dimensions of God.

Blessed be you, impenetrable matter: you who, interposed between our minds and the world of essences, cause us to languish with the desire to pierce through the seamless veil of phenomena.

Blessed be you, mortal matter: you who one day will undergo the process of dissolution within us and will thereby take us forcibly into the very heart of that which exists.

Without you, without your onslaughts, without your uprootings of us, we should remain all our lives inert, stagnant, puerile, ignorant both of ourselves and of God. You who batter us and then dress our wounds, you who resist us and yield to us, you who wreck and build, you who shackle and liberate, the sap of our souls, the hand of God, the flesh of Christ: it is you, matter, that I bless.

I bless you, matter, and you I acclaim: not as the pontiffs of science or the moralizing preachers depict you . . . but as you reveal yourself to me today, in your totality and your true nature.

You I acclaim as the inexhaustible potentiality for existence and transformation wherein the predestined substance germinates and grows.

> *I acclaim you as the universal power which brings together and unites, through which the multitudinous monads are bound together and in which they all converge on the way of the spirit.*
>
> *I acclaim you as the melodious fountain of water whence spring the souls of men and as the limpid crystal whereof is fashioned the new Jerusalem.*
>
> *I acclaim you as the divine milieu, charged with creative power, as the ocean stirred by the Spirit, as the clay molded and infused with life by the incarnate Word. . . .*
>
> *Raise me up then, matter, to those heights, through struggle and separation and death; raise me up until, at long last, it becomes possible for me in perfect chastity to embrace the universe.*[68]

In Teilhard de Chardin we find an exceptional example of the harmonious integration between his work as a researcher in geology and paleontology and his contemplative experience, together with the desire to renew Christian theology in an era marked by non-religious science. Aside from his intense and coherent life, his work as a scientist and his manifestations of faith, Teilhard de Chardin's best letter of introduction as a true modern mystic of matter is in his writings, in which he reveals himself as a "devotee" of matter as well as a deeply spiritual person living completely in harmony. The French Jesuit scientist and mystic wants to be *faithful to God* while being *faithful to the earth*. In one of his most eloquent confessions, he writes:

---

[68] Pierre Teilhard de Chardin, "Hymn to Matter," in *Escritos del tiempo de guerra* (Madrid: Taurus, 1966), 457–459; in English, see *Pierre Teilhard de Chardin: Writings* (Maryknoll, NY: Orbis Books, 1999), 44–45.

> I love the Universe, its energies, its secrets, and its hopes, and because at the same time I am dedicated to God, the only Origin, the only Issue and the only Term. I want thee pages to be instinct with *my love of matter and life*, and *to reconcile it*, if possible, with the unique *adoration* of the *only absolute and definitive Godhead*.
>
> ... If we are to be united in Christ, must we dissociate ourselves from the forward drive inseparable from this intoxicating, pitiless cosmos that carries us along ... ?
>
> That, above all, is the message I wish to communicate: *the reconciliation of God and the world*.
>
> ... I stepped down into the most hidden depths of my being.... With terror and intoxicating emotion, I realized that *my own poor trifling existence was one with the immensity of all that is and all that is still in the process of becoming*.[69]

Cuénot, a distinguished scholar of Teilhard, aptly articulates the Teilhardian pursuit that underpins his life's work, seamlessly integrating his paleontological research, theological reflections, contemplative practices, didactic pursuits, and even his "pastoral" endeavors.

> We therefore see *a new mystique* elaborating itself before our eyes. Throughout his thousands of years of life, man has felt himself torn between his upward aspirations towards "Heaven" and the terrestrial values of the Earth beneath ... Far from accepting the idea that the Earth is cooling down, we can believe that it is *taking fire* and burning with a new mystic blaze.[70]

---

[69] Ibid., 26–27 and 37.
[70] Cuénot, *Ciencia y fe en Teilhard de Chardin*, 100–101; in English, *Science and Faith in Teilhard de Chardin*.

As Teilhard himself confesses, he loved and studied nature not primarily as a scientist, not even as a sage, but as a "worshipper" seeking to "see clearly into its heart." That is why his spirituality is not sustained by a Platonic and dualistic separation from matter, nor is it something contrary and detrimental to the spirit, but precisely from "a deeper penetration into the universe," an immersion in the "ocean of matter," as he states in the "Hymn to Matter" quoted above or in his eloquent "The Spiritual Power of Matter":

> *Son of earth, steep yourself in the sea of matter,* bathe in its fiery waters, for it is the source of your life and your youthfulness.
>
> You thought you could do without it because the power of thought has been kindled in you? . . . Well, you were like to have perished of hunger.
>
> . . . *Purity does not lie in separation from, but in a deeper penetration into the universe.* It is to be found in the *love of that unique, boundless Essence* which penetrates the inmost depths of all things and there, from within those depths.[71]

The mystic and scientist even speaks of loving matter to the point of *adoring it*, not as idolatry or pantheism, but recognizing the presence of God in everything, of seeing in it the *diaphany* or transparency of the divine, and in this way extending the commandment of love to nature and all that exists:

> And why, indeed should I not worship it, the stable, the great, the rich, the mother, the *divine*? Is not matter, in its own way, *eternal and immense*? Is it not matter whose absence our imagination refuses to conceive, whether in the furthest limit of space or in the endless recesses of time?

---

[71] "The Spiritual Power of Matter," in *Escritos del tiempo de guerra*, 453. This work ends with the "Hymn to Matter," which brings the book to a close.

Is it not the one and only universal substance, the ethereal fluidity that all things share without either diminishing or fragmenting it?

Is it not the absolutely fertile generatrix, the Terra Mater, that carries within her the seeds of all life and the sustenance of all joy? Is it not at once the common origin of beings and the only end we could dream of, the primordial and indestructible essence from which all emerges and into which all returns, the starting point of all growth and the limit of all disintegration?[72]

The "Hymn to Matter" is included in *The Spiritual Power of Matter*, collected in Teilhard's work *Hymn of the Universe* (Jersey, August 1919). The "Hymn" is the response of man kneeling before the interpellation posed by Matter. Matter, which Teilhard here writes with a capital letter, is *The Divine Milieu*—the title of another of his most important works—charged with creative power, through which the creative spirit of God springs forth, manifested above all in Jesus of Nazareth. God is the immanent motor of evolution and the transcendent origin of all creative forces. The mission of the Spirit is "the *unification of the multiple*" through the renewal of matter, in a process of constant ascension. Matter becomes that which "nourishes" the Spirit in its ascensional effort: this is its "spiritual power." The destiny of nature is not to be mastered and used arbitrarily by man, but to lead man to union with God. Humanity thus needs to achieve a harmonious balance with the cosmos, an integral ecological balance, to achieve personal equilibrium.

Mass on the World

In addition to the *Hymn to Matter*, the other text that especially shows the brilliant sensitivity of this scientific mystic in the face

---

[72] Teilhard de Chardin, *Escritos del tiempo de guerra*, 42.

of Reality, the contemplative Christian perspective and harmony with the cosmos, is the *Mass on the World*. Both express more powerfully than any other Christian writing the "spiritual power of matter." The *Mass on the World* was written by Teilhard in 1923, on the occasion of a scientific expedition to the desert of Ordos (China). Faced with the impossibility of celebrating the Eucharist on an appointed liturgical day (the Transfiguration), he decided to celebrate it by meditating on the Eucharistic Presence in the universe: "The effect of the priestly act extends beyond the consecrated host to the cosmos itself . . . *The entire realm of matter is slowly but irresistibly affected by this great consecration.*"[73] The theologian N. M. Wildiers says in the "Introduction" to this beautiful text by Teilhard: "His faith in the Eucharistic mystery was not only ardent: it was as precise as it was firm. But this faith is justly strong and realistic enough to enable him to discover the consequences, or, as he said, the *prolongations* and *extensions of that faith.*" This union with the whole of the universe is nothing other than an extension of the most sincere Pauline thought, expressed by Paul of Tarsus in his discourse at the Areopagus: "In Him we live and move and exist" (Acts of the Apostles, 17:28). The universe is full of God, imbued with Christ.

The offering

My paten and my chalice are the depths of a soul laid widely open to all the forces which in a moment will rise up from every corner of the earth and converge upon the Spirit. Grant me the remembrance and the mystic presence of all those whom the light is now awakening to the new day.

. . . This restless multitude, confused or orderly, the immensity of which terrifies us; this ocean of humanity whose slow, monotonous wave-flows trouble the hearts

---

[73] "Introduction" to the "Mass on the World," in Pierre Teilhard de Chardin, *Himno del Universo* (Madrid: Taurus, 1971), 11–36.

even of those whose faith is most firm: it is to this deep that I thus desire all the fibres of my being should respond. All the things in the world to which this day will bring increase; all those that will diminish; all those too that will die.

. . . But the offering you really want . . . is nothing less than the growth of the world borne ever onwards in the stream of universal becoming. . . . Receive, O Lord, this all-embracing host which your whole creation, moved by your magnetism, offers you at this dawn of a new day.

Teilhard offers the entire cosmos unto God, that matter which is the *divine milieu*, which *is in God*, in intimate relationship with Him, as we have stated above. He feels deeply united to the cosmos by means of that "overwhelming sympathy for all that stirs within the dark mass of matter." Teilhard knows himself to be *one with All That Is*. That is the mystique of ecospirituality which we seek here.

A BRIEF CONCLUSION

An *eco-theology* and *eco-spirituality* imply not only thinking of the world and the Divinity together and demanding care for creation, but go beyond that. They are a way of situating oneself in the world, seeing the whole of Reality in a complex, interrelated way; Reality that is at once one and plural, harmonious and lucid as well as unpredictable, with light and darkness, in which we confidently place ourselves with everything. This involves seeing ourselves as a *relationship*, as an *inseparable part of the Whole*. For this, we need to mature every day, to learn to *open ourselves up* to that Whole, to the total Reality. And we need to do so with the humility of which St. John of the Cross spoke: "To come to the knowledge *you have not* you must go by the way in which *you know not* . . . in which *you are not*."

This totalizing vision of Reality leads us toward a new theology and a new radical ecosophical spirituality, since its foundation lies in the total communion and harmony of humans with the cosmos and with God, overcoming all dualism. We are an indivisible part of Reality; as the "butterfly effect" manifests, everything good and everything bad we do affects it, just as it also affects us, for better or for worse. Moreover, we cannot grow spiritually if it is not with this body that we have and *are*, and with this earth that makes up our body. This spirituality is in the best tradition of Christian mysticism and of all religions.

We can end this exploration of science, philosophy, theology, and spirituality with a quote from Teilhard de Chardin, who—as we have also maintained—advocates for viewing Reality as an integrated Whole, in which we are fundamentally integrated:

> Poets, philosophers, and mystics—the long procession of those who have been initiated into the vision and *cult of the Whole*—have left behind them a central wake which we can follow unmistakably from our own days right back to the most distant horizons of history . . . the essentially modern work of philosophic criticism and scientific research which has been carried out for the last two or three centuries in every field of terrestrial knowledge, is all leading in the same direction . . . to a magnification and solidification of *the universe as one bloc.*
>
> . . . the vital question for Christianity today is to decide what attitude believers will adopt towards this *recognition of the value of the Whole*, this "preoccupation with the Whole." Will they open their hearts to it, or will they reject it as an evil spirit?[74]

---

[74] Teilhard de Chardin, *Como yo creo*, 69 and 72.

Bibliography

Abbott, Michael M., and Hendrick C. Van Ness. *Termodinámica*. Mexico: McGraw-Hill, 1975.

Agudelo, Guillermo, and José Guillermo Alcalá. "La complejidad." In *Evolución: Un nuevo paradigma*, edited by Máximo Sandín. Madrid: Instituto de Investigación sobre Evolución Humana, 2003.

Amor Ruibal, Angel María. *Los problemas fundamentales de la filosofía y el dogma.* new ed. 10 vols. Santiago de Compostela: Seminario Conciliar, 1914–1936, 1995–1999.

Barreiro, Xosé Luis. *Mundo, hombre y conocimiento en Amor Ruibal.* Santiago de Compostela: Pico Sacro, 1978.

Bartholomew I. *On Earth as in Heaven. Ecological Vision and Initiatives of Ecumenical Patriarch Bartholomew.* Edited by John Chryssavgis. New York: Fordham University Press, 2012.

Batchelor, Martine, and Kerry Brown, eds. *Buddhism and Ecology*. New Delhi: Motilal Banarsidass, 1995.

Bergson, Henri. *Creative Evolution*. Westport: Greenwood Press, 1944.

———. *La evolución creadora.* Madrid: Espasa-Calpe, 1973.

Boff, Leonardo. *Cry of the Earth, Cry of the Poor.* Maryknoll, NY: Orbis Books, 2002.

———. *Ecología. Grito de la tierra, grito de los pobres,.* Madrid: Trotta, 1996.

———. *Ecology and Liberation: A New Paradigm.* Maryknoll, NY: Orbis Books, 1995.

———. "El Cristo Cósmico: Una espiritualidad del universo." https://www.atrio.org/2016/09/el-cristo-cosmico-una-espiritualidad-del-universo.

———. *El despertar del águila*. Madrid: Trotta, 2000.

———. *El Tao de la liberación. Una ecología de la transformación*. Madrid: Trotta, 2006.

———. *Evangelio del Cristo cósmico. Hacia una nueva conciencia planetaria*. Madrid: Trotta, 2009.

———. *Francis of Assisi, Francis of Rome: A New Springtime for the Church*. Maryknoll, NY: Orbis Books, 2014.

———. *Francis of Assisi: A Model for Human Liberation*. Maryknoll, NY: Orbis Books, 1996.

———. *Francisco de Asís. Ternura y vigor*. Santander: Sal Terræ, 1990.

———. *Holy Trinity, Perfect Community*. Maryknoll, NY: Orbis Books, 2000.

———. *Jesucristo el Liberador*. Colombia: Indo-American Press, 1977.

———. *Jesus Christ Liberator: A Critical Christology for Our Time*. Maryknoll, NY: Orbis Books, 1978.

———. *La dignidad de la Tierra. Ecología, mundialización, espiritualidad*. Vol. 2000, Madrid: Trotta, 2000.

———. *La Santísima Trinidad es la mejor comunidad*. Madrid: Paulinas, 1990.

———. *La Trinidad, la sociedad y la liberación*. Madrid: Paulinas, 1987.

———. *Liberar la Tierra. Una ecología para un mañana posible*. Madrid: San Pablo, 2018.

———. *O Evangelho do Cristo Cósmico*. Petrópolis: Editora Vozes, 1971.

———. "Teología de la liberación y ecología: alternativa, confrontación o complementariedad?" *Revista internacional de teologia*, no. 261 (1995): 93–105.

———. "Teologia della liberazione ed ecologia: Una lotta comune per la sinfonía del creato." *Adista*, no. 44 (June 1996).

———. *Trinity and Society*. Maryknoll, NY: Orbis Books, 1996.

———. *Una ética de la Madre Tierra. Cómo cuidar la Casa Común*. Madrid: Trotta, 2017.

Boff, Leonardo, Fritjof Capra, and Elizabeth May. *Voices from the Earth Charter Initiative responding to Laudato si'*. Costa Rica: Universidad Técnica Nacional, 2018.

Boff, Leonardo, and Anselm Grün. *Becoming New: Finding God within Us and in Creation*. Maryknoll, NY: Orbis Books, 2019.

———. *Lo divino en el ser humano y en el universo. Camino hacia la unificación*. Madrid: Trotta, 2019.

Boff, Leonardo, and Mark Hathaway. *The Tao of Liberation: Exploring the Ecology of Transformation*. Maryknoll, NY: Orbis Books, 2009.

Boff, Leonardo, Alex Zanotelli, and Gaël Giraud. *Cuidar la madre tierra. Comentario a la encíclica Laudato si' del papa Francisco*. Madrid: Sanpablo, 2015.

Bonaventure of Bagnoregio. *The Life of St. Francis of Assisi*. Charlotte, NC: TAN Books, 2010.

———. *Obras Completas*. Madrid: Biblioteca de Autores Cristianos, 1945.

Borghesi, Massimo. *Jorge Mario Bergoglio. Una biografía intelectual*. Madrid: Encuentro, 2018.

Bourgerol, Jacques Guy. *Introducción a San Buenaventura*. Madrid: Biblioteca de Autores Cristianos, 1964.

Bradley, Ian. *Dios es verde. Cristianismo y medio ambiente*. Santander: Sal Terræ, 1993.

———. *God Is Green: Christianity and the Environment*. London: Darton, Longman & Todd, 1990.

Briard, Jacques. "Bâle et Seoul: générosités, limites et enjeux d'Églises." *Lumen vitæ* 4, no. 1 (1993).

Brooks, David. "Fracking and the Franciscans." *The New York Times*, June 23 2015. https://www.nytimes.com/2015/06/23/opinion/fracking-and-the-franciscans.html.

Calabrò, Pablo. *Le cose si toccano. Raimon Panikkar e le scienze moderne*. Milan: Diabasis, 2011.

Capra, Fritjof. *El tao de la física*. Málaga: Sirio, 2000.

———. *Sabiduría insólita*. Barcelona: Kairós, 2003.

———. *The Tao of Physics*. Boulder: Shambhala, 2010.

Castellani, Brian, and Lasse Gerrits. *Map of the Complexity Sciences*. York: Art & Science Factory, 2021. https://www.art-sciencefactory.com/complexity-map_feb09.html.

Cavana, María Luisa, Alicia Puleo, and Cristina Segura. *Mujeres y ecología. Historia, pensamiento, sociedad*. Madrid: Al-Mudayna, 2004.

Chao Rego, Xosé. *Camiño verde. Ecoloxía e creación*. Santiago: Irimia, 1996.

———. "Creación." In *10 palabras claves en religión*, edited by Andrés Torres Queiruga: Verbo Divino, 1992.

———. *Na fronteira do misterio. Credo para xente non credula*. Vigo: SEPT, 1995.

Charlier, Catherine. "L'Alliance avec la nature selon la tradition hébraïque." In *Religion et écologie*, edited by Danièle Hervieu-Léger. Paris: CERF, 1993.

Charpak, George. *Siate saggi, diventate profeti*. Milan: Codice, 2004.

Cilliers, Paul. *Complexity and Postmodernism: Understanding Complex Systems*. London: Routledge, 1988.

Corbí, Marià. *El conocimiento silencioso. Las raíces de la cualidad humana*. Barcelona: Fragmenta, 2017.

Coste, René. "Justicia, paz, salvaguardia de la creación." *Concilium*, no. 236 (1991).

Cousins, Ewert. *Christ of the 21st Century*. New York: Element, 1992.

Crossan, John Dominic. *The Historical Jesus: The Life of a Mediterranean Jewish Peasant*. Edinburgh: T&T Clark, 1992.
Cuénot, Claude. *Ciencia y fe en Teilhard de Chardin*. Barcelona: Plaza & Janés.
———. *Nuevo léxico de Teilhard de Chardin*. Madrid: Taurus, 1968.
———. *Science and Faith in Teilhard de Chardin*. London: Garnstone Press, 1967.
D'Ors, Pablo. *Biografía del silencio*. Madrid: Siruela, 2012.
Davies, Paul. "La flecha del tiempo." *Investigación y Ciencia*, no. 314 (November 2002).
Deleuze, Gilles. *Nietzsche And Philosophy*. New York: Columbia University Press, 2006.
———. *Nietzsche y la filosofía*. Barcelona: Anagrama, 2006.
Delio, Ilia. *Christ in Evolution*. Maryknoll, NY: Orbis Books, 2008.
Denzinger, Heinrich, and Peter Hünerman. *El Magisterio de la Iglesia*. Barcelona: Herder, 2000.
Descartes, René. *Discourse on Method*. London: Penguin Classics, 1964.
DesJardins, Joseph R. *Éthique de l'environnement. Une introduction à la philosophie environnementale*. Quebec: Presses de l'Université du Québec, 1995.
Díaz, Carlos. *Ecología y pobreza en Francisco de Asís*. Oñate: Editorial Franciscana Arantzazu, 1986.
Dodd, Charles Harold. *Las parábolas del Reino*. Madrid: Cristiandad, 1974.
———. *The Parables of the Kingdom*. Glasgow: Fontana Books, 1961.
Eckhart, Meister. *El fruto de la nada*. Madrid: Siruela, 2001.
Eddington, Arthur Stanley. *The Nature of the Physical World*. New York: Macmillan, 1928.
Fernández, Gustavo. "La mirada ecológica del culto celta." Mystery Planet, https://mysteryplanet.com.ar/site/la-mirada-ecologica-del-culto-celta/.

Ferrater Mora, Josep. *Diccionario de filosofía*. Barcelona: Ariel-RBA, 2005.

Fornet-Betancourt, Raúl "Ciencia, tecnología y política en la filosofía de Raimon Panikkar." In *La filosofía intercultural de Raimon Panikkar*, edited by Ignasi Boada. Barcelona: Pòrtic, 2004.

Francis. *Beloved Amazonia*. Maryknoll, NY: Orbis Books, 2020.

———. *Una gran esperanza, la custodia de la creación*. Vatican City: Libreria Editrice, 2019.

Galilei, Galileo. *Carta a Cristina de Lorena y otros escritos*. Madrid: Alianza, 1987.

Galimberti, Marina. "Écoféminisme: Utopie ou nécessité?" http://www.penelopes.org:80/archives/pages/beijing/.

Gandhi, Mahatma. *An Autobiography: The Story of My Experiments with Truth*. Ahmedabad, India: Navajivan Publishing House, 1993.

Ganoczy, Alexandre. "Perspectivas ecológicas de la doctrina cristiana de la creación." *Concilium*, no. 236 (1991).

Gembillo, Giuseppe. *Da Einstein a Mandelbrot. La filosofia degli scienziati contemporanei*. Florence: Le Lettere, 2009.

———. *Filosofía de la complejidad*. Buenos Aires: Editora Latinoamericana, 2018.

———. "Fuoco! La chimica "fonte" della complessità." *Complessità* IV, no. 1-2 (2009): 70–74.

George, Susan. "La ecología, principal apuesta para el siglo XXI." *Le Monde diplomatique*, November 16, 1996.

Gershenson, Carlos. "How Can We Think Complex?" In *Managing Organizational Complexity: Philosophy, Theory and Application*, edited by Kurt Richardson. Charlotte: Information Age, 2005.

Gibellini, Rosino. "El debate teológico sobre la ecología." *Concilium*, no. 261 (1995).

Girardi, Giulio, Jesús Espeja, and Enrique Dussel. *Cristianismo, justicia y ecología*. Madrid: Utopía, 1994.

Greshake, Gisbert. *El Dios Uno y Trino. Una teología de la Trinidad.* Barcelona: Herder, 2002.

Grupo de Sostenibilidad y Ética Cristiana de Cristianismo y Justicia. "El año que la ecología se convirtió (oficialmente) en un asunto católico." 2015, https://blog.cristianismeijusticia.net/2015/01/30/el-ano-que-la-ecologia-se-convirtio-oficialmente-en-un-asunto-catolico.

Guardans, Teresa. *La verdad del silencio.* Barcelona: Herder, 2009.

Guattari, Félix. *Las tres ecologías.* Valencia: Pre-textos, 1996.

Harle, Tim. "Complexity and Theology Readings." Susanna Wesley Foundation, 2017, https://susannawesleyfoundation.org/wp-content/uploads/2017/02/Complexity-and-Theology-for-Keith-Elford-SWF-latest.pdf.

Heisenberg, Werner. *Physics and Philosophy.* London: Harper Perennial, 1963.

Hervieu-Léger, Danièle, ed. *Religion et écologie.* Paris: CERF, 1993.

Hey, Tony, and Patrick Walters. *The Quantum Universe.* Cambridge: Cambridge University Press, 1987.

Heylighen, Francis. "Cybernetics and Second Order Cybernetics." In *Encyclopedia of Physical Science & Technology*, edited by Robert Allen Meyers. San Diego: Academic Press, 2001.

———. "The Science of Self-Organization and Adaptivity." In *The Encyclopedia of Life Support Systems*, edited by Douglas Kiel. Oxford: Eolss Publishers, 2002.

Heylighen, Francis, Paul Cilliers, and Carlos Gershenson. "Complexity and Philosophy." In *Complexity, Science and Society*, edited by Jan Bogg and Robert Geyer. London: CRC Press, 2007.

Higgins, Michael. *The Jesuit Disruptor: A Personal Portrait of Pope Francis.* Toronto: House of Anansi, 2024.

Husserl, Edmund. *Formal and Transcendental Logic: Essay on a Critique of Logical Reason.* Dordrecht: Springer Dordrecht, 1969.

Huxley, Aldous. *La filosofía perenne.* Buenos Aires: Sudamericana, 1977.

———. *The Perennial Philosophy: An Interpretation of the Great Mystics, East and West.* New York: Harper Perennial Modern Classics, 2009.

Ivereigh, Austen. *The Great Reformer: Francis and the Making of a Radical Pope.* New York: Henry Holt, 2014.

Jeremias, Joachim. *Unknown Sayings of Jesus.* Eugene, OR: Wipf and Stock, 2008.

John of the Cross. *Vida y obras completas.* Madrid: Biblioteca de Autores Cristianos, 1973.

Kasper, Walter. *The God of Jesus Christ.* Chestnut Ridge, NY: Crossroad Publishing, 1986.

Krause, Karl Christian Friedrich. *The Ideal of Humanity and Universal Federation.* South Yarra, Australia: Leopold Classic Library, 2016.

Latour, Bruno. *Nous n'avons jamais été modernes. Essais d'anthropologie symétrique* Paris: La Découverte, 1991.

———. *Reassembling the Social: An Introduction to Actor-Network Theory.* Oxford: Oxford University Press, 2007.

———. *We Have Never Been Modern.* Cambridge, MA: Harvard University Press, 1993.

Leclerc, Éloi. *El cántico de las criaturas.* Oñate: Editorial Franciscana Arantzazu, 1977.

Lenoir, Frédéric. *Francisco, la primavera del Evangelio.* Madrid: PPC, 2014.

Lovelock, James. *Gaia. Una nueva visión de la vida en la Tierra.* Barcelona: Orbis, 1982.

———. *Gaia: A New Look at Life on Earth.* Oxford: Oxford University Press, 2000.

Lucena, Antonio. "La ecología y las grandes religiones." In *Ecología y cristianismo. XV Congreso de Teología*, edited by Various. Madrid: Evangelio y Liberación, 1995.

Luise, Raffaele. *Raimon Panikkar. Profeta del dopodomani*. Milan: San Paolo Edizioni, 2014.
Machado, Antonio. "Proverbios y cantares I." In *Poesías completas*. Madrid: Espasa-Calpe, 1973.
Maitland, Sara. *Viaje al silencio*. Barcelona: Alba, 2010.
Manzanera, Juan. "Ecología y espiritualidad." In *Ecología y cristianismo. XV Congreso de Teología*. Madrid: Evangelio y Liberación, 1995.
Marcos, Sylvia. "La sacralidad de la tierra. Perspectivas mesoamericanas." *Concilium*, no. 261 (1995): 45–58.
Marcuse, Herbert. *El hombre unidimensional. Ensayo sobre la ideología de la sociedad industrial avanzada*. Barcelona: Seix Barral, 1971.
———. *One-Dimensional Man: Studies in the Ideology of Advanced Industrial Society*. Boston: Beacon Press, 1991.
Markale, Jean. *Druidas. Tradiciones y dioses de los celtas*. Madrid: Taurus, 1989.
Martínez-Brocal, Javier. *El Papa de la misericordia*. Barcelona: Planeta, 2015.
Massein, Paul. "Pratityasamutpada." In *Diccionario de las religiones*, edited by Paul Poupard. Barcelona: Herder, 1987.
McDonagh, Sean. *On Care for Our Common Home: Laudato Si'*. Maryknoll, NY: Orbis Books, 2016.
McFague, Sallie. *Modelos de Dios. Teología para una era ecológica y nuclear*. Santander: Sal Terræ, 1987.
———. *Models of God: Theology for an Ecological, Nuclear Age*. Minneapolis: Fortress Press, 1987.
Melloni, Javier. *Vislumbres de lo Real*. Barcelona: Herder, 2007.
———. *Voces de la mística*. Vol. I, II, Barcelona: Herder, 2009, 2012.
Meza Rueda, José Luis. "Ecosofía: otra manera de comprender y vivir la relación hombre-mundo." *Cuestiones Teológicas* 37, no. 87 (2010).

Miguélez, Xosé Antón. *Tenemos carta de Dios*. Barcelona: Centre de Pastoral Litúrgica, 1996.

Moltmann, Jürgen. *Creating a Just Future: The Politics of Peace and the Ethics of Creation in a Threatened World*. London: SCM Press, 1989.

———. *La justicia crea futuro. Política de la paz y ética de la creación en un mundo amenazado*. Santander: Sal Terræ, 1992.

———. *The Trinity and the Kingdom*. Minneapolis: Fortress Press, 1993.

Morales, Xavier. *La relativité de Dieu. La contribution de la "Process Theology" à la théologie trinitaire*. Paris: CERF, 2017.

Morin, Edgar. *El método*. Madrid: Cátedra, 1981–2006.

———. "Il metodo del metodo." *Complessità* IV, no. 1-2 (2009).

———. *La Naturaleza de la Naturaleza*. El Método. Vol. I, Madrid: Cátedra, 2008.

———. *Leçons d'un siècle de vie*. Paris: Denöel, 2021.

———. *Les sept savoirs nécessaires pour une éducation du futur*. Paris: UNESCO, 1999.

———. *Method: Towards a Study of Humankind*. New York: Peter Lang, 1992.

———. *Mis demonios*. Barcelona: Kairós, 1995.

———. *The Nature of Nature*. Method: Towards a Study of Humankind. Vol. I, New York: Peter Lang, 1992.

———. *Seven Complex Lessons in Education for the Future*. Paris: UNESCO, 1999.

Naess, Arne. "Self-Realization in Mixed Communities of Humans, Bears, Sheep, and Wolves." *Inquiry*, no. 22 (1979): 1–4.

Neihardt, John G. *Black Elk Speaks. Being the Life Story of a Holy Man of the Oglala Sioux*. Lincoln: University of Nebraska Press, 1961.

Nelson Wieman, Henry. "A Philosophy of Religion." *The Journal of Religion* 10, no. 1 (1930).

Newell, Allen. *A Guide to the General Problem-Solver Program GPS.* Santa Monica: Rand Corporation, 1963.

Nhâ't Hanh, Thich. *Bouddha et Jésus sont des frères.* Gordes: Reliés, 2001.

———. *Buddhism and Ecology.* London: Cassell, 1992.

———. *Going Home: Buddha and Jesus as Brothers.* New York: Riverhead Books, 1999.

O'Murchu, Diarmuid. *Quantum Theology.* New York: Crossroad Publishing, 2004.

O'Murchu, Diarmuid. *Teología cuántica. Implicaciones espirituales de la Nueva Física.* Quito: Abya Yala, 2014.

Osorio, Sergio Néstor. *Bioética y pensamiento complejo, un puente en construcción.* Bogotá: Universidad Nueva Granada, 2008.

Panikkar, Raimon. "Autobiografía intelectual. La filosofía como estilo de vida." *Anthropos*, no. 53-54 (1985).

———. *The Cosmotheandric Experience: Emerging Religious Consciousness.* Maryknoll, NY: Orbis Books, 1993.

———. *Cultural Disarmament: The Way to Peace.* Louisville: Westminster John Knox Press, 1995.

———. *De la mística. Experiencia plena de la vida.* Barcelona: Herder, 2005.

———. *Ecosofía. La sabiduría de la Tierra.* Edited by Jordi Pigem. Barcelona: Fragmenta, 2021.

———. *Ecosofía. Para una espiritualidad de la tierra.* Madrid: San Pablo, 1994.

———. *El concepto de naturaleza. Análisis histórico y metafísico de un concepto.* Madrid: Instituto de Filosofía Luis Vives, 1972.

———. "El indeterminismo científico." *Anales de Física y Química*, no. 396 (1945).

———. *El silencio del Buddha. Una introducción al ateismo religioso.* Madrid: Siruela, 1999.

———. *Espiritualidad hindú. Sanâtana dharma.* Barcelona: Kairós, 2004.

———. "¿Está el fulcro de la filosofía comparativa?" In *Sobre el diálogo intercultural*, 71–94. Salamanca: San Esteban, 1990.
———. *La experiencia de Dios*. Madrid: PPC, 1994.
———. *La experiencia filosófica de la India*. Madrid: Trotta, 1997.
———. *La intuición cosmoteándrica. Las tres dimensiones de la realidad*. Madrid: Trotta, 1999.
———. *La nueva inocencia*. Estella: Verbo Divino, 1993.
———. *La puerta estrecha del conocimiento. Sentido, razón y fe*. Barcelona: Herder, 2008.
———. *La Trinidad. Una experiencia humana primordial*. Madrid: Siruela, 1998.
———. *Misterio y revelación. Hinduismo y cristianismo, encuentro entre dos culturas*. Madrid: Marova, 1971.
———. *Mysticism, Fullness of Life*. Maryknoll, NY: Orbis Books, 2014.
———. *Ontonomía de la Ciencia. Sobre el sentido de la ciencia y sus relaciones con la filosofía*. Madrid: Gredos, 1961.
———. *Paz e interculturalidad. Una reflexión filosófica*. Barcelona: Herder, 2002.
———. *Paz y desarme cultural*. Santander: Sal Terræ, 1993.
———. *Pensamiento científico y pensamiento cristiano*. Santander: Sal Terræ, 1994.
———. *The Rhythm of Being. The Gifford Lectures*. Maryknoll, NY: Orbis Books, 2010.
———. *The Silence of God: The Answer of the Buddha*. Maryknoll, NY: Orbis Books, 1989.
———. *Sobre el diálogo intercultural*. Salamanca: San Esteban, 1990.
———. *The Trinity and the Religious Experience of Man; Icon-Person-Mystery*. Maryknoll, NY: Orbis Books, 2009.
Panikkar, Raimon, and Hans Peter Dürr. *L'amore fonte originaria dell'universo. Un dialogo su scienza della natura e religione*. Rome: La Parola, 2011.
Pannenberg, Wolfhart. *Anthropology in Theological Perspective*. Edinburgh: T&T Clark, 1999.

Peacocke, Arthur. *Creation and the World of Science*. Oxford: Oxford University Press, 1979.

Peeters, Denise. "Pour une théologie à l'école de l'écologie." *Lumen vitæ* 48, no. 1 (1993): 51–65.

Pérez Martínez, Alfredo. "La obra de Stuart Kauffman. Aportaciones a la biología del siglo XXI e implicaciones filosóficas." Universidad Complutense de Madrid, 2005.

Pérez Prieto, Victorino. "Cuidado de la casa común. Una ciudad que cuida de la creación." *Faro*, no. 1 (2017): 30–37.

———. *Dios, Hombre, Mundo: La trinidad en Raimon Panikkar*. Barcelona: Herder, 2008.

———. *Do teu verdor cinguido. Ecoloxismo e cristianismo*. La Coruña: Espiral Maior, 1997.

———. *Ecologismo y cristianismo*. Santander: Sal Terræ, 1999.

———. "Ecoloxismo, feminismo e cristianismo. Unha relación indispensable." *Encrucillada*, no. 163 (2009): 302–12.

———. "El pensamiento cristiano es trinitario, simbólico y relacional. Encuentros con Raimon Panikkar." *Iglesia viva*, no. 223 (2005): 63–84.

———. "A filosofia como sabedoria do amor. Raimon Panikkar." *Humanística e Teologia* I, no. 34 (2013): 145–64.

———. *La búsqueda de la armonía en la diversidad. El diálogo ecuménico e interreligioso desde el Concilio Vaticano I*. Estella: Verbo Divino, 2014.

———. "La ecoteología en el quehacer teológico del siglo XXI." En el décimo aniversario del Equipo de Investigación Ecoteología, de la Facultad de Teología Pontificia Universidad Javeriana de Bogotá, 2012, http://www.ecoteologiapuj.blogspot.com/2012/10/mensaje-de-victorino-perez-prieto.html.

———. "La interioridad en las tradiciones religiosas no cristianas." In *Hacia una teología de la interioridad*, edited by Elena Andrés and Carlos Esteban Garcés, 95–140. Madrid: PPC, 2019.

———. "Los tres ojos del conocimiento en San Buenaventura. De la reductio Bonaventuriana al pensamiento complejo de Edgar Morin y la perspectiva cosmoteándrica de Raimon Panikkar." In *Perspectivas sobre el pensamiento de san Buenaventura de Bagnoregio y otros estudios*, edited by Julio César Barrera, Luis Fernando Benítez and Andrés Felipe López. Bogotá: Universidad de San Buenaventura, 2018.

———. "Los tres ojos del conocimiento: Ciencia, Filosofía y Teología." *Complessità* XIII, no. 1-2 (2018): 46–72.

———. *Más allá de la fragmentación de la teología, el saber y la vida: Raimon Panikkar*. Barcelona: Tirant lo Blanch, 2008.

———. "Nel cuore di un cristianesimo ecologista: l'intima connessione tra materia, coscienza e infinito." *Adista*, no. 5 (2013).

———. "Raimon Panikkar y Xavier Zubiri en diálogo: realidad cosmoteándrica y respectividad." In *Panikkar hoy*, edited by Ignasi Moreta, 159–200. Barcelona: Fragmenta, 2022.

———. "Raimon Panikkar, Xabier Zubiri y Amor Ruibal. Un pensamiento marcado por la relación: del "correlacionismo ontológico" y la "respectividad" a la "perspectiva cosmoteándrica"." *Ilu. Revista de Ciencias de las Religiones*, no. 23 (October 2018): 217–38.

———. "Reseña: "La Trinidad y un mundo entrelazado. Relacionalidad en las ciencias físicas y la teología"." [In es]. *Análisis* 47, no. 87 (2016): 443–49.

Pérez Prieto, Victorino, and José Luis Meza Rueda. *Diccionario panikkariano*. Barcelona: Herder, 2016.

Pigem, Jordi. *Ángeles o robots. La interioridad humana en la sociedad hipertecnológica*. Barcelona: Fragmenta, 2018.

———. *GPS (Global Personal Social). Valores para un mundo en transformación*. Barcelona: Kairós, 2011.

Pikaza, Xabier. *El desafío ecológico. Creación bíblica y bomba atómica*. Madrid: PPC, 2004.

Politi, Marco. *Francisco entre lobos. El secreto de una revolución*. Mexico: Fondo de Cultura Económica, Mexico, 2015.

Polkinghorne, John. *Ciencia y teología*. Santander: Sal Terræ, 2000.

———. *La Trinidad y un mundo entrelazado. Relacionalidad en las ciencias físicas y la teología*. Estella: Verbo Divino, 2013.

———. *Science and Theology: An Introduction*. Minneapolis: Fortress Press, 1998.

———. *The Trinity and an Entangled World: Relationality in Physical Science and Theology*. Grand Rapids: William B. Eerdmans Pub. Co., 2010.

Potter, Van Rensselaer. *Bioethics: Bridge to the Future*. Saddle River, NJ: Prentice-Hall, 1971.

———. *Bioética puente, bioética global y bioética profunda, Cuadernos del Programa Regional de Bioética*. Bogotá: Organización Panamericana de la Salud, 1998.

———. *Global Bioethics, Building on the Leopol Legacy*. Michigan: Michigan State University Press, 1988.

Prigogine, Ilya. *Introducción a la termodinámica de los procesos irreversibles*. Madrid: Selecciones Científicas, 1974.

———. *Introduction to the Thermodynamics of Irreversible Processes*. New York: Wiley, 1968.

Prigogine, Ilya, and Isabelle Stengers. *La nueva alianza. Metamorfosis de la ciencia*. Madrid: Alianza, 1990.

———. *Order Out of Chaos: Man's New Dialogue with Nature*. London: Verso, 2018.

Primavesi, Anne. *Del Apocalipsis al Génesis. Ecología, feminismo y cristianismo*. Barcelona: Herder, 1995.

———. *From Apocalypse to Genesis: Ecology, Feminism and Christianity*. Minneapolis: Fortress Press, 1991.

Radford Ruether, Rosemary. *Ecotheology. Voices from South and North*. Geneva: World Council of Churches, 1994.

———. *Gaia and God: An Ecofeminist Theology of Earth Healing*. San Francisco: HarperOne, 1994.

———. *New Woman, New Earth: Sexist Ideologies and Human Liberation.* New York: Seabury Press, 1975.

———, ed. *Women Healing Earth: Third World Women on Ecology, Feminism, and Religion.* Maryknoll, NY: Orbis Books, 1996.

Riechmann, Jorge. *Redes que dan libertad: introducción a los nuevos movimientos sociales.* Barcelona: Paidós, 1994.

Rifkin, Jeremy. *Entropy: A New World View.* New York: Viking Press, 1980.

Robinson, Keith, ed. *Deleuze, Whitehead, Bergson: Rhizomatic Connections.* New York: Palgrave Macmillan, 2009.

———. "Towards a Metaphysics of Complexity." *Interchange* 36, no. 1-2 (2005).

Rodríguez, José Vicente. "San Juan de la Cruz y la ecología." *Revista de Espiritualidad*, no. 182 (1987).

Ruiz de la Peña, Juan Luis. *Teología de la creación.* Santander: Sal Terræ, 1986.

Russell, Robert, Arthur Peacocke, and Nancey Murphy, eds. *Chaos and Complexity: Scientific Perspectives on Divine Action.* Vatican City: Vatican Observatory Publications, 1997.

Sacchi, Annachiara. "Entrevista a Leonardo Boff, exponente destacado de la teologia de la liberación. El ecoceno como alternativa al Antropoceno." Rebelión, 2020, https://rebelion.org/el-ecoceno-como- alternative-to-anthropocene/.

Sampedro, José Luis. *El río que nos lleva.* Havana: Arte y Literatura, 1989.

Sanz, Enrique, ed. *Cuidar de la Tierra, cuidar de los pobres. Laudato si' desde la teología y con la ciencia.* Santander: Sal Terræ, 2015.

Scannone, Juan Carlos. *El papa del pueblo.* Madrid: PPC, 2017.

Schmitt, Charles B. "Perennial philosophy: From Agostino Steuco to Leibniz." *Journal of the History of Ideas* 27, no. 4 (1966): 505–32.

Schneider, Eric D., and Dorion Sagan. *Into the Cool: Energy Flow, Thermodynamics, and Life.* Chicago: University of Chicago Press, 2006.

Schweitzer, Albert. *Civilization and Ethics.* London: Unwin Books, 1961.

Shiva, Vandana. "Ecofeminismo, derechos de la naturaleza, suma kawsay. Diálogo con mujeres ecuatorianas y conferencia." Seminario de Feminismo Nuestroamericano, 2010, http://seminariodefeminismonuestroamericano.blogspot.com/2013/04/vandana-shiva-ecofeminismo-derechos-de.html.

———. *Staying Alive: Women, Ecology, and Development.* Berkeley: North Atlantic Books, 2016.

Sicre, José Luis. "La creación, don de Dios." In *Ecología y cristianismo. XV Congreso de Teología,* edited by Various. Madrid: Evangelio y Liberación, 1995.

Simonnet, Dominique. *L'Écologisme.* Paris: PUF, 1994.

Smuts, Jan. *Holism and Evolution.* New York: MacMillan Company, 1926.

Swansburg, John. "The Self-Made Man: The Story of America's Most Pliable, Pernicious, Irrepressible Myth." Slate, 2017, https://www.slate.com/articles/news_and_politics/history/2014/09/the_self_made_man_history_of_a_myth_from_ben_franklin_to_andrew_carnegie.html.

Teilhard de Chardin, Pierre. *Christianity and Evolution.* London: Harcourt, 1969.

———. *Ciencia y Cristo.* Madrid: Taurus, 1968.

———. *Como yo creo.* Madrid: Taurus, 1970.

———. *The Divine Milieu Explained: A Spirituality for the 21st Century.* Mahwah, NJ: Paulist Press, 2007.

———. *El medio divino.* Madrid: Taurus, 1967.

———. *Escritos del tiempo de guerra.* Madrid: Taurus, 1966.

———. *Himno del Universo.* Madrid: Taurus, 1971.

———. *Pierre Teilhard de Chardin: Writings*. Maryknoll, NY: Orbis Books, 1999.
Thomas of Celano. *Escritos y biografías*. Madrid: Biblioteca de Autores Cristianos, 1971.
———. *The Life of St. Francis and the Treatise of Miracles*. Phoenix: Tau Publishing, 2017.
Torres Queiruga, Andrés. "Amor Ruibal." In *Dicionario enciclopedia do pensamento galego*. Vigo: Consello da Cultura Galega, 2008.
———. "Amor Ruibal, pensador no cambio de século." In *O pensamento luso-galaico-brasileiro (1850-2000)*. Lisbon: Imprensa Nacional–Casa da Moeda, 2009.
———. *Creo en Dios Padre. El Dios de Jesús como afirmación plena del hombre*. Santander: Sal Terræ, 2001.
———. *El Dios de Jesús. Aproximación en cuatro metáforas*. Santander: Sal Terræ, 1991.
———. *Recuperar la creación*. Vigo: SEPT, 1996.
Various. *Ecología y cristianismo. XV Congreso de Teología*. Madrid: Evangelio y Liberación, 1995.
———. *El desafío ecológico. Ecología y humanismo*. Salamanca: Universidad Pontificia, 1989.
———. *La mística en el siglo XXI*. Madrid: Trotta, 2002.
———. "No hay cielo sin tierra." *Concilium*, no. 236 (1991).
Weber, Renée. *Diálogos con científicos y sabios. La búsqueda de la unidad*. Barcelona: La Liebre de Marzo, 1990.
White, Lynn. "The Historical Roots of Our Ecological Crises." *Science*, no. 155 (1967).
Whitehead, Alfred North. *Proceso y realidad*. Buenos Aires: Losada, 1956.
Wilber, Ken. *The Atman Project: A Transpersonal View of Human Development*. Wheaton, IL: Quest Books, 1996.
———. *Cuestiones cuánticas. Escritos místicos de los físicos más famosos del mundo*. Barcelona: Kairós, 1987.

———. *The Eye of Spirit: An Integral Vision for a World Gone Slightly Mad*. Boulder: Shambhala, 2001.

———. *Los tres ojos del conocimiento*. Barcelona: Kairós, 1994.

———. *Quantum Questions: Mystical Writings of the World's Great Physicists*. Boulder: Shambhala, 1984.

———. *Up from Eden: A Transpersonal View of Human Evolution*. Wheaton, IL: Quest Books, 2007.

Wyllie, Irvin G. *The Self-Made Man in America: The Myth of Rags to Riches*. New York: The Free Press, 1966.

Zubiri, Xavier. *Nature, History, God*. Lanham, MD: University Press of America, 1981.

Index

absolute zero temperature, 27. *See also* second law of thermodynamics
abstraction, 25, 79
Abyss, 13–14
actor-network theory, 8*n*10
Adam, 4, 120–22, 219
adamâh, 4, 115, 122
Adorno, Theodor, 59
a-duality, 99. *See also* advaita
advaita, 43, 99, 205*n*24, 211
agape, 198
Algunos problemas limítrofes entre ciencia y filosofía (Panikkar), 78
Al-Jîlî, Abd al-Karim, 43
alter-globalization, 110, 113
Amazonian Church, 181–82
Amor Ruibal, Ángel, 48–49
androcentrism, 148, 151
Angelus Silesius, 44
anima, 149
animism, 102
animus, 149
ANT. *See* actor-network theory
anthropocentrism, 12, 80–81, 89, 107, 119, 142–44, 148, 151
anthropo-ethics, 74
anti-ecologism, 110*n*21, 123

Aparecida Document (CELAM), 156–58
Aquinas, Thomas, 14, 39, 144, 205–6, 219
Aranguren, José Luis, 4
Aristotle, 47, 204
arrow of time, 32
Ascent of Mount Carmel (John of the Cross), 60*n*60, 216
atomism, 203–4
Augustine of Hippo, 39, 41, 219–20, 231
Avatamsaka. *See* Indra's Net, 98
Aztecs, 16, 106

Babylonians, 116, 121, 127
Bacon, Francis, 145, 196
Bartholomew I, 154
Basel Convention (2005), 173
Basel Ecumenical Conference (1989), 153
Basil of Caesarea, 160
Beloved, God as, 225, 228–29, 231–32
Beloved Amazonia (Pope Francis), 181*n*52
Benedict XVI, 155, 157, 159
Bergson, Henri, 21, 29, 36, 53, 55, 92

Bernard of Clairvaux, 41, 44, 199
Bernardone, Pietro, 225
Berry, Thomas, xiv
Bhagavad Gita, 41, 99
biodiversity, 170
bioethics, 50–52
biosphere, xii, 71–72, 136n46, 155
Black Elk, 106
Boff, Leonardo
  on Abyss, 14
  on cosmic Christ, 137–40
  on ecology, 114, 217
  on Francis of Assisi, 225
  on immanence, 210
  and liberation theology, 150–51
  on Trinity, 202
  on unified theories, 13
Bohm, David, xi, 216
Bohr, Niels, 2, 12, 17, 92
Boltzmann, Ludwig, 33
Bonaventure, 5n6, 44, 174, 205–6, 219, 225
Book of Tao. See *Daodejing*
Bradley, Ian, 130, 141, 144, 224
Brahman, 43, 98
Brewin, Kester, 191
Brooks, David, 165
Brunner, Emil, 92
Buddha, 76, 100–101
Buddhism, 3, 18, 43, 75–76, 82, 100–102, 218
Bultmann, Rudolf, 146
Buñuel, Luis, 6

Cáceres, Berta, 110
Calabrò, Paolo, 94
Callon, Michel, 8n10

Calvin, John, 144
Canticle of the Creatures (St. Francis), 128, 222, 226–27
Capra, Fritjof, 2, 9–10, 45
Cardenal, Ernesto, 2, 17, 128, 189, 212, 216
Caritas in veritate (Benedict XVI), 157
Carnot's theorem, 28
Cartesianism, 26, 31, 36, 48, 93, 145
Castellani, Brian, 34n19
Castillo, José María, 147
Catechism of the Catholic Church, 184, 186, 202
Catherine of Genoa, 41
Catherine of Siena, 41
Celtic peoples, 102–3
Centesimus annus, 156
Chalcedonian Creed, 134n45
Chao Rego, Xosé, 145, 148
chaosmos, 1, 12, 62, 73
Charpak, George, 94
Chief Seattle, 105, 108, 190
Chipko Movement, 112
Christ
  as Bridegroom, 231n67
  cosmic, 133–40, 144, 209
  as ecologist, 129, 131
Christianity and Science, 192
Christic, 137–38, 140
Christogenesis, 136, 140
Christology, 140, 191
christosphere, 136n46
Church Fathers, 43, 204–5
Cilliers, Paul, 38
circumincessio, 205n24
Civilisation et barbarie (Morin), 57
Clausius, Rudolf, 27n5, 28n6, 79

Index

Clement of Alexandria, 39, 43
climate crisis. *See* ecological crisis
Cloud of Unknowing, 41
colligite fragmenta, 77, 85
common home, 141, 158–59, 161, 164, 184–85, 187
Complex Christ, The (Brewin), 191
complexity
   and bioethics, 50–51
   and complex thought, 56, 62–63
   defining, 8, 24–25
   and evolution, 34–36, 46, 73
   and knowledge, 68–69
   and ontonomy, 83
   and reductionism, 46–48
   and thermodynamics, xi–xii, 22–23, 26, 29, 32
   and Trinity, 191
   and uncertainty, 73
complexity theory, 8, 23–24, 35, 93–95, 151
complex thought, 56, 58, 60, 63, 66, 74, 167, 191, 216
complexus, 8, 24, 59
consciousness, 7n9
   in Buddhism, 102
   and cosmotheandric knowledge, 90
   and ecosophy, 87, 89
   and ecospirituality, 213
   in Hinduism, 99
   and metanoia, 163
   in mysticism, 214, 218–19
   and panentheism, 209
   and Reality, 4–5, 15, 18, 36
   universal, 136n46
conservation of energy, principle of, 27. *See also* first law of thermodynamics
conversion, 76, 172, 180
Coomaraswamy, Ananda, 39, 41
Copernicus, 25, 117
correlationism, 48–49
Cosmic Canticle (Cardenal), 2, 17, 128, 189
cosmic Christ, 133–40, 144, 209
cosmogenesis, 12, 33, 137n50, 140, 209
cosmos
   and balance, 237–40
   biblical concept of, 116, 121–22, 128
   and Buddhism, 100–101
   vs. chaosmos, 1, 12
   and Divinity, 48, 91, 210–12
   and ecology, 115, 148–51, 155, 157, 166, 213, 217–18, 225–27
   and entropy, 25, 28, 46
   and mysticism, 230–31
   and quantum physics, 11, 13, 23–24
   and thermodynamics, xi, 34
Cosmotheandric Experience, The (Panikkar), 76, 190
cosmotheandric intuition, 75, 89–90
Cosmotheandric Intuition, The (Panikkar), 74
cosmotheandrism, xiii, 53, 82, 89–90, 94, 134, 211
Council of Chalcedon, 134
Council of Constantinople II, 134
Coyne, George, x

Creation Is a Most Beautiful Gift of God (Pope Francis), 185
creationism, 118
Creative Evolution (Bergson), 21, 29
Cuénot, Claude, 137, 235

Daniel, 128
Daodejing, 18, 97
Darwin, Charles, 108
Das Kapital (Marx), 186n56
Dear Amazonia (Pope Francis), 181
D'Eaubonne, Françoise, 112
deep ecology, xiii, 52, 88, 102, 112, 225
Deleuze, Gilles, 3, 37, 55
"Demise of Democritus, The," 204
De perennis philosophia, 39
Descartes, René, 30, 46–47, 87, 145, 196
determinism, 26, 67
Deus meus et omnia, 142, 227, 230
Deuteronomy, 123–24
Dewey, John, 92
Dhammapada, 41, 100
dharma, 100
dialectic, 65, 77
dialogic, 58, 65, 77
Diamond Sutra, 41
Dickie, John, 144
Dionysius the Areopagite, 41, 219
Discourse on Method (Descartes), 145
disorder
  in biblical thought, 121, 123, 157
  and complexity, 29, 32–33, 95
  and entropy, 27
  and Reality, 24–25
dissipative structures, 29, 33, 47
Divine Complexity, 192
Dogen, 43
dominion, ix, 71, 121, 195–97, 227
dominium terræ, 147
dualism, 42, 70, 87, 119, 143, 178
Dwelling Place for Wisdom, A (Panikkar), 76
Dyson, Freeman, ix

Earth Overshoot Day, 172
Earth Summit (1992), 173
Ecclesiastes, 129
ecocide, 114, 184
ecofeminism, 19, 110–13, 149–50, 213
ecogenocide, 114
ecological crisis, ix–x, 61, 109, 141–42, 153–54, 158, 161–62, 169, 185, 187, 192, 196, 217
ecologism, 108, 110n21, 113, 148–49, 206, 213, 217
ecology, 9, 14
  and Buddhism, 102
  in Catholic thought, 152n24, 155–56, 158, 164–65, 227
  and cosmos, 115, 148–51, 155, 157, 166, 213, 217–18, 225–27
  deep, xiii, 52, 88, 102, 112, 225
  and ecocide, 184–85
  vs. ecofeminism, 111
  vs. ecologism, 108
  vs. ecosophy, 87–88, 179

and ecotheology, 191
and education, 183
and holistic thought, 115
Ecology and Liberation (Boff), 151
ecopacifism, 19, 107, 110–11, 190, 213
Ecosofia (Panikkar), 76
ecosophical, 227
ecosophy, 36, 85, 87–89, 179, 190, 217–18, 240
ecospirituality, x, xiii, 19, 190, 213, 215, 222, 228, 239
ecotheology, 19, 148, 190–91, 193, 239
Eddington, Arthur, 16, 29, 31–32, 45, 92
Eden, 120, 122, 219
Einstein, Albert, 7, 12, 29, 45, 47
El concepto de naturaleza (Panikkar), 76
Elements of Chemistry (Lavoisier), 33
energy
  conservation of, 27
  dissipation of, xi, 27, 29, 32–33
  and entropy, 27–28, 32–33, 47
  matter as, 11
  as quanta, 9
  and work, 31
Enlightenment, 145
entropy, xi, 25, 27–28, 32–34, 46–47, 79, 95
Enuma Elish, 121
environmentalism, 100, 108–10, 112–14, 145, 148–49, 152–53, 227
Ephesians, 135
epistemology, 61

equilibrium, 29, 32, 34, 104, 193, 208
eros, 199–200
essentialism, 23, 151
eternal philosophy. *See* perennial phisilophy
etropé, 27*n*5
Evangelium vitae (John Paul II), 156
evolution
  and Buddhism, 100
  and complexity, 34–36, 46, 73
  and cosmogenesis, 12
  and creationism, 118
  and entropy, 27–29
  and indeterminacy, 31
  in Teilhard de Chardin, 136*n*46, 137–38, 140, 237
  and uncertainty, 38
Experience of God, The (Panikkar), 76
Eyeless in Gaza, 40

feminism, 110–12, 148–49, 197
Fichte, Johann Gottlieb, 209*n*32
first eye, 41, 218–19
Fornet-Betancourt, Raúl, 84
Fourier, Joseph, 33
Fox, George, 41
Francis (Pope)
  on Amazon, 182–84
  on common home, 161–62, 187
  importance of ecology, 155, 158–59, 164, 169
  on interconnectedness, 175–76, 178
  on seamless fabric of reality, x, 9, 177

on structures of sin, 185
on technocracy as oppression, 160, 167–68, 172
on water as human right, 170
Francis de Sales, 41
Francis of Assisi, 19, 142, 156, 164, 221–22, 224–27, 229–30
Franklin, Benjamin, 6n7
From Apocalypse to Genesis (Primavesi), 149
Future of Creation - Future of Humanity, 155

Gaia, divinizing, 212
Gaia and God (Ruether), 149
Gaia hypothesis, 89, 212
Galeano, Eduardo, 181
Galilei, Galileo, 117
Gandhi, Mahatma, 99, 111n22
Ganoczy, Alexandre, 122n38
Gembillo, Giuseppe, 46
General Problem Solver, 64n66
Genesis, 116, 120–22, 143, 150
geocentrism, 117
geosphere, 136n46
German Bishops' Conference, 155
Gerrits, Lasse, 34n19
Gershenson, Carlos, 38
Gertrude of Helfta, 44
Gibellini, Rosino, 147
Gifford Lectures, 92
Girardi, Giulio, 113–14
gnosis, 39
Gnosticism, 133n44, 140, 219
Golden Letter (Gertrude of Helfta), 44
González de Cardedal, Olegario, 147

González Faus, Ignacio, 147
Gracia, Diego, 50
Grand Unified Theory, 13
"Great Hope, A" (Pope Francis), 184
Gregory of Nazianzus, 204
Gregory of Nyssa, 39, 44, 204
Greshake, Gisbert, 204–5
Guardini, Romano, 162
Guattari, Félix, 88
Guénon, René, 39

Habermas, Jürgen, 84
Hadewijch of Antwerp, 44
Haeckel, Ernst, 108
Haught, John, 192
Hegel, Friedrich, 5, 65
Heidegger, Martin, 48, 55, 84
Heisenberg, Werner, 10, 12, 16, 33, 45, 47–48, 78, 92–93
heliocentrism, 117
Hellenic culture, 116, 128
Hesse, Hermann, 224
heteronomy, 19, 83–84
Heylighen, Francis, 38
Hindu thought, 17, 38, 43, 75–76, 98–99, 112, 211, 218
Hinlicky, Paul, 192
"Historical Roots of Our Ecological Crisis, The" (White), ix, 141–42
holism, 36, 64, 114
hologrammatic principle, 64
holon, 64
hólos, 114
Homeland Earth (Morin), 57
Hosea, 126, 198
Hugo of St. Victor, 5n6, 205, 219
"Human Energy," xii

humanism, 50, 108, 217
human rights, 153, 170
Husserl, Edmund, 48, 84
Huxley, Aldous, 22, 39–42
"Hymn to Matter" (Teilhard de Chardin), 236–37
hypostatic union, 134

Ibn'Arabi, 43
Ibn Gabirol, Solomon, 43
ice melt, ix
Ideal of Humanity, The (Krause), 209n32
idolatry, x, 126–27, 236
illumination, 4, 174
Imitation of Christ, The (à Kempis), 41
immanence, 3n1, 42, 55, 91, 119, 173, 198, 203, 210–11
Inca culture, 104
incarnation, 133, 226
indeterminacy principle. *See* uncertainty principle
Indra's Net, 97–98
"Initiatives œcuméniques pour la sauvagarde de la création" (Lautwan), 152n24
integral ecology, 158, 166, 173, 181, 183, 185
interconnectedness, 86, 88, 92, 125, 176, 196, 212–13
interdependence, xi, 59, 88, 114, 153n27, 175, 178, 184, 190, 197, 202, 213
International Society for Science and Religion, 203
Introduction à la pensée complexe (Morin), 57
Invisible Harmony (Panikkar), 76

Isaiah, 126–27, 131
Islam, 43, 142

James, William, 45, 92
Jaspers, Karl, 84
Jeremiah, 127–28
Jeremias, Joachim, 140
Jerónimo de la Cruz, 229
Job, 128–29
John (Evangelist), 85, 131, 134
John of the Cross, 19, 41, 60, 137, 174, 199, 216–17, 219–21, 229–31, 239
  and consciousness, 219
  erotic imagery in, 199
  on knowledge, 220
  love for nature, 229–31
  on mystery of Reality, 217
John Paul II, x, 155–57, 159, 177, 186, 224
John XXIII, 40
Josselin, Ralph, 131
Joule, James Prescott, 27
Juan de Santa Ana, 229
Judaism, 120n37, 136
Jung, Carl, 45, 220
Justice Creates the Future (Moltmann), 146

kabas, 121
Kabbalah, 43
Kabir, 41
Kant, Immanuel, 54
karma, 100
karuna, 100
Kasper, Walter, 205n24
Kauffman, Stuart, 191
Kelvin (Lord), 28n6
Kempis, Thomas à, 41

Ketuvim, 120*n*37
Kim Sou-Hwan, Stephen, 153
kosmology, 117*n*33
kosmos, 118
Krause, Karl Christian Friedrich, 209
Kyrios, 133

Laborem exercens (John Paul II), 156
La complexité humaine (Morin), 57
Lady of Aparecida, 158
"La entropía y el fin del mundo," 78–79
La intuición cosmoteandrica (Panikkar), 75
Lankavatara Sutra, 41
La nueva inocencia (Panikkar), 75–76
Laozi, 18, 41–42, 97–98, 108
Latin American Bishops' Conference (2008), 156, 158
Latour, Bruno, 8, 177
Laudate Deum (Pope Francis), 187
Laudato si' (Pope Francis)
　on biblical wisdom, 119
　and Catholic commitment to ecology, 155, 158, 161, 163
　and integral ecology, 166, 173
　on interrelatedness, x–xi, 152, 176, 179, 181
　on need for ecospirituality, x–xi
　on socioeconomics, 167, 171
Laudes creaturarum. See *Canticle of Creatures*
Lautwan, Françoise, 152*n*24

Lavoisier, Antoine, 33
Law, John, 8*n*10
Law, William, 41
laws of thermodynamics, xi, 26–34
Leclerc, Éloi, 226
Leçons d'un siècle de vie (Morin), 3*n*1, 56–57, 63
Leibniz, Gottfried Wilhelm, 30, 37, 39
Lello, Thiago de, 181
Lenoir, Frédéric, 159
Le paradigme perdu (Morin), 57
Les sept savoirs nécessaires (Morin), 58*n*56
Let Us Be Protectors of Creation (Pope Francis), 185
Leviticus, 123, 176
liberation theology, 148, 150, 186, 197
Limbaugh, Rush, 165
Linnaeus, Carl, 108
logos, 58, 118, 134
Lorenz, Edward, 24
Lovelock, James, 212
Löwy, Michael, 158, 165

Machado, Antonio, 7, 60
macrocosm, 8, 27, 202
Magisterium, 163–64
Mammon, 72, 126
Maragall, Joan, 222
Marcel, Gabriel, 92
Marcuse, Herbert, 84, 168
Marx, Karl, 186*n*56
Mass on the World (Teilhard), 238
matter
　as energy, 11–12
　freedom of, 94

and heat, 33–34
inert, 94, 218
materiality of, 218
and Omega Point, 136–37
in quantum physics, 9, 11
and Reality, 93–94, 207
and spirit, 83, 87, 89, 106, 119, 126, 143, 190, 211, 213
spiritualization of, 224
in Teilhard de Chardin, 234–39
Mauss, Marcel, 58
Mayer, Julius von, 27
Mayor Zaragoza, Federico, 66
McFague, Sallie, 149, 194–95, 199, 201, 206
mechanistic model, 9
Mechthild of Magdeburg, 44
Meister Eckhart, 41, 44, 174
Melloni, Javier, 216
Menchú, Rigoberta, 114
Merton, Thomas, 44
Mes démons (Morin), 1, 55, 57
metanoia, 163, 180
Method, The (Morin), 56–57, 59–60
Metz, Johann Baptist, 146
microcosms, 8, 27, 202
Miguélez Díaz, Xosé Antón, 200
"Missionary Disciples Custodians of the Common Home" (CELAM), 158
Misterio y revelación (Panikkar), 76
Models of God (McFague), 149
Moltmann, Jürgen, 92, 123, 146, 195, 201, 204–5
monism, 42, 53, 70, 87, 193, 208
Monod, Jacques, 210
Moraes, Vinicius de, 181

Morin, Edgar
on chaosmos, 12, 25
and complex thought, 8, 51, 56–66, 74, 216
on cosmogenesis, 33
and Panikkar, 77
on progress, 67–68, 70–71
on Reality, 3n1
"Mount of Perfection, The" (John of the Cross), 60n60
My Demons. See *Mes démons* (Morin)
mysticism
Christian, 44, 174, 220, 240
and cosmos, 230–31
in Huxley, 40
in John of the Cross, 229
Judaism, 43
in Panikkar, 220
and quantum physics, 9
and Reality, 5, 81, 211, 214
Sufism, 43
in Teilhard de Chardin, 137
unitive, 43
mystikós, 43
Myth, Faith and Hermeneutics (Panikkar), 76

Naess, Arne, 88
Nagarjuna, 18, 43
Narrow Gate of Knowledge, The (Panikkar), 22
Nasr, Seyyed Hossein, 162
Natalis Solis Invicti, 131
naturalism, 108–9
nefesh hayya, 122
neo-perennial philosophy, 39
Neri, Philip, 41
Neruda, Pablo, 181

network theory, 34
Nevi'im, 120n37
Newell, Allen, 64n66
Newman, John Henry, 144
Newton, Isaac, x, 30–31, 46
Nhâ't Hanh, Thich, 3, 101–2
Nicholas of Cusa, 41, 44
nidana, 101
Nietzsche, Friedrich, 55
Noah, 119
Nobel, Alfred, 64n66
nomos, 84
non-duality, 6, 42–44, 99, 134, 173, 218, 227
noosphere, 136n46
noumenon, 15
Nova Methodus (Leibniz), 30
nulla æsthetica sine ethica, 3

Octogesima adveniens (Paul VI), 156
Of Mysticism (Panikkar), 76
oikos, 193
Omega Point, xii, 136–37
O'Murchu, Diarmuid, 10–12
One-Dimensional Man (Marcose), 168
ontological relativity, 48–49
Ontonomía de la ciencia (Panikkar), 76, 83–84
ontonomy, 19, 83–84
order
　and entropy, 27–28, 32–33
　and Reality, 24–26, 95, 133n44
　and rta principle, 99–100
Order out of Chaos (Prigone), 1, 21
Origen of Alexandria, 39
original sin, 122n39

Original Source of Beings, 13–14
Ortega y Gasset, José, 48, 75

Pachamama, 104
Pali Canon, 100n4
panentheism, 209–11
Panikkar, Raimon
　cosmotheandrism, 53, 134
　on divinization, 174, 212
　and ecologism, 148
　ecosophy, 36, 88–89, 179, 190, 218
　on entropy, 79, 95
　Gifford Lectures, 92
　on identity, 76–77
　kosmology, 117n33
　and metanoia, 163
　and Morin, 77
　on mysticism, 214, 220
　ontonomy, 19, 83–85
　and panentheism, 210
　on pantheism, 208
　and perennial philosophy, 39
　on Reality, 3n1, 5, 8, 48–49, 80–82, 86–87, 90–91, 93–95
　on relativity, 101, 205
　on science, 16, 78–79
　on superficiality, 2, 4
　on theistic frameworks, xiii
　and Whitehead, 55
Pannenberg, Wolfhart, 146
pan-relationality, 226
pantheism, 43, 162, 167, 173, 208–9, 227, 236
Parliament of Religions (1993), 155
Parousia, 137

Index

pars pro toto-totum in parte, 85–86
Paul VI, 155–56, 229n65
Peacocke, Arthur, 92, 146
Peeters, Denise, 112n24
Pensamiento científico y pensamiento cristiano (Panikkar), 76
Penser global (Morin), 57
Pentateuch, 123
perennial philosophy, 10, 22, 38–43, 45
perichôrêsis, 176, 205n24
permanence, 31, 54
philia, 200
Philosophiæ naturalis (Newton), 30
philosophia perennis. *See* perennial philosophy
Pickard, Stephen, 191
Pico della Mirandola, Giovanni, 39
Pigem, Jordi, 64n66, 164, 168, 172
Pikaza, Xabier, 147
Planck, Max, 33
Plato, 219, 236
pleroma, 135
Plotinus, 43, 219
Polkinghorne, John, 92, 190–91, 203–4
polycentric thought, 71
positivism, 29
Potter, Van Rensselaer, 36, 50–52
Pour sortir du xxè siècle (Morin), 57
Prabhavananda (Swami), 40
pratityasamutpada, 43, 82, 100–101
Priestercodex, 120
Prigogine, Ilya, 1, 8, 21, 24–26, 28–29, 31, 33, 47–48, 94

Primavesi, Anne, 149
process philosophy, 53
Protecting Human Life (Pope Francis), 185
Psalms, 124–26, 176
Pseudo Dionysius Areopagite, 44
Ptolemy, 117
Puebla document, 186–87
purification, 174

quanta, 9, 11
Quantum Field Theory, 13
quantum mechanics, 9, 26, 31, 94
quantum physics, 8–11, 13, 23–24, 151, 191, 203
Quantum Questions (Wilber), 14
Querida Amazonia. *See Dear Amazonia* (Pope Francis)

radah, 121
Rahner, Karl, 146, 203, 212
Ramakrishna, 39, 41
Ramanuja, 43
Ramayana, 98
randomness, 21, 32, 65. *See also* uncertainty
Reality
  absolute, 86
  and consciousness, 4–5, 15, 18, 36
  and disorder, 24–25
  and matter, 93–94, 207
  Morin on, 3n1
  and mysticism, 5, 81, 211, 214
  non-duality of, 43–44, 134, 227
  and order, 24–26, 95, 133n44
  Panikkar on, 3n1, 5, 8, 48–49, 80–82, 86–87, 90–91, 93–95

as seamless fabric, x–xi, 7–9, 19, 38, 54, 75, 89, 137, 155, 159, 175, 177, 194, 225
reconciliation, 134, 192, 235
Recuperar la creación (Torres Queiruga), 148
reductionism, 36, 46–47, 59, 64, 85, 212
Reflections on the Motive Power of Fire (Carnot), 28n6
Reflexiones autobiográficas (Panikkar), 1
Reinventing the Sacred (Kauffman), 192
relational ontology, 203–4
relational thinking, 58, 114
relativity, 43, 49–50, 82, 101, 196
religation, 217, 222
res cogitans, 47
resurrection, 136, 138–39
Richard of St. Victor, 205
Ricœur, Paul, 48, 92
Rig-veda, 97–98
Robinson, Keith, 37
Romans (Scripture), 97, 135, 178
rta principle, 43, 99–100
ruah, 122
Ruether, Rosemary Radford, 149, 197
Ruiz de la Peña, Juan Luis, 148
Rumi, 41
Russell, Bertrand, 52, 55
Ruysbroeck, Nicholas, 41

Sagan
  Carl, ix
  Dorion, 22, 26
salvation, 4, 16, 79, 98, 100, 102, 136, 143, 199
Sampedro, José Luis, 93

sanātana dharma, 38
Sartre, Jean-Paul, 48
Scheler, Max, 48, 224
Schering, Ernst, 229n65
Schillebeeckx, Edward, 146
Schneider, Eric D., 22, 26
Scholasticism, 39
Schrödinger, Erwin, 12, 16, 45
Schweitzer, Albert, 92, 146
scientism, 14, 83, 86
seamless fabric of Reality, x–xi, 7–9, 19, 38, 54, 75, 89, 137, 155, 159, 175, 177, 194, 225
Second Axial Age, 77
second eye, 41, 218–19
second law of thermodynamics, xi, 21, 26–27, 29, 32, 34
Seeking the Church (Pickard), 191
sefirot, 43
self-organization, 12, 47, 65
Seoul document, 153
Shankara, Adi, 41, 43
Shaw, John Clifford, 64n66
Shiva, Vandana, 112, 213
Silence of God, The (Panikkar), 76
Simeon the Stylite, 6
Simon, Herbert A., 64
Simón del desierto (Buñuel), 6
sin, structures of, 185–86
Smuts, Jan, 36, 114
Sollicitudo rei socialis (John Paul II), 156
space-time, 87, 137, 189
sparsa colligo, 58, 77
Spinoza, Baruch, 36, 43, 52, 208, 210
spirit, and matter, 83, 87, 89, 106, 119, 126, 143, 190, 211, 213

Spiritual Canticle (John of the Cross), 217, 228–32
Spiritual Foundations for the Care of Creation (Pope Francis), 185
Steuco, Agostino, 39
Stevens, Isaac, 105
Stoicism, 133n44
structures of sin, 185–86
Suess, Eduard, xii
Sufism, 43
superficiality, 2–4, 6–7
Swimme, Brian, 13
Synod of the Amazon (2019), 180–83
systems theory, 56–57

ta aisthêta, 219
Tacitus, 102
Tagore, Rabindranath, 41
tai chi, 43
ta mystika, 219
Tanakh, 120n37, 128
ta noêta, 219
Taoism, 18, 42–43
Tao of Physics (Capra), 2
Tauler, Johannes, 41
technocracy, 164, 167–69, 181
"Técnica y tiempo," 79
Teilhard de Chardin, Pierre
  and Christogenesis, 138, 140
  on evolution, 136n46, 137–38, 140, 237
  on matter, 234–39
  as mystic, 215, 221–22, 234–35
  and Omega Point, xii, 136–37
  and pantheism, 208, 210, 236–37
Teresa of Ávila, 41, 199, 222, 229n65

theandrism, 134, 211
theo-anthropo-cosmic, 89–90
theocentrism, 81, 119
theophany, 44
Theory of Everything, 190, 204
theory of theory, 60–61
Theos, 91
theosophy, 208
thermodynamics, xi, 21–23, 26–29, 31–34, 79
  classical, 30
  and complexity, xi–xii, 22–23, 26, 29, 32
  and cosmos, xi, 34
  laws, xi, 26–34
thermogenesis, 33
third eye, 5, 41, 218–20
third law of thermodynamics, 47
Thomas (Coptic Gospel), 140
Thomas of Celano, 224
Thomson, W. *See* Kelvin (Lord)
Tillich, Paul, 92, 198
Tolstoy, Leo, 111n22
Torah, 120n37
Torres Queiruga, Andrés, 147, 197, 199
Touraine, Alain, 56
"Towards a Metaphysics of Complexity" (Robinson), 37
"Towards an Alliance for Justice, Peace and the Integrity of Creation," 153
Trinitarian theology, 190–91, 203–4, 206
Trinity and World Religions, The (Panikkar), 76

Unamuno, Miguel de, 75
uncertainty principle, 10, 24, 31–33, 47–48, 59, 78

UN Conference on Sustainable Development (2012), 173
UNESCO, 65–66
Unified Theory, 13
United Nations Environment Program (UNEP), 164
Unknown Christ of Hinduism, The (Panikkar), 76
Upanishads, 17–18, 41
utopian ideology, 108–9

Valmiki, 98
Valverde, José María, 4
Vancouver Conference of Ecumenical Council of Churches (1983), 153
Varela, Luis Miguel, 22, 26, 29
Vedanta Society, 40
Vedas, 43
Vedic Hinduism, 99
Vigil, José María, 11–12
visistadvaita, 43
Vivekananda (Swami), 39

Watts, Alan, 39
wave mechanics, 9
Weil, Simone, 44

"What Is Happening to Our Common Home" (Pope Francis) 169
White, Lynn, ix, 107, 141–42, 223
Whitehead, Alfred North, 35–37, 52–55, 60, 92, 198–99
Wieman, Henry Nelson, 54n49
Wilber, Ken, 14–15, 39, 45
Wildiers, N. M., 238
William of Saint-Thierry, 44
Wisdom, 128
World Council of Churches, 153
World Day of Peace (1990), 156
World Day of Prayer for the Care of Creation (2015), 185
Wounded Knee, 106

Zambrano, María, 75
Zechariah, 131
zeroth law of thermodynamics, 27
Zhuangzi, 41
Zizioulas, John, 204
Zorastrianism, 143
Zubiri, Xavier, 48–49, 75